D1239413

From Patrician to Professional Elite

From Patrician to Professional Elite

*The Transformation of the
New York City Bar Association*

MICHAEL J. POWELL

Russell Sage Foundation   New York

The Russell Sage Foundation

The Russell Sage Foundation, one of the oldest of America's general purpose foundations, was established in 1907 by Mrs. Margaret Olivia Sage for "the improvement of social and living conditions in the United States." The Foundation seeks to fulfill this mandate by fostering the development and dissemination of knowledge about the political, social, and economic problems of America. It conducts research in the social sciences and public policy and publishes books and pamphlets that derive from this research.

The Board of Trustees is responsible for oversight and the general policies of the Foundation, while administrative direction of the program and staff is vested in the President, assisted by the officers and staff. The President bears final responsibility for the decision to publish a manuscript as a Russell Sage Foundation book. In reaching a judgment on the competence, accuracy, and objectivity of each study, the President is advised by the staff and selected expert readers. The conclusions and interpretations in Russell Sage Foundation publications are those of the authors and not of the Foundation, its Trustees, or its staff. Publication by the Foundation, therefore, does not imply endorsement of the contents of the study.

Library of Congress Cataloging-in-Publication Data

Powell, Michael J.
    From patrician to professional elite.

    Bibliography: p.
    Includes index.
    1. Association of the Bar of the City of New York—
History. I. Title.
KF334.N4A8454 1988   340'.06'07471 88-32476
ISBN 0-87154-686-8

Cover and text design: William Bennett

10 9 8 7 6 5 4 3 2 1

To Susan, Oliver, and Toby

Contents

List of Tables

List of Figures

Acknowledgments

In the lengthy process of researching and writing this book, I have incurred many debts, both personal and institutional. I regard myself extremely fortunate to have had from the outset of the project the support and encouragement of two exceptional mentors, John P. Heinz and Edward O. Laumann. Engaged at the time in their ground-breaking research on the Chicago bar, Jack Heinz and Edward Laumann suggested that I undertake this study in order to permit a comparison of the organized bar in Chicago and in New York. Their intellectual and personal support has been both generous and unflagging, and I appreciate it greatly.

Without the institutional support of the American Bar Foundation, this study could not have been undertaken or completed. Thanks are especially due to Spencer L. Kimball, executive director of the Foundation at the beginning of the study, who extended the Foundation's financial support during the initial period of data collection and early analysis, and to Jack Heinz, who continued this support during his tenure as executive director, making possible further analysis and extensive revisions to the original dissertation upon which this book is based. As well as providing financial support, the American Bar Foundation was a congenial and stimulating environment in which to work. Many colleagues at the Foundation, especially Charles Cappell, Barbara Curran, Janet Gilboy, Robert Nelson, Katherine Rosich and Rayman Solomon, provided encouragement and help along the way. Brian Frankl assisted with the data collection and Clara Carson provided expert technical assistance. Special thanks are due to Terry Halliday, who read much of the manuscript and furnished ideas, constructive criticism, and personal support in generous proportions.

This book arose from my graduate work in the department of sociology at the University of Chicago, and I wish to acknowledge my intellectual debts to Charles Bidwell, Donald Levine, Edward Laumann, Barry Schwartz, and Edward Shils. To the late Morris Janowitz I owe a special personal and intellectual debt. Not only did he take me under his wing, but his insistence on the need for the systemic analysis of major societal institutions undergirds this inquiry.

I also owe a special debt of gratitude to the leaders of the Association of the Bar of the City of New York who allowed me to come into their association and examine it from the inside. Without their willingness to be open to external scrutiny this book could not have been written. In particular, thanks are due to Merrell E. Clark, Jr., president at the time I began the study, and to Oscar Ruebhausen, his successor, for their helpfulness and suggestions. Ron Monroe, Gene Waters, and the late Paul B. DeWitt were extremely generous with their time and assistance. Thanks also to the many members of the Association who allowed me to interview them; they graciously answered my questions. I would like to acknowledge especially the assistance of Leonard M. Leiman and Ezra Levin.

Thanks also to Priscilla Lewis of the Russell Sage Foundation, who provided encouragement and support as well as helpful editorial advice.

Of course, none of these individuals or institutions bears responsibility for what follows. That is mine alone.

Finally, I would like to acknowledge the moral and material support of my parents over many years of study. My greatest debt, however, is to Susan, Oliver, and Toby, who have given love, understanding, and encouragement without measure. To them I gratefully dedicate this book.

Introduction

The Association of the Bar of the City of New York (ABCNY) is not an ordinary bar association. That is immediately apparent to those who enter its doors on West 44th Street in midtown Manhattan. Completed in 1896, and listed as one of New York's historic buildings, the "house" of the ABCNY, as it is affectionately referred to by its members, is an impressive edifice. Built in the grand Victorian manner, it has a cavernous entrance hall or foyer, flanked by imposing marble columns and surrounded by tastefully decorated reading rooms. The foyer leads to a wide marble staircase. Upstairs at one end is a large meeting room the walls of which are lined with heavy oil portraits of past presidents. At the other end, smaller committee rooms furnished with highly polished tables and leather chairs surround an open lobby. The oriental rugs, period-piece furniture, antique vases, and rich velvet draperies contribute to the overall impression of dignity, importance, and wealth, an impression not unlike that presented by the old exclusive social clubs of the city. Far from being simply a functional office building, as are so many headquarters of professional associations, the house of the ABCNY is a testament to its distinctive upper-class history.

In addition to having the appearance and atmosphere of an exclusive, upper-class social club, the ABCNY is located in the midst of what could be called the "club district," given the number of social clubs located there. Next to the ABCNY are the Century Association, an exclusive literary club, and the Princeton University Club. Immediately behind are the New York Yacht and Harvard University clubs. Within easy walking distance are the University and Yale clubs. In the past, committees of the ABCNY frequently would begin their meetings with dinner at one of these neighboring clubs before settling down to the business of the profession. It is not surprising, then, that to many members of the New York bar the ABCNY appeared, for much of its history, to be more an upper-class legal club for the establishment of the bar than a professional association open to all lawyers in good standing.

Upper-class culture and leadership were not the only remarkable features of the ABCNY. It was also the first of the modern bar associations, and its formation in 1870 set in motion a movement whereby local, state, and national bar associations were established throughout the United States. The leaders of the infant ABCNY played a significant role in this movement. They were instrumental in the formation of the New York State Bar Association (NYSBA) in 1876 and the American Bar Association (ABA) in 1878. The ABCNY served as a model for bar associations founded in other cities throughout the late nineteenth century. By 1916 more than six hundred bar associations at all levels of government had been established across the United States.

Although only a local metropolitan bar association, the ABCNY enjoyed a national reputation from the beginning. In large part this reflected the national prominence of its leaders in both law and politics. Among the ABCNY's early presidents were William M. Evarts, who successfully defended President Andrew Johnson against impeachment in the United States Senate; James C. Carter, who led the opposition to the movement to codify the American law in the early twentieth century; and Elihu Root, onetime secretary of state, who chaired the ABA committee in the 1920s that gave impetus to the national demand for higher educational requirements for admission to the bar. Over the 110 years from its founding until 1980, two of the ABCNY's presidents were United States presidential candidates; one was a former justice of the United States Supreme Court; five were former or future secretaries of state (most recently, of course, Cyrus Vance, who went directly from the presidency of the ABCNY to being Jimmy Carter's secretary of state); and several others served as cabinet members in various national administrations. Furthermore, a significant minority of the ABCNY's membership was composed of nonresident members from all over the United States who gave to the Association a national hue.

The national standing of the ABCNY, and its nationwide membership, reflected the historic position of New York as the dominant commercial and financial center of the United States. Consequently, noted New York advocates developed national reputations, and the large law firms on Wall Street became national firms serving corporate clients whose interests knew no city limits or state borders. The New York legal establishment represented in the ABCNY, then, was not a local elite, as the legal elites of other cities tended to be, but a national elite, a fact that endowed the ABCNY with a significance extending far beyond the five counties of New York City.

Most of the early bar associations were exclusive organizations in their early years. Formed by "the better and best elements of the profession," the Chicago Bar Association (CBA) initially charged high admission fees and annual dues, and the Boston Bar Association was described as "originally and for a long time . . . a conservative and selective group." [1] Moreover, the ABA for many years held its annual meetings at Saratoga Springs, a favorite summer enclave of the upper class that attracted, largely, members of the Northeastern establishment and the Southern gentry who could afford to escape the summer heat and enjoy the benefit of the waters. [2] What was distinctive about the ABCNY, however, was that whereas these other associations soon abandoned their exclusive, aristocratic stance, to become "open" bar associations welcoming as members all lawyers in good standing, the ABCNY remained a selective, upper-class organization into the post–World War II period. In 1950 the ABCNY still had a rigorous admissions process in place and included only about one fifth of the New York bar in its membership. Indeed, as late as 1973, journalist Paul Hoffman referred to the ABCNY as the "organization of the Brahmins of the bar." [3]

Such retention of selective membership, and the elite status that followed, when other bar associations had long adopted more inclusive policies to increase their size and revenue, raised some tantalizing research questions. Why would the leadership of the ABCNY seek to maintain its selectivity? What were the assets that exclusiveness and high social standing bestowed upon the ABCNY? To what extent did these assets outweigh the disadvantages of unrepresentativeness?

Research on the organized bar in Chicago in the late 1970s, as part of the larger Chicago Bar Project at the American Bar Foundation, had indicated the considerable difficulties that inclusive associations experienced in reaching decisions on important matters of substance and in

---

1. Jerold S. Auerbach, *Unequal Justice: Lawyers and Social Change in Modern America* (New York: Oxford, 1976), p. 63; Roscoe Pound, *The Lawyer from Antiquity to Modern Times* (St. Paul: West Publishing, 1953), p. 259.

2. Auerbach, *Unequal Justice*, p. 63.

3. Paul Hoffman, *Lions in the Street* (New York: Saturday Review Press, 1973), p. 203.

mobilizing their membership.[4] Composed of diverse interests and viewpoints, representative associations such as the CBA were often hamstrung by internal dissensus and therefore were unable to make decisive contributions on controversial matters of professional policy. Founders of a "counter" bar association in Chicago in 1969—the Chicago Council of Lawyers—viewed it as impossible to work for reform through the inclusive CBA because the very elements within the profession or legal system that needed reform, according to them, were well represented within the CBA itself.[5] Indeed, many of the reform initiatives within the CBA, including the idea of the Chicago Bar Project, originated with a select, "elite" committee of leading practitioners and law professors, the Committee on the Development of Law.[6]

The young founders of the Chicago Council of Lawyers pointed to the ABCNY as a model of a bar association that was able to engage in reform of the legal system. In addition, the ABCNY operated a professional lawyer discipline system, had endorsed civil rights legislation in the early 1960s, and strongly supported federal funding of legal services for the indigent. The implication was that a selective "elite" model of organizing, such as that of the ABCNY, was able to act more decisively and intervene more effectively in policy-making.

The invitation to study the ABCNY and its effectiveness in influencing policy outcomes, then, provided an opportunity to examine the validity of the suggestion that a relatively homogeneous membership combined with elite status could better effect change than could a heterogeneous, representative association. As a consequence, throughout the book there is always an implicit, and oftentimes explicit, comparison of the elite ABCNY with the representative CBA in order to test the hypothesis of the superiority of the elite model of organizing.

At one level, then, the ABCNY presented a rare opportunity to examine the internal dynamics and organizational structure of an elite association. At another level, my knowledge of the Chicago bar, and research on the Chicago Council of Lawyers, raised questions about the extent of elite influence in an increasingly heterogeneous profession, an issue of central importance to the debate over the class basis

---

4. For a brief description of the Chicago Bar Project and a discussion of the difficulties consequent to comprehensiveness and inclusiveness, see John P. Heinz, Edward O. Laumann, Charles L. Cappell, Terence C. Halliday, and Michael H. Schaalman, "Diversity, Representation, and Leadership in an Urban Bar: A First Report on a Survey of the Chicago Bar," *American Bar Foundation Research Journal* (1976): 717–785.

5. Michael J. Powell, "Anatomy of a Counter-Bar Association: The Chicago Council of Lawyers," *Amerian Bar Foundation Research Journal* (1979): 501–541.

6. Heinz et al., "Diversity, Representation, and Leadership," p. 719.

of modern professionalism. Those who hold to an elite view of the legal profession, such as social historian Jerold Auerbach, assign enormous influence and power to its upper-class members in its historical development.[7] According to this view, the ABCNY had been a vehicle through which the upper-class minority of the New York bar controlled the nonelite majority.

With its large and ethnically diverse bar, and several local, inclusive county bar associations in addition to the ABCNY, New York City was an excellent site to examine the validity of hypotheses of elite or upper-class dominance. Was the selective ABCNY, with all its resources of prestige and wealth, able to determine professional policy and effect reforms of the legal system? Or did the nonelite majority of the profession have resources of its own with which to oppose and thwart elite initiatives? Examination of the effectiveness with which the ABCNY was able to support and implement its policies and programs would address these central questions about the role and influence of the corporate legal elite in the legal profession.

On beginning my research on the ABCNY in the late 1970s, however, I found its identity as an upper-class institution much less certain than it had seemed from a distance. Its intimidating admissions process had been relaxed, resulting in a younger and more diverse membership. Its greater diversity was demonstrated by the new members of the governing board, the Executive Committee, elected unopposed in 1980. They included two Italian Catholic lawyers, one of whom practiced immigration law and the other criminal defense, a woman from the New York branch of the national legal clinic of Jacoby and Meyers, and the general counsel of a large corporation. Not one was from the traditional recruiting grounds of the Wall Street firms, and three of the four new members of the ABCNY's governing board were definitely not Anglo-Saxon, Protestant males. With such visible changes in leadership composition, the ABCNY no longer appeared an upper-class organization; the question was whether it remained an elite association at all, or had become an inclusive body on the model of the CBA.

The entire post–World War II period was one in which there was increased pressure for the full incorporation of all elements of the American population into the mainstream, culminating in the civil rights and feminist movements of the 1960s and 1970s. Ascriptively defined groups, such as racial and ethnic minorities and women, whose members had been effectively excluded from many central institutions of American society, sought the removal of barriers to their

---

7. Auerbach, *Unequal Justice.*

participation through the mobilization of their political and legal rights. This political movement reached its peak in the mid-1970s with affirmative-action programs, school busing, fair-housing and employment legislation, federal regulation of the rights of the disabled, and antidiscrimination suits, although it had commenced with *Brown* v. *Board of Education* in 1954 and the Civil Rights Act ten years later. Demands for increased access and participation were not restricted to the public domain but extended into the private associational sphere. It became very difficult for private clubs and associations to continue openly to exclude from their membership persons on grounds of race, ethnicity, religion, or gender. As Talcott Parsons noted in a perceptive essay on the implications of "the egalitarian trend of the 'rights' complex," these shifts in the normative order occurred over a relatively short time span and have been dramatic in their impact.[8] Clearly, the ABCNY could not stand apart from these pressures for greater inclusiveness, especially as the legal profession itself experienced rapid growth during these decades, with a significantly higher proportion of women entering the bar.

Recognition that the ABCNY had changed in response to pressures for greater inclusiveness raised a new set of research questions about organizational adaptation to environmental change, the prospects for patrician professionalism, and, at the macro level, the survival of elite institutions in modern mass society. In the first instance, I was interested in the extent, management, and organizational effects of change. If the membership of the ABCNY had indeed become more representative of the bar at large, were there ways in which internal diversification and growth could be managed without necessarily leading to fundamental change in the elite character of the Association? In other words, was there a middle ground the ABCNY could find between class-based exclusiveness and mass-based inclusiveness? I also was interested in the consequences of membership change for the organizational structure and decision-making processes of the ABCNY. Did greater membership diversity, and the consequent representation within the ABCNY of conflicting interests, increase the level of internal dissensus to the extent that its ability to reach decisions was hindered? I address these questions about the extent, direction, and consequences of compositional and organizational change in the ABCNY in the post–World War II decades in Chapters Two, Three, and Four.

---

8. Talcott Parsons, "Equality and Inequality in Modern Society, or Social Stratification Revisited," in Edward O. Laumann (ed.), *Social Stratification: Research and Theory for the 1970s* (Indianapolis: Bobbs-Merrill, 1970), p. 18.

If questions about the direction of membership and organizational change are considered first, consideration of the implications of these changes for the role of the elite association in a highly differentiated occupational system quickly follows. Chapter Five examines the extent of the moral authority of the ABCNY in the postwar decades in the face of a heterogeneous bar, and discusses the new directions in which its new membership took it. With changes in its membership, and the likelihood of increased internal dissensus, was the ABCNY still able to exercise moral leadership within the profession? Chapter Six returns to the question we began with, that is, whether an elite professional association such as the ABCNY is better able to exercise influence over policy-making, to bring knowledge to the assistance of governance, as Terence Halliday puts it, than is a heterogeneous and representative association such as the CBA.[9] This question is addressed through an examination of the effectiveness of explicit attempts by the ABCNY to influence the direction of legal change not just in narrow matters of professional politics but in wider spheres of public policy. Throughout, comparison is made with the CBA, and the conditions that facilitate the successful exercise of influence by an elite association in a differentiated system are outlined.

There remains a second order of questions at the macrosociological level. Not only did the apparent changes in the ABCNY's composition in response to pressures for greater inclusiveness raise the issue of the place of elites in differentiated professional structures; they also made it necessary to examine the larger conundrum of the persistence and continued role, if any, of elite associations and institutions in democratic, mass societies. This macrosocial question has been of concern to social theorists at least since the French Revolution destroyed the established order in France and raised the specter of democratization. Alexis de Tocqueville, for instance, observing the recurrence of revolution in nineteenth-century France, viewed the advance of equality as an unstoppable tide. It would mean not only the extension of the political franchise but the end of legal differences in statuses and privileges and the undermining of the traditional deference order based on inherited position.[10] While acknowledging that the equalitarian trend had its positive features, Tocqueville was overwhelmingly pessimistic about its consequences for the quality of life and culture, seeing it as opening the way to the tyranny of the majority.

---

9. Terence C. Halliday, *Beyond Monopoly: Lawyers, State Crises and Professional Empowerment* (Chicago: University of Chicago Press, 1987).

10. Alexis de Tocqueville, *Democracy in America* (New York: Alfred Knopf, 1945).

Contemporary critics of mass society have echoed Tocqueville's conservative complaint, fearing that the emergence of modern mass media and communications systems has hastened the removal of differences of all kinds and facilitated the dominance of mass culture.[11] Furthermore, as the periphery moved closer to the center of society, elite groups risked losing their distinctiveness and autonomy of action. Karl Mannheim, writing in the 1930s with the menace of fascism before him, coined the unattractive term "de-distantiation" for such decreased distance between elite and mass that arose from "the open character of democratic mass society, together with its growth in size and the tendency toward general public participation."[12]

In addition to de-distantiation, Mannheim saw democratization as negatively affecting societal elites in several ways. First, he anticipated the emergence of a plurality of elites in democratic societies. Whereas to Suzanne Keller the plurality of elites strengthens the integration of society, to Mannheim it results in interelite conflict that makes the process of governance much more difficult.[13] As Mannheim put it: "The more elites there are in a society, the more each individual elite tends to lose its function and influence as a leader, for they cancel each other out."[14] Moreover, noting that it was "the important contribution of modern democracy that the achievement principle increasingly becomes the criterion of social success," Mannheim was concerned that the movement from dependence upon birth and inherited position as criteria for recruitment into societal elites would mean higher turnover in membership and therefore decreased elite continuity and stability.[15] Since Mannheim's time, egalitarian trends not only have encouraged the increased prominence of achievement principles but also have led to affirmative action programs whereby individuals from nonelite ascriptive groups are elevated into elite positions. The operation of both achievement mechanisms and affirmative-action requirements has the potential of resulting in heterogeneous elite groups the members of which no longer share common backgrounds and interests, with the possible consequence of greater intraelite conflict and stalemate.

Writing in the early 1960s, Digby Baltzell also saw a crisis of moral authority and leadership. The reasons lay not so much in the disinte-

---

11. See, for example, William Kornhauser, _The Politics of Mass Society_ (New York: Free Press, 1959).

12. Karl Mannheim, _Man and Society in an Age of Reconstruction_ (New York: Harcourt, Brace, 1940), p. 86.

13. Suzanne Keller, _Beyond the Ruling Class: Strategic Elites in Modern Society_ (New York: Random House, 1963).

14. Mannheim, _Man and Society in an Age of Reconstruction_, p. 86.

15. Ibid., p. 89.

gration of societal elites, due to inexorable democratization, as in the petrification of the existing white Anglo-Saxon Protestant (WASP) establishment due to its unwillingness "to share and improve its upper-class traditions by continuously absorbing talented and distinguished members of minority groups into its privileged ranks."[16] Baltzell pointed to the pervasive anti-Semitism of the WASP upper class as an indication of the emergence of a caste-like mentality that undermined the moral authority of the old American class-based elite. Not so pessimistic as Mannheim, Baltzell contended that an upper-class elite could sustain its moral authority by adopting a guarded meritocractic outlook and incorporating new elites of achievement as they arose without reference to their social origins. Indeed, in direct contrast to Mannheim, who feared the diversification of elite membership, Baltzell argued that "in order for an upper class to maintain a continuity of power and authority, especially in an opportunitarian and mobile society such as ours, its membership must, in the long run, be representative of the composition of society as a whole."[17]

It may be that the ABCNY, by incorporating more diverse elements of the New York bar in the postwar decades, was unconsciously following Baltzell's prescription, thereby ensuring its continued moral leadership of the bar, rather than succumbing to fundamental democratization and internal stalemate. Whether upper-class or elite associations can persist in a democratic society, or in a heterogeneous occupational system such as the legal profession, and whether they continue to exercise moral authority, is an important empirical and theoretical question both for those who fear the surge of egalitarian sentiment, as did Tocqueville and Mannheim, and for those who welcome the downfall of class-based elites as an advance for democracy and equality.

Modern professional associations have functioned for more than a century almost completely removed from public scrutiny, generally subject only to the sympathetic examination of amateur centennial historians. Although social scientists have recognized the centrality of the learned professions, or knowledge-based occupations, to modern postindustrial society, the organizations of these professions have largely escaped scholarly attention. The one notable exception is the detailed study of the membership composition, leadership, and structure of the American Medical Association in the interwar years published by

---

16. E. Digby Baltzell, *The Protestant Establishment: Aristocracy and Caste in America* (New York: Vintage, 1964), p. x.

17. Ibid., p. xi.

Oliver Garceau in 1941.[18] Path-breaking though it was, Garceau's study had not been updated or followed by any similar studies of other major professional associations until Terence Halliday's and Charles Cappell's analyses of the internal organization, policy initiatives, and legislative influence of the CBA.[19] More often, scholars have generalized about the collective bodies of the professions without first undertaking the empirical research necessary to sustain those generalizations. For example, Auerbach suggests throughout his history of the modern American legal profession that large-firm, corporate lawyers have dominated the organized bar and determined the direction of professional development.[20] Yet nowhere does he present a detailed analysis of the composition of the leadership of the major professional associations to verify this important assertion. Even Magali Larson, in her much-noted work on the rise of professionalism, emphasizing the historical efforts of the professions to establish monopoly control over their work, glosses over the specifics of the composition, structure, and policies of the very entities presumably responsible for the formulation and advocacy of the collective interests of the professions.[21] Clearly, professional associations were central to the whole professionalization process, yet they have not been subjected to close scrutiny by the students of that process.

Although perhaps of peripheral importance in the everyday work lives of most members, professional associations have played a significant role in shaping and defining the larger context within which the professional operates. Additionally, their advocacy of professional interests has influenced the development of public policy in central institutions of modern society such as law and health. As Everett Hughes, whose work on professionalism has helped shape the field, perceptively observed, "Lawyers not only give advice to clients and plead their cases for them; they also develop a philosophy of law–of its na-

---

18. Oliver Garceau, *The Political Life of the American Medical Association* (Cambridge: Harvard University Press, 1941).

19. Halliday, *Beyond Monopoly*. Charles L. Cappell, *A Legal Elite: Investigations into Professional Politics and the Production of Law* (Ph.D. dissertation, University of Chicago, 1982). See also Terence C. Halliday and Charles L. Cappell, "Indicators of Democracy in Professional Associations: Elite Recruitment, Turnover, and Decision Making in a Metropolitan Bar Association," *American Bar Foundation Research Journal* (1979): 697–767; Charles L. Cappell and Terence C. Halliday, "Professional Projects of Elite Chicago Lawyers, 1950–1974," *American Bar Foundation Research Journal* (1983): 291–340.

20. Auerbach, *Unequal Justice*.

21. Magali Sarfatti Larson, *The Rise of Professionalism: A Sociological Analysis* (Berkeley: University of California Press, 1977).

ture and functions, and of the proper way to administer justice."
Hughes goes on to note that "every profession considers itself the
proper body to set the terms in which some aspect of society, life or
nature is to be thought of, and to define the general line, or even the
details of public policy concerning it."[22] It is the professional associations that formulate and advocate these positions in the wider polity.
For example, it is clear that the particular shape of the National Health
Service in Britain owed much to the intervention of the Royal Colleges
and the British Medical Association in the policy-making process.[23]
Closer to home, the adoption of the private insurance model for reim-
bursement for medical expenses by the federal government in the development of Medicare and Medicaid was largely the result of the intervention of professional interests.[24] Similarly, the final structure of
the federal program to provide legal assistance to indigents reflected
the concerns of the organized bar as represented by the ABA.[25] Professional associations, then, have contributed to the development of policy in areas of critical importance to contemporary society.

That national professional associations should have exercised considerable influence over public policy should not be surprising because
they enroll as members many thousands, in some cases hundreds of
thousands, of highly educated, articulate, and well-to-do professionals.
Although they are smaller, local metropolitan associations may also enjoy substantial resource abundance. The ABCNY, for instance, in 1980
had more than 12,000 members and an annual income in excess of
$3,000,000. Its assets, including its buildings, were valued at more than
$5,000,000. The number and range of its active committees that could
respond to requests for assistance or initiate policy development in particular areas is staggering. In 1980 the ABCNY had no fewer than
eighty-five standing and special committees meeting regularly, making
reports, discussing developments in the law and legal practice, monitoring the courts, drafting bills, and writing amicus briefs. These committees address a bewildering array of legal matters, some of apparently minor, technical import and others of broad substantive policy.
Some of these committees intervene regularly, and as a matter of
course, in legislative and administrative processes. Committees on

---

22. Everett C. Hughes, *The Sociological Eye* (Chicago: Aldine, 1971), p. 376.
23. Harry Eckstein, *Pressure Group Politics* (London: Allen and Unwin, 1960).
24. Rosemary Stevens, *American Medicine and the Public Interest* (New Haven: Yale University Press, 1971).
25. Earl Johnson, *Justice and Reform: The Formative Years of the OEO Legal Services Program* (New York: Russell Sage Foundation, 1974).

State and Federal Legislation prepare frequent reports on proposed legislation, monitoring its substantive content as well as its technical adequacy, while the Committees on Securities Regulation and Trade Regulation comment on a regular basis on proposals for rule changes emanating from the Securities Exchange Commission and the Federal Trade Commission. Taken together, the ABCNY has considerable resources of expertise, connectedness, wealth, and prestige that can be mobilized in pursuit of its goals.

Furthermore, the most consequential and immediate manifestations of collective professional influence are apparent at the local and state levels, rather than at the national, where issues of paramount importance to practitioners are typically determined. The regulation of professional activity is dependent upon legislative and judicial action at the state level. Though the ABA may develop a new code of ethics, it is of no effect unless adopted by state supreme courts and promulgated as court rules. In considering what provisions to include, state supreme courts are much more likely to pay attention to the representations of local and state associations in their immediate environment than to the recommendations of a distant national association. For this reason, local practitioners are more likely to feel primary loyalty to, and to actively participate in, local or state associations. Not only do they influence the conditions under which they work, and provide a mechanism for collective action, but they also facilitate the development of collegial ties that can lead to referrals and enhance a practitioner's career and practice. For members of the corporate, large-firm elite of the New York bar, the ABCNY has generally been the object of their primary loyalty and identification, although many also maintain memberships in the State Bar Association and the ABA.

Following the Chicago School tradition of institutional analysis, then, this book presents an in-depth examination of the articulation of a consequential local institution with its changing societal environment. Although institutional analysis of this genre begins with a detailed case study of a significant local organization as exhibited in Everett Hughes's analysis of the Chicago Real Estate Board, Philip Selznick's study of the early years of the Tennessee Valley Authority, and James Jacobs's examination of the changing patterns of administration of Stateville prison in Illinois, it traces the broader macrosocial implications of the patterns of stasis and change that it finds.[26] Thus

---

26. Everett C. Hughes, *The Chicago Real Estate Board: The Growth of an Institution* (New York: Arno Press, 1979); Philip Selznick, *TVA and the Grass Roots* (Berkeley: University of California Press, 1949); James B. Jacobs, *Stateville: The Pentitentiary in Mass Society* (Chicago: University of Chicago Press, 1977).

Hughes's analysis explores professionalization as a strategy for up-wardly mobile occupations and of the dynamics of interoccupational competition, Selznick's case study led to an appreciation of the impli-cations for organizational goals of processes of co-optation, and Ja-cobs's historical account demonstrated how broad societal changes penetrate even the walls of total institutions. Yet institutional analysis remains faithful to the entity under study. In Jacobs's words, institu-tional analysis is more "concerned with the complexity of particular types of institutions than with the more abstract properties of formal organizations" and consequently draws as heavily on political sociol-ogy as on the sociology of organizations.[27]

The studies cited above remain case studies even though their sig-nificance goes far beyond their cases. This book also unapologetically presents a case study with the contention that detailed examinations of particular cases are necessary to supplement the broad sweep of his-torical generalization and the aggregate depictions of social change pre-sented by time series analysis: Neither of these "gets inside" organiza-tions and institutions to unravel the mechanics and politics of adaptation. With respect to the sociology of the professions, as Halli-day contends, it is only by the intensive case study of professional organizations "that core issues, such as collective professional action, internal professional politics, and the mobilization of professional knowledge can be satisfactorily addressed."[28]

Also in the Chicago tradition, I have not been wedded to any one methodology but rather committed to achieving as full an understand-ing of the processes of change in the ABCNY as possible. Hence I em-ployed a variety of data-collection methods, including simple random surveys of membership records at three points in time, in-depth per-sonal interviews with knowledgeable insiders and external observers, and a detailed analysis of internal and public documents. During my research I was based at the ABCNY and invited to many of its ongoing activities and thus had the rare opportunity of observing at firsthand an elite association in action. The fusion of these several methods of investigation made possible a well-rounded appreciation of the com-plexities of institutional change in a way that the use of any one method could not allow. Examination of processes of adaptation and change requires a developmental rather than a synchronic perspective, and so the analysis presented here covers the post–World War II dec-ades, set against the background of the ABCNY's century-long history,

27. Jacobs, *Stateville*, p. 1.
28. Halliday, *Beyond Monopoly*, p. xviii.

with a particular focus on the 1970s, the decade in which the velocity of change was greatest.

This book, then, is not just an analysis of the processes of organizational change as illustrated by a particular organization, though it is at least that; nor is it solely an examination of the exercise of power by a professional elite, though it is also that. It goes further to examine the means by which an upper-class institution can persist and maintain its elite identity in modern mass society. At the same time, this study investigates the conditions under which elite associations can exercise influence in pluralist structures. The ABCNY was the manifestation of the Northeastern establishment in the highly differentiated and stratified New York bar. Investigation of its varying articulation with an increasingly heterogeneous profession and a changing normative order, together with an examination of its influence capabilities, speaks to an enduring problem of modern democracies: What place remains, if any, for elite institutions in ostensibly democratic and egalitarian societies?

PART ONE

Patrician Professionalism

Chapter One

Urban Reform, Patrician Professionalism, and Social Control

In the latter half of the nineteenth century a new American establishment was forged from the union of the old colonial upper class and the new families of wealth spawned by the industrial age.[1] Whereas the old upper class was essentially defined by lineage and, particularly in the South, ownership of large estates, the new upper class was based upon the possession of wealth as it was accumulated by the great industrialists and financiers of the nineteenth century. Parvenu families such as the Carnegies and the Rockefellers, the Mellons and the Vanderbilts, were quickly accepted and incorporated into this new aristocracy. While the old upper class was largely regional in nature, composed of established families of local note, the new upper class took on a national character as the industrial empires built by its members knew no local or regional limits, and as newly constructed national systems of communication and transportation encouraged its integration. Yet it was heavily biased toward the Northeast, especially with the eclipse of the South following the Civil War and the rise of the industrial cities in the North. In particular, New York City, the preeminent financial and commercial center of the reconstituted nation, was its base.[2] Even though it contained internal divisions that hindered its exercise of power, this Northeastern establishment came to dominate the Republican party and exercise an inordinate influence on national and local affairs well into the twentieth century.[3]

---

1. E. Digby Baltzell, *The Protestant Establishment: Aristocracy and Class in America* (New York: Vintage Books, 1964).

2. For a discussion of the place of New York in the national system of cities in the latter half of the nineteenth century, see David C. Hammack, *Power and Society: Greater New York at the Turn of the Century* (New York: Russell Sage Foundation, 1982).

3. See E. Digby Baltzell, *Philadelphia Gentlemen: The Making of a National Upper Class* (Glencoe, Ill.: The Free Press, 1958).

Threatened by rapid urbanization and an influx of immigrants, the old New England gentry and the new industrial and financial magnates combined to establish a variety of exclusive upper-class associations during the latter decades of the nineteenth century. The exclusive country clubs of the suburbs and men's clubs of the cities, the fashionable summer resorts, the boarding preparatory schools, and the Social Register were new upper-class institutions that gave cohesiveness and identity to this new associational aristocracy. These "patrician protective associations," as Baltzell refers to them, were formed primarily for the purpose of sheltering the upper class from the undesirable elements flooding into the Northeastern cities.[4] They also served to transmit upper-class culture and assimilate newcomers. Behind the walls of these exclusive associations the upper class could maintain its cultural and ethnic homogeneity.

The inclusiveness of this new upper class was strictly limited to persons whose ascriptive characteristics and religious affiliations were the same as those of the old New England families: white and Anglo-Saxon by birth, and Protestant by baptism (WASP). The exclusive upper-class suburbs and summer resorts and country clubs explicitly kept out those without the right parentage and religion no matter what their wealth or position. Successful Jewish financiers and businessmen found the doors of the prestigious city clubs closed to them, forcing them to form their own. Indeed, the late nineteenth and early twentieth centuries saw a resurgence of anti-Semitic sentiment among the WASP establishment coincidental with the rising flood tide of immigration.[5] The new American upper class may have been more open than its European equivalents, but it was open only to those who were white, of North European stock, and Episcopalian, Presbyterian, or Congregationalist.

At the same time as this new American upper class was being consolidated, the modern professions, especially of medicine and law, rose into positions of dominance in the occupational hierarchy. Though law and physic were professions of long standing, their status in mid-nineteenth-century America had been far from secure. Medicine was divided into warring sects, each promising to outperform the others in their competition for clients and recognition, but none demonstrating

---

4. Baltzell, *The Protestant Establishment*, p. 113; for an analysis of the rise of the New England preparatory schools and their role in the consolidation of a national upper class, see Steven B. Levine, "The Rise of American Boarding Schools and the Development of a National Upper Class," *Social Problems* 28 (1980): 63–91.

5. For an extensive discussion of anti-Semitism among the American upper class, see Baltzell, ibid.

any proven ability to heal or save. Practitioners of these various sects, including the so-called regulars who were eventually to come out on top, generally enjoyed little deference and low incomes.[6] At the same time, law had been transformed by the egalitarian pressures of Jacksonian democracy from a relatively exclusive practice based on the English guild model into an open occupation that welcomed all men of good character.[7] The high status and excellent financial rewards of medical or legal practice so evident in the mid-twentieth century were not apparent in pre–Civil War America.

In the latter decades of the nineteenth century the classic professions of law and medicine underwent a renaissance, and new fields of expertise claimed professional status. It was in these decades that the age of "professional dominance," as Illich critically characterizes the modern world, was born.[8] Both old and new professions sought collective upward mobility through the adoption of entrance requirements and the raising of standards. An essential element of this process of professionalization was the formation of professional associations to regulate conduct and promote the interests of the professions. There was a flurry of association building during these decades, with the major professions establishing organizations at the local, state, and national levels. These new associations played an important role in the development and propagation of a professional culture and the definition of the values that would underpin it. They defined the boundaries of acceptable professional conduct and, by creating ethical codes in which this definition was encapsulated, attempted to impose their definition upon their constituencies. Noting that these associations were invariably formed by elite members of the professions, oftentimes members of the Northeastern establishment, some commentators on the rise of the modern professions have linked their purposes to the needs and interests of the new upper class. Indeed, they have seen these associations as imposing a restrictive class-based view of professionalism and in so doing serving the interests of the upper class.[9]

---

6. Paul Starr, *The Social Transformation of American Medicine* (New York: Basic Books, 1982).

7. Roscoe Pound, *The Lawyer from Antiquity to Modern Times* (St. Paul, Minn.: West Publishing Co., 1953).

8. Ivan D. Illich, ed., *Disabling Professions* (London: M. Boyars, 1977).

9. Jerold S. Auerbach, *Unequal Justice: Lawyers and Social Change in Modern America* (New York: Oxford University Press, 1976); Magali Sarfatti Larson, *The Rise of Professionalism: A Sociological Analysis* (Berkeley: University of California Press, 1977).

URBAN REFORM AND PROFESSIONAL ORGANIZATION

The ABCNY was founded in 1870 in response to revelations of widespread political and judicial corruption in New York City, and the legal shenanigans associated with competition for control over the nation's railroads. Tammany Hall and the Irish Democrats had controlled city government and the local judiciary since midcentury. Rumors of corruption on a grand scale circulated frequently, so much so that lawyer and diarist George Templeton Strong complained bitterly in 1868 that "the New Yorker belongs to a community worse governed by lower and baser blackguard scum than any other city in Western Christendom."[10] Although this extreme statement demonstrated the anti-Irish feelings of the old upper-class establishment, which had lost control of city government, it was not just misplaced mugwumpery. Evidence of the misappropriation of vast amounts of money from the public treasury surfaced later during the trial of Tammany Hall's Boss Tweed.

Furthermore, immediately after the Civil War an intense struggle began among railroad entrepreneurs wanting to consolidate their lines, eliminate competition, and develop coherent systems of track, a struggle that continued for much of the remainder of the nineteenth century. In New York there were two particularly bitter battles for control of the state's railroads in the latter part of the 1860s involving the colorful speculators Jim Fisk and Jay Gould and many of the city's leading lawyers.[11] Both of these resulted in well-publicized scandals in which legislators, judges, and lawyers were all implicated. Legislators were bribed to pass legislation favoring particular railroads, judges issued multiple and conflicting injunctions throwing lines into receivership, and lawyers made extensive use of *ex parte* contacts with partial judges in order to gain favorable findings.[12] To many observers the frequent abuse of legal process and procedures by lawyers acting for the railroads in these struggles, and the connivance of judges in this abuse, made a mockery of the law and threatened its integrity and legitimacy.

---

10. Quoted in George Martin, *Causes and Conflicts: The Centennial History of the Association of the Bar of the City of New York* (Boston: Houghton Mifflin, 1970), p. 3. Martin's centennial history is excellent, and much of this material relating to the founding of the ABCNY comes from it.

11. For a brief discussion of these struggles to consolidate the state's railroads, see Martin, *Causes and Conflicts*, pp. 3–15.

12. *Ex Parte* means on one side only, or from one party. A judicial proceeding is said to be *ex parte* when it is granted at the instance of one party only and without notice to, or contestation by, any other party adversely interested (*Black's Law Dictionary*, 1979, p. 517).

In reaction to numerous complaints about the manipulation and corruption of the legal system, the *New York Times* on June 20, 1869, called for the formation of "a permanent, strong and influential association of lawyers for mutual protection and benefit."[13] Noting that individual lawyers are powerless to resist the influence of judges, the *Times* concluded that united action and organization on the part of highly respected members of the bar were necessary if lawyers were to stand up to the judiciary and to the political machine that elected them. There was no immediate response by the city's prominent lawyers, but following a second plea by the *Times* some months later,[14] and after a particularly nasty physical conflict over a strategic section of upstate New York track demonstrated once again the abuse of legal process by prominent members of the bar, a "call for organization" circulated privately among leading members of the New York bar, eventually leading to an organizational meeting and the founding of the ABCNY.[15]

At this meeting, attended by nearly two hundred "of the decent part of the profession," the proposers of the new association made clear their intentions.[16] Foremost among them was the restoration of "the honor, integrity and fame of the profession in its two manifestations of the Bench and Bar." With the recent railroad imbroglios clearly on their minds, the future members of the ABCNY applauded vigorously when the practice of getting *ex parte* writs through backdoor access to compliant judges was attacked. While a specific reform agenda was not proposed, a passionate speech by Samuel J. Tilden, a prominent lawyer and reform politician, expressed the reformist intentions of many of those present. Calling for an aggressive association of lawyers, Tilden proclaimed that the bar "can have reformed constitutions, . . . a reformed judiciary, . . . the administration of justice made pure and honorable" if only it would assert itself. If New York was to remain the commercial and monetary capital of the United States, Tilden contended, "it must establish an elevated character for its Bar, and a reputation throughout the country for its purity in the administration of justice."[17]

Despite Tilden's strident call to action, the new association did not immediately commit its energies to reform but, instead, was content

---

13. Martin, *Causes and Conflicts*, p. 12.

14. Ibid., p. 15.

15. Ibid.

16. This account of the meeting to organize the ABCNY is drawn from Martin, *Causes and Conflicts*, chap. 3.

17. Quoted in Martin, *Causes and Conflicts*, p. 38.

during its first eighteen months of existence to establish itself in a commodious and comfortably furnished brownstone home complete with rare books, busts of eminent lawyers, and a librarian. As a consequence, *The Albany Law Journal* complained in March 1871 that the influence of the new association "is seen neither in court nor legislature, nor in the morals or manners of the bar."[18] It soon was to become, however, actively involved in the urban reform movement. Members of the ABCNY led the fight against Tammany Hall and the Tweed Ring in the mid-1870s and, indeed, prosecuted Tweed and his cronies in the city's courts.[19] Leaders of the ABCNY were also instrumental in founding the Committee of Seventy, an organization of leading business and professional men committed to unmasking corruption and improving city government. One of the most prominent of the urban reformers of this period, Dorman B. Eaton, was a lawyer and a founding member of the ABCNY. For the remainder of the century elite corporate lawyers were to be found in large numbers in the urban reform movements.[20]

For its part, the ABCNY took the lead in pressing for the impeachment of several judges, all of whom owed their positions to Tweed and Tammany Hall and whose judicial conduct reflected that debt, and in lobbying for a constitutional amendment to change the way judges were selected. While successful in unseating the three Tammany judges accused of improper conduct, the ABCNY was unsuccessful in its efforts to have judges appointed rather than elected, a change that would have significantly weakened Tammany's control over the judiciary.[21] The ABCNY and its members, then, played a major part in what historians have referred to as the "genteel reform" movement of the 1870s, in which patrician leaders sought to regenerate city government.[22] By the 1880s, however, leadership in the urban reform movement had passed to new citizens' organizations in which lawyers often played dominating roles but with the ABCNY in the background. Yet, its reputation as a "good government" organization established, the

---

18. Ibid., p. 47.

19. For an account of the ABCNY's involvement in reform activities, see Martin, *Causes and Conflicts*, chaps. 5 and 6.

20. Robert W. Gordon, "Legal Thought and Legal Practice in the Age of American Enterprise, 1870–1920," in Gerald L. Geison, ed., *Professions and Professional Ideologies in America* (Chapel Hill: University of North Carolina Press, 1983), p. 80.

21. Martin, *Causes and Conflicts*, chap. 6.

22. See, generally, David C. Hammack, *Power and Society*. Also, Gerald W. McFarland, "Partisan of Non-Partisanship: Dorman B. Eaton and the Genteel Reform Tradition," *Journal of American History* 54 (1968): 806–822; John G. Sproat, *The Best Men: Liberal Reformers in the Gilded Age* (New York: Oxford University Press, 1968).

ABCNY from time to time in the future took up cudgels against Tammany Hall—particularly over the selection of judges.

The formation of the ABCNY and other metropolitan bar associations, and of the American Bar Association (ABA) in 1878, was motivated in large part by the reformist intent of established patrician lawyers.[23] Why was the chaotic state of the law and the low standard of conduct of judges and lawyers such a prominent concern for them when leading lawyers themselves regularly took advantage of overlapping jurisdictions, inconsistent statutes, and partial judges in representing their clients? After all, the lions of the New York bar, including the president-to-be of the ABCNY, William M. Evarts, the president of the New York Law Institute, Charles O'Conor, and the leading law reformer of the time, David Dudley Field, were arrayed on both sides of the infamous railroad battles, engaging in the very activities said to undermine respect for the law.[24]

One answer is that of Max Weber, who emphasized the importance, to the advance of capitalism, of a formally rational and predictable legal system.[25] According to this view, calculability of outcomes was critical to investors and financiers, with the uncertainties introduced by the intervention of the personalistic rule of machine politicians decidedly unsettling. Ideally, the legal system should display the same attributes as bureaucracy in the system of rational-legal domination characteristic of advanced capitalism: the predominance of rules, the separation of personal predilections from public responsibilities, and the exclusion of personal obligations and ties. If decisions are based upon the systematic and consistent application of rules and precedents, without the distortion introduced by personal prejudices or obligations, then the calculability of their outcomes is greatly enhanced and rational investment decisions and planning are possible. Corporate lawyers, then, could be expected to work for the rationalization of the legal system, particularly as it was the established economic interests they represented that stood to benefit most from the consistent rule of law.

The problem with this account, intuitively attractive though it may be, is that there is little indication that established economic interests

---

23. John A. Matzko, " 'The Best Men of the Bar': The Founding of the American Bar Association," in Gerard W. Gawalt, ed., *The New High Priests: Lawyers in Post–Civil War America* (Westport, Conn.: Greenwood Press, 1984.)

24. Robert W. Gordon, " 'The Ideal and the Actual in the Law': Fantasies and Practices of New York City Lawyers, 1870–1910," in Gawalt, *The New High Priests*, pp. 56–57.

25. Max Weber, *On Law in Economy and Society* (New York: Simon and Schuster, 1954), pp. 350–351.

actually desired law reform. Rather, as Harry Scheiber shows, business entrepreneurs viewed the inconsistent, unreformed nature of law as a positive advantage.[26] It afforded them cover through its ambiguity and inconsistency, and allowed them to hinder and delay legal decisions unfavorable to their interests. Presenting an alternative explanation, Robert Gordon notes that a substantial number of elite corporate lawyers in the late nineteenth century had patrician Whig aspirations "to play a distinctive role in American society, . . . mediating between capital and labor, between private acquisitiveness and democratic redistributive follies," aspirations that played themselves out in the urban and judicial reform movements of the time.[27] Decrying the breakdown of the liberal order as manifested in the embarrassing lack of uniformity in the law and of impartiality in its application, these Tocquevillean lawyer-aristocrats sought to repair the situation through the restoration of the liberal legal ideal in which the boundaries of private and public action were clearly demarcated, individual rights well-defined and certain, and procedures regular and consistent. To achieve these ends it was necessary not only to promote law reform—the scientific refinement of the law so that its general principles were clarified and anomalies and anachronisms excised—but also to free the legal system from the particularism and partiality brought about by political interference most frequently manifested in the patronage appointment, or machine-controlled, election of judges.

Furthermore, the scientific reform of the legal system would extricate the reformers from the predicament in which they found themselves as agents for private interests taking advantage of the inconsistencies of the law and the particularism of judges at the very time they preached the virtues of the common law. As Gordon observes, "It is difficult to escape the conclusion that the reformers' program was partially embraced as a cure for their own condition."[28] If legal rights were certain, jurisdictional inconsistencies removed, and procedures clear and universal in their application, "the advantages accruing from illegitimate tactics would simply disappear, and lawyers could keep their clients within the law."[29]

In an earlier essay, Gordon demonstrates how elite lawyers could achieve this happy condition through an examination of the reform of the corporate reorganization law carried out by eminent New York

---

26. Harry Scheiber, "Federalism and the American Economic Order, 1789–1910," *Law and Society Review* 10 (1975): 57–118.

27. Gordon, " 'The Ideal and the Actual,' " p. 56.

28. Ibid., p. 57.

29. Ibid.

practitioners in the 1880s.[30] Practice in this area had been very disorderly and unseemly, with creditors and their lawyers rushing to the courtroom to have *ex parte* injunctions issued and friendly receivers appointed by partial judges. The room for corruption was unlimited. By the end of the 1880s, however, the procedures in reorganization practice had been centralized and rationalized, and a systematic and predictable process put in place. Elite reorganization lawyers no longer had to race to the courthouse and use illegitimate tactics. But the rationalization of the system benefited the corporate insiders, the management, who received judicial protection and priority in the settlement of claims. Elite lawyers had reformed the system, removing much of the chaos and reducing the unseemly competition for favors, but in so doing had institutionalized the advantage of their most important clients.

Law and judicial reform were concerns that mobilized leading lawyers into forming bar associations in the 1870s and which continued to exercise them well into the twentieth century. Bar associations such as the ABCNY established law reform committees to draft and promote clearly stated uniform laws and legislative committees to monitor and comment on the draftsmanship and consistency of impending legislation. They also continued to press for the "merit selection" of judges as a way to diminish the particularistic control of political machines over the courts, and in the meantime attempted to act as gatekeepers to the bench by evaluating and reporting on the qualifications of candidates nominated by the political parties for election to judicial positions.[31]

BEST MEN OF THE BAR
AND PATRICIAN PROFESSIONALISM

Critical treatments of the urban reform movement of the late nineteenth century have seen it as motivated as much by anti-immigrant and anti-ethnic bias as by a genuine concern over corruption and the quality of city government. As Gordon observes, "reform in the name of scientific professionalism was among other things an ideology of middle-class, native-born whites."[32] Although it might produce more efficient urban government it could also be used to keep power out of

---

30. Gordon, "Legal Thought and Legal Practice," pp. 101–103.

31. It was not just the patrician ABCNY that sought to separate the legal and political spheres, but also the more broadly based Chicago Bar Association. See Terence C. Halliday, *Beyond Monopoly: Lawyers, State Crises and Professional Empowerment* (Chicago: University of Chicago Press, 1987).

32. Gordon, " 'The Ideal and the Actual,' " p. 53.

efficient urban government it could also be used to keep power out of the hands of new immigrant groups and other undesirables. In a similar vein, revisionist accounts of the professionalization process and the formation of professional associations in the late nineteenth century stress their origins in the nativist, anti-immigrant sentiment of the Protestant elite.[33] Indeed, one did not have to scratch far below the genteel surface to find the anti-Irish feelings of the Anglo-Protestant elite that founded the ABCNY. Noted diarist and founding member, George Templeton Strong, referred to the city's leaders as "blackguard Celtic tyrants" who are members of "a race not remarked for its love of other people's liberties,"[34] and one of the ABCNY's early presidents, Joseph H. Choate, suggested to the Friendly Sons of Saint Patrick in an after-dinner speech that should the multitude of Irishmen in the United States return home and take up arms they could throw out the British and at last "Ireland would be for Irishmen and America for Americans."[35]

The anti-Irish sentiment of the founders of the ABCNY was reflected in the selection of the first president of the ABCNY, a choice demonstrating that professional standing was not the only, or most important, consideration in the selection of leaders. Social origins and background characteristics were also crucial criteria. Perhaps the most obvious candidate for the position was Charles O'Conor, one of the outstanding advocates of his day and a leader of the bar. At the time he was president of the New York Law Institute, the only collegial organization of lawyers in New York to survive the leveling trends of the Jacksonian period, albeit merely in the form of a library and meeting place. But O'Conor was the son of poor Irish immigrants who had to work his way through school and into the practice of law, not attending an Ivy League college or law school along the way. Never fully accepted among the social elite of the city, and not prone to show deference to them, O'Conor's name does not even appear among the subscribers to the "call for organization." Although O'Conor became a member almost immediately after the ABCNY was formed, he was never to hold any leadership office.[36]

In direct contrast to O'Conor, William M. Evarts, who was elected unopposed as the first president of the ABCNY and occupied the office for the first decade of its history, was descended from an old Protestant

---

33. Auerbach, *Unequal Justice;* Larson, *The Rise of Professionalism;* Randall Collins, *The Credential Society* (New York: Academic Press, 1979).

34. Quoted in Hammack, *Power and Society,* p. 8.

35. Quoted in Martin, *Causes and Conflicts,* p. 178.

36. For a brief biography of O'Conor, see Martin, *Causes and Conflicts,* pp. 22–24.

New England family and graduated from Yale University and Harvard Law School.[37] Furthermore, he was a leading figure in the Republican party of Lincoln and Seward and was active on the national political scene. Evarts had all the right credentials for the position: He was an outstanding lawyer with a national reputation and, importantly, he had the "correct" social background. By their nomination of Evarts, the organizers indicated the type of association they had in mind. Though he may have been atypical of members of the ABCNY in terms of his national prominence, Evarts was highly typical in terms of his Anglo-Saxon, Protestant background. Aspiring to play the role of Tocquevillean lawyer-aristocrats, the leaders of the New York bar and of the ABCNY in the latter decades of the nineteenth century were generally not of aristocratic origins. Rather, like Evarts, they were the sons of upstate New York and New England gentry, the descendents of small-town Protestant ministers, doctors, and lawyers.[38]

Once in New York, however, and having achieved a modicum of professional success and reputation, these sons of upstate gentry quickly became part of the patrician elite of the city. Graduates of Ivy League colleges and law schools, they were welcomed in the most exclusive clubs of the city and were invariably listed in the *Social Register,* a directory to New York's Protestant establishment. Indeed, every one of the twenty lawyers who served as president of the ABCNY from its beginnings in 1870 until 1920 was listed in the New York *Social Register,* along with the leading families of the city. The leaders of the ABCNY may not have been born aristocrats but they were certainly part of the upper-class establishment of New York City. As the ABCNY's centennial historian admitted of its early leaders: "They genuinely loved Harvard and Yale, and many of them loved the Protestant church."[39]

That membership in the ABCNY would be restricted to an elite group of the New York bar was made clear at its inception. The original "call for organization," inviting interested persons to an initial meeting, was circulated only to a select group of leading lawyers. No attempt was made to publicize the first meeting, to draw it to the attention of all lawyers interested in the cause of reform whatever their eminence or background. Indeed, the notice sent out to subscribers to the "call," informing them of the meeting place and time, suggested they "preserve this notice and present it at the door."[40] The intention

---

37. For an account of Evarts's career, see Martin, *Causes and Conflicts,* pp. 23–27.
38. Gordon, " 'The Ideal and the Actual,' " p. 56.
39. Martin, *Causes and Conflicts,* p. 179.
40. Ibid., p. 28.

clearly was to keep out those without invitations. As George Martin notes: "The proposed association gave promise of being not only active, agreeable and talented but also exclusive."[41]

Membership was to be restricted to "the more worthy of the profession," thereby contributing to the restoration of status distinctions in the bar, distinctions that had been demolished by mid-century Jacksonian democracy. Earlier in the century there had been stringent requirements for admission to the bar, together with the stratification of the profession into three ranks—attorneys, solicitors, and counselors.[42] All this was swept away by the new constitution for New York State adopted in 1846 whereby judges were to be elected, not appointed, and requirements for admission to the bar reduced to the barest minimum. Status distinctions among lawyers also disappeared so that, as one speaker bemoaned at the organizing meeting, "Every man, from the merest tyro to the greatest and most renowned amongst us, was put on the same footing."[43] While the patrician leaders of the New York bar no longer controlled admission to the profession, by forming an exclusive association in which membership was restricted to those deemed worthy they could distance themselves from the mass of lawyers "seen in almost all our courts, slovenly in dress, uncouth in manners and habits, ignorant even of the English language, jostling and crowding and vulgarizing the profession."[44] Comments such as these, which were commonplace in the late nineteenth century, clearly manifested the nativist, anti-immigrant sentiment of the patrician leaders of the bar who founded the ABCNY and served as its leaders. Although presenting itself as a professional association open to all who were worthy, the neophyte ABCNY appeared to many to be of the same ilk as the other "patrician protective associations" formed in the latter decades of the nineteenth century to provide shelter from the invasion of undesirables.[45]

Following an expressly elitest organizing philosophy, the new association did not actively solicit new members from the expanding New York bar but rather constructed an elaborate admissions process that could only serve to discourage many potential applicants at the same time that it ensured the preservation of the ABCNY's homogeneity. Candidates for membership had to be sponsored, that is, proposed and seconded by existing members, and they were required to provide four

41. Ibid.
42. Ibid., pp. 31–34.
43. Ibid., p. 33.
44. Quoted in Matzko, "The Best Men of the Bar," p. 78.
45. See Baltzell, *The Protestant Establishment*.

references from among the existing membership as to their standing in the bar and their character. In addition, the candidate had to list a further two members of the Association from whom the Committee on Admissions could seek further references if necessary. If a candidate could find the necessary sponsorship, he was still subject to screening and interview by the Committee on Admissions. The committee was not the final stage in the process, however, as it only made recommendations as to the acceptability of candidates. The final say as to whether to admit a candidate rested with the members at large who, assembled in a members' meeting, voted on the admission of those recommended by the committee. A lawyer seeking membership, then, had to have the support of eight current members, pass the screening of the Committee on Admissions, and receive the positive vote of the membership. Moreover, he had to have the wherewithal to pay the fifty-dollar admission fee and the annual dues of forty dollars, not inconsiderable sums at that time.

Requirements such as these, far from encouraging new membership, served to restrict the ABCNY to a small, homogeneous group of lawyers known to one another and with similar social and legal qualifications. In 1871 the New York bar was estimated to total almost 4000 persons and yet the ABCNY had enrolled only 462 members, little more than 10 percent. Suggesting that the ABCNY would only be effective in achieving reform if it lowered its dues and welcomed all reputable lawyers into membership, *The Albany Law Journal* complained that the Bar Association "partakes too much of the character of a close corporation, or of what the people call a ring, to bring into sympathy with it any considerable number of the lawyers of the city."[46] There was the clear implication in the ABCNY's membership policy that not all lawyers, even those in good standing, were worthy of admission. The extended admissions procedures served to keep a suitable distance between the "best men" of the bar, who were included in the ABCNY, and the unworthy masses who were unwelcome. Undisturbed by such criticism, the ABCNY maintained its restrictive admissions procedures for a hundred years, until the 1970s, in fact, and thereby reproduced over the years its exclusive character. Not only were its leaders for the next century prominent lawyers, members of the most exclusive social clubs, and frequently listed in the Social Register, but its membership also constituted a select minority of the New York bar. As a consequence, the ABCNY has been accurately viewed for much of its history

---

46. Martin, *Causes and Conflicts*, p. 48.

as representing the WASP, upper-class elite of the city and manifesting patrician professionalism within an increasingly diverse bar.

THE RISE OF THE LARGE LAW FIRM

The founders and early leaders of the ABCNY, men like Evarts, Carter, and Choate, were eminent advocates and noted orators who made their reputations in the courtroom defending a variety of clients. They did not solely represent businesses or practice only business law. Both Evarts and O'Conor, for instance, were involved in sensational divorce and immorality trials.[47] In the decades following the formation of the ABCNY, however, the professional identity of the leaders of the New York bar and of the ABCNY began to change. In the late nineteenth century, accompanying the emergence of the large business corporation and the growing importance of business and corporate law was the appearance of the large law firm, organized to serve efficiently the multiple legal needs of the new financial and industrial behemoths. Rather than law firms being simply a convenient combination of lawyers sharing office space and overhead costs, who otherwise practiced relatively independently, the new large firms emphasized the specialization and interdependence of its members. Revenues were pooled and distributed among the members of the firm on a percentage basis, and associates were hired straight from law school as salaried associates with the possibility of an eventual promotion to partner. The legal needs of the corporate clients of these firms required office work rather than litigation, consisting "mostly of drafting instruments such as charters, leases, mortgages, bond indentures, and reorganization plans to comply with such [state corporation] laws."[48] Consequently, the dominant figures in this new legal institution were not advocates of the old school but "office lawyers," men who rarely ventured into courtrooms but sat on corporate boards and advised heads of corporations and banks.

In his study of the emergence of the large law firm, Wayne K. Hobson argues that large law firms with their rationalized organizational structure and recruitment practices became essential only when "industrial corporations requiring continuous legal supervision" became the main clients of business lawyers.[49] Consequently, from the twenty embryonic large firms in New York in the 1890s with five or more partners

---

47. Evarts defended Henry Ward Beecher against charges of adultery in a famous trial, and O'Conor several times represented parties in divorce disputes.

48. Gordon, "Legal Thought and Legal practice," p. 73.

49. Wayne K. Hobson, "Symbol of the New Profession: Emergence of the Large Law Firm, 1870–1915," in Gawalt, ed., *The New High Priests*, p. 8.

and associates, there emerged several very large firms, or "law facto-ries," such as Cravath, Swaine, & Seward and Sullivan & Cromwell in the twentieth century coincident with the emergence of very large ag-glomerations of capital such as the Pennsylvania Railroad and United States Steel. Cravath, Swaine, & Seward (later Cravath, Swaine & Moore), the archetypical large firm, already included nineteen lawyers in 1908 and expanded to ninety-four by 1940.[50] Though New York was not the only city in which large law firms emerged around the turn of the century, it did have the greatest concentration of them, reflecting its position as the nation's financial and commercial center. By 1915 there were fifty-one firms in New York with five or more partners or associates and fourteen with ten or more members.[51] In other cities there were not enough large firms to form a self-contained elite of the bar drawn from their members, but in New York, by the early years of the twentieth century, there was a sufficient density of these lawyers to form a new professional elite. Consequently, the elite of the bar in other large cities remained relatively heterogeneous in terms of the types of practice represented within it while that of New York became increasingly homogeneous, with large-firm lawyers dominant.

Not all the members of this new elite around the turn of the century were from the large law factories such as Cravath, Swaine, & Seward and Sullivan & Cromwell, but most were corporation lawyers rather than trial lawyers. Francis Lynde Stetson and Elihu Root, for instance, who had withdrawn from trial work entirely in the 1890s to concentrate on advising business clients on matters of finance and corporate reor-ganization, did not care to practice in very large firms and insisted on limiting the growth of their own firms.[52] But their practices and clien-tele were little different from those of Paul Cravath and William Crom-well, and after their retirement their firms followed the same organi-zational path. Significantly, Stetson and Root were elected presidents of the ABCNY soon after the turn of the century, as were other cor-poration lawyers and founders of large corporate firms such as John L. Cadwalader, Lewis Cass Ledyard, and George W. Wickersham. From this time onward the leadership of the ABCNY came overwhelmingly from the ranks of the senior partners of the large firms.

This new professional elite of corporate lawyers that led the ABCNY in the twentieth century was no less WASPish than its predecessor. Indeed, it may have been more exclusive and restrictive because it was

---

50. Collins, *The Credential Society*, p. 152. For a detailed account of the development of the Cravath firm, see Robert T. Swaine, *The Cravath Firm and Its Predecessors 1819–1947* (New York: Ad Press, 1947).

51. Hobson, "Symbol of the New Profession," tables 2 and 3, pp. 11, 18.

52. Martin, *Causes and Conflicts*, pp. 188–191.

more difficult for ethnic outsiders to gain entry to an elite defined by partnership in a few select firms than it was to earn professional standing as successful trial lawyers. Institutionalized when nativist sentiment was at its peak, and upper-class, native-born Americans were establishing exclusive clubs, neighborhoods, and summer resorts to which they could retreat from the increasingly heterogeneous city, the large law firm became yet another exclusive organization from which undesirable ethnic newcomers could be excluded. Just as big business became "a new preserve of the older Americans, where their status and influence could continue and flourish . . . ," so too did the large law firms that served them. Both "restricted access to those who presented proper ethnic and social credentials."[53] Hiring new members directly from Harvard, Yale, and Columbia, the leaders of the large law firms were able to ensure that the "best men"—for they were all men—who entered their portals were of North European stock and Protestant persuasion like themselves. It was this homogeneous professional elite, with "a predilection to aristocratic demeanour,"[54] that dominated the ABCNY in the twentieth century, maintaining its patrician culture and attempting to impose upon the profession at large, and the wider legal system, its values and norms.

POLICING THE BAR AND SCREENING THE JUDICIARY

The ABCNY provided not only a refuge for native-born WASPs from the hurly-burly of an increasingly heterogeneous and crowded profession, but also a vehicle through which the WASP legal establishment could exert influence over the profession and the legal system. Concerned with the conduct of lawyers and the independence and quality of the judiciary, the leaders of the ABCNY founded in 1870 committees on grievances (to hear grievances against lawyers) and the judiciary to address these areas. Through these committees the ABCNY sought to improve the standards of the bar and the bench through the investigation of complaints against lawyers and judges and the initiation of disciplinary action or impeachment proceedings where warranted. The Committee on the Judiciary also later commenced the practice of screening lawyers nominated for judicial positions by the political parties in an attempt to keep unqualified candidates off the bench. In establishing these committees the ABCNY was taking the moral high ground and asserting that, although representing a minority of the

---

53. Auerbach, *Unequal Justice, p. 21.*
54. Hobson, "Symbol of the New Profession," p. 14.

members of the New York bar, it could and would define acceptable standards of professional and judicial conduct and act to discipline those lawyers or judges who brought the bar and bench into disrepute.

Although established in 1870, the Committee on Grievances did little until the late 1870s, when the ABCNY agreed to investigate and press charges against an attorney who had bribed a witness.[55] In doing so, the ABCNY's committee was establishing an important precedent, for in the past only the courts had initiated proceedings against lawyers for misconduct. Despite de facto recognition by the New York courts as a legitimate agency to investigate complaints against lawyers, and to prosecute if necessary, following the success of this initial action, the grievance committee remained relatively inactive until the middle of the 1880s. A major question that needed to be resolved was whether the committee had authority to investigate and act upon complaints brought against nonmembers as well as members of the Association. In 1884 the question was answered when members of the ABCNY voted to extend the committee's purview to include all lawyers practicing in Manhattan and the Bronx, whether or not members. In the first year after this new bylaw was adopted the committee received twelve complaints, nine of which were brought against nonmembers of the ABCNY, demonstrating the immediate impact of the expansion in the committee's reach.[56]

In taking upon itself this responsibility and authority, the ABCNY did not usurp the role of some other agency but rather stepped into a vacuum. No other agency was actively engaged in regulating the conduct of lawyers. Although the courts certainly had the power to do so, they lacked the resources or desire to police the profession. Generally, to the extent that the courts were concerned about lawyers' conduct at all, their interest was limited to what took place in court and to activities directly related to courtroom proceedings. Laypersons complaining about the treatment they had received in a lawyer's office had great difficulty in getting anyone to listen to their complaints, much less to act upon them. The ABCNY's establishment of the Committee on Grievances, and the assertion of its intent to investigate complaints against all lawyers, represented a substantial change not just in the number of complaints received but also in the kinds of misconduct subject to investigation and discipline. Now there was a body that would hear complaints against lawyers, "not so much for their actions in

---

55. The following outline of the development of the Committee on Grievances is drawn from Martin, *Causes and Conflicts*, chap. 20.

56. Ibid., p. 360.

courtrooms as for their actions, or failures to act, outside them."[57] In future years, the vast majority of discipline actions brought against lawyers related to non-courtroom offences such as the conversion of clients' funds, client neglect, and client solicitation.[58]

By 1892, as Martin observes, the chief purpose and activity of the grievance committee was clear: "It would receive complaints against lawyers from any source, it would investigate them, and where disciplinary action seemed appropriate it would petition the Supreme Court to act."[59] Although only the Court had the authority to suspend or disbar an attorney, the committee, and through it the ABCNY, exercised considerable discretionary authority in determining which complaints to investigate and which to dismiss as being unfounded or outside the committee's compass. It also had the authority to initiate investigations without prior complaints having been received, an authority that was used infrequently because of the committee's limited resources, but was still a potential source of power over the bar at large. Thus in the 1930s, when the ABCNY launched an intensive investigation of client solicitation on the part of personal injury lawyers, otherwise known as ambulance chasers, it was the grievance committee that heard and prosecuted charges brought against individual attorneys. The grievance committee, then, provided the patrician ABCNY with the means by which it could clamp down on particular practices it deemed unprofessional and particularly undesirable.

In successfully establishing a grievance committee that would investigate complaints and bring charges against lawyers, the ABCNY was a pioneer in professional self-regulation, providing a model for other associations to emulate. Soon thereafter most local, metropolitan, and state bar associations formed discipline committees and, following the ABCNY, asserted their right to investigate complaints against all lawyers in their regions, whether members or not. While the commitment of many local and metropolitan bar associations to lawyer discipline was largely rhetorical, the ABCNY took the responsibility seriously and allocated substantial organizational resources to it. As early as 1906 the grievance committee hired its first full-time attorney, and by 1912 it had developed into a sizable operation that absorbed as much as 25 percent of the ABCNY's annual expenditures and employed five attorneys and

---

57. Ibid.

58. See Jerome E. Carlin, *Lawyers' Ethics: A Survey of the New York Bar* (New York: Russell Sage Foundation, 1966); S. Arthurs, "Discipline in the Legal Profession in Ontario," *Osgoode Hall Law Journal* 7 (1970): 261.

59. Martin, *Causes and Conflicts*, p. 361.

several clerks.[60] In committing such resources to the committee, the ABCNY was responding to its increased work load as the number of complaints it received rose dramatically after the turn of the century, reaching a peak of 907 in 1912.[61] That same year the committee held 140 "trials" or hearings resulting in 56 recommendations for discipline. Although the final number of lawyers disciplined has always been a small percentage of those about whom complaints are received, and a very small proportion of the total number of lawyers in practice, from the perspective of the ABCNY the commitment of time and resources to lawyer discipline was substantial. The 140 trials in 1912 represented almost three hearings per week, which required the attendance of members of the committee to consider the charges and decide as to disposition. Despite the grievance committee's slow start, then, by World War I it had become a major component of the ABCNY and an important fixture in the New York bar.

The Committee on Judiciary began its active life in 1872 by successfully bringing charges against three judges accused of improper conduct who were closely associated with Boss Tweed and Tammany Hall.[62] Two of the judges were impeached and removed from office by the senate of the state legislature; the third resigned from office prior to the hearings. Following this success the ABCNY sought to bypass Tammany Hall by having judges appointed by the governor instead of elected in what was the first of many unsuccessful attempts to have an appointive system replace that of popular election. In New York, the election of judges typically meant the unopposed election of candidates nominated by the political parties because of their political loyalties, oftentimes irrespective of their legal acuity or experience. The electoral system enabled the political parties to exercise considerable influence over the judiciary, and was an important source of patronage for Tammany Hall, which used judicial positions as rewards for its supporters. The ABCNY's consistent efforts to replace the election of judges with an appointive system reflected its long-term interest both in removing the legal system from the patrimonial authority of the party bosses and in improving the quality of the bench by institutionalizing a merit selection process.

---

60. Ibid., p. 366. Compare the ABCNY's commitment of resources to that of the Chicago Bar Association, which did not appoint even a full-time investigator to grievance work until 1965. See Michael J. Powell, "Divestiture; The Cession of Responsibility for Lawyer Discipline," *American Bar Foundation Research Journal* (1986): 31–54.

61. Martin, *Causes and Conflicts*, p. 364.

62. Ibid., chap. 6.

Failing in its efforts in 1873 to have the election of judges replaced by appointment, the judiciary committee thereafter concentrated its energies on screening the candidates proposed by the political parties in the hope of influencing the outcomes of the electoral process and on investigating complaints of misconduct made against sitting judges. In adopting these two tasks, the judiciary committee refused to restrict itself to Manhattan and the Bronx, as did the grievance committee, but rather insisted on reviewing candidates for judicial positions, and investigating complaints about judicial conduct, in all five counties of New York—Brooklyn, the Bronx, Queens, and Staten Island as well as Manhattan—even though the ABCNY had very few members who practiced in counties other than New York or who were familiar with their courts. It continued to review candidates from these counties even when local county bar associations began their own evaluations and made plain their opposition to what they viewed as the ABCNY's intrusion on their turf. In claiming citywide jurisdiction, the ABCNY was in effect discounting the evaluations of the local county associations and asserting that it alone possessed the knowledge and moral virtue to screen adequately candidates for local and state benches. Later in the twentieth century the ABCNY unsuccessfully attempted to persuade the leaders of the political parties to allow its committee to screen candidates before nomination with the understanding that the parties would nominate only those the ABCNY found to be qualified.[63] In attempting to make these arrangements, the ABCNY sought to install itself as a gatekeeper controlling access to the local and state benches.

There was some incongruence in the ABCNY's active role in screening judicial candidates and investigating complaints against judges: It presumed to act as gatekeeper and moral arbiter for conduct in arenas in which few of its members practiced. As we have noted, the ABCNY was increasingly dominated by large-firm, corporate lawyers. Karl Llewellyn observed that in the early twentieth century this large-firm elite moved "mass-wise" out of the courts and into a largely office practice, advising corporate executives rather than litigating.[64] Few lawyers from large firms were likely to seek judicial positions in the local and state courts as they carried relatively low salaries and little prestige in the corporate lawyers' world. In contrast, for local lawyers practicing in the "personal plight" sphere where there was a rapid turnover of clients, income often uncertain, and retirement benefits rare, a local or

---

63. Ibid., chap. 18.

64. Karl N. Llewellyn, *The Bramble Bush: On Our Law and Its Study* (Dobbs Ferry, N.Y.: Oceana, 1981). See also Martin, *Causes and Conflicts*, pp. 191–192.

state judgeship offered financial security and high standing in local communities. The elite corporate lawyers of the judiciary committee, then, passed on the qualifications of candidates for benches before which they never appeared and investigated the conduct of judges in courts with which they were unfamiliar. Such distance from the objects of their investigation and evaluation undoubtedly facilitated objectivity and protected committee members from any judicial retaliation, but to members of the local bars in the five counties it manifested the attempt of the patrician, large-firm elite of the bar to impose its criteria and standards upon their courts and judiciary.

Why was the work of the judiciary and grievance committees of such importance to the ABCNY? The judiciary and grievance committees were prestigious committees within the Association; membership on them was a stepping-stone to leadership positions. Apart from the library, there were no other areas of activity into which the ABCNY consistently channeled so much energy and so many resources. Its grievance work became the model of the nation, earning plaudits even in the midst of severe criticism of the adequacy of the organized bar's efforts in this area in the 1960s.[65] Why should the ABCNY be concerned about the quality of judges and standards of conduct in courts in which few of its members practiced? And why should it seek to regulate the conduct of lawyers with whom its members rarely dealt and whose misdeeds did not harm them directly?

One answer is that these committees and their work were the means by which the patrician WASP elite controlled the mass of the New York bar, a bar that was increasingly composed of members of recent immigrant ethnic groups. To many observers, the ethical strictures of the profession enforced by the ABCNY were biased against the urban, small-firm, or solo practitioner struggling to make a living out of the law.[66] For instance, immortalizing a past reality of the small-town lawyer whose reputation spreads by word of mouth in a *Gemeinschaft* society, the Canon of Ethics adopted by the American Bar Association in 1908 and subsequently enforced by the ABCNY's grievance committee proscribed client-getting activities such as the advertising, self-promotion, and solicitation that might be necessary for a young lawyer to establish a practice in a *Gesellschaft* city of strangers. Practitioners in the less rewarding "personal plight" hemisphere of the law, usually in-

---

65. See American Bar Association, Report of the Special Committee on Evaluation of Disciplinary Enforcement (June, 1970). This report pointed to the ABCNY's Committee on Grievances as one of the few in the nation that was at all effective.

66. Auerbach, *Unequal Justice*, pp. 40–53; Philip Schuchman, "Ethics and Legal Ethics," *George Washington Law Review* 37 (1968–1969): 244–269.

volving personal injury, divorce, and criminal defense work, were often caught up in an ongoing scramble for clients whom typically they represented on a one-shot basis. In contrast, large-firm lawyers usually had a more stable clientele of business corporations with recurring legal needs. Even so, large-firm lawyers engaged in their own subtle form of client solicitation by cultivating contacts and friendships with persons likely to bring corporate business to their law firms. In prosecuting lawyers accused of soliciting personal injury clients through ambulance chasing while ignoring these more subtle forms of solicitation, the grievance committee attempted to regulate the nonelite segments of the bar whose practices the patrician elite found distasteful.[67]

Increasingly, especially in the large urban areas, personal plight practitioners were of recent immigrant background, frequently Southern or Eastern European in origin and Jewish or Catholic in religion. As the ethical code of the profession appeared to be weighted against these small-firm and solo practitioners, and as they were more likely than WASP corporate lawyers to be the targets of disciplinary action, Auerbach argues strongly that the officially approved ethical norms and disciplinary apparatus of the organized bar were largely directed against the growing numbers of ethnic lawyers.[68] Certainly, the ABCNY's construction and operation of a substantial disciplinary machine emphasized the distance between the upper-class, WASP members who exercised this form of social control and the ethnic "underclass" of the New York bar, which frequently constituted its target.

There was also an ethnic dimension to screening judicial candidates, because many of the candidates for the local and state benches were members of recent immigrant ethnic groups who were being recognized by the local political machine and rewarded for their support. Judgeships were part of the patronage system. As with the ABCNY's exercise of lawyer discipline, the work of its judiciary committee was directed largely at nonmembers, many of whom were from New York's immigrant communities. In attempting to exercise control over the

---

67. The ABCNY led several crusades against ambulance chasers. For a description of such a crusade, see Martin, *Causes and Conflicts,* pp. 374–376. One must recognize, however, that the solicitation of personal injury cases was rather different in its potential effects on clients from the solicitation of business clients at a golf club. Whereas the business client is sophisticated and capable of looking after itself, the personal injury client solicited immediately after an accident is frequently in no condition to make commitments, especially when these commitments deliver to the lawyer up to 50 percent of any award on a contingent fee basis. More often than not, these clients were left with very little from an award once medical expenses and legal fees were paid. Ambulance-chasing did result in abuses and the exploitation of poorly educated clients.

68. Auerbach, *Unequal Justice,* pp. 40–53.

New York bar and judiciary, then, the ABCNY can be viewed as the archetype of the upper-class WASP bar association, using its resources to dominate the ethnic underclass of the bar.

Yet such a conspiratorial picture conveys only part of the reality. In the 1870s, the initial targets of the ABCNY's investigations were not all members of ethnic communities by any means. The first lawyer the ABCNY sought to discipline, at some risk to its own internal harmony, was one of its own founding members, David Dudley Field.[69] Field was a very prominent lawyer, a Protestant, and a founder of Shearman and Sterling, one of New York's preeminent law firms. His actions in the railroad consolidation struggles of the late 1860s were regarded by many members of the ABCNY as beyond the pale, and these members initiated proceedings against Field despite his standing in the bar. Similarly, one of the three judges the ABCNY was instrumental in having removed from the bench hailed from an upstate New York Protestant family and graduated from Yale University, despite his close ties to Boss Tweed and Tammany Hall.[70] That the grievance committee was not averse to tackling a leading member of the Wall Street bar was demonstrated by its investigation and prosecution of Thomas L. Chadbourne in 1921 on charges of representing clients with a serious conflict of interest.[71] Chadbourne had been a member of the ABCNY since 1904, was a well-known corporate lawyer with important political connections, and the head of an established Wall Street firm. Chadbourne was represented before the grievance committee by the noted Wall Street lawyer, William D. Guthrie, later to be president of the ABCNY, but the grievance committee nevertheless decided to bring charges against Chadbourne in the courts notwithstanding considerable controversy within the ABCNY over the case. On occasion, then, the ABCNY has investigated the conduct of its own WASPish members even though the majority of those disciplined almost certainly have been ethnic small-firm or solo practitioners who were not members of the Association.

It is also clear that an important concern among the leaders of the ABCNY in establishing and sustaining these committees was the effect of recurrent revelations of judicial corruption and lawyer misconduct upon the legitimacy of the legal system and the standing of the legal profession. Certainly, the patrician founders of the ABCNY felt it was their obligation to engage in reform activities directed at both bench

---

69. Martin, *Causes and Conflicts,* chap. 7.
70. Ibid., p. 76.
71. Ibid., pp. 368–369.

and bar. Although it was an elite minority presuming to judge the non-elite majority, it was also attempting to establish and maintain standards for lawyers and judges, something no other agency was doing. Once the grievance committee's activities became known, the rapidly increasing number of complaints the ABCNY received from dissatisfied clients indicated that there was a demand for its services. However inadequate and limited the work of the grievance committee in these years, it provided a means of redress, previously unavailable, for clients who had been cheated by their lawyers. Given the commitment with which the leaders of the ABCNY pursued the tasks of lawyer discipline and judicial evaluation, it is hard to avoid the conclusion that they were motivated in large part by a sense of obligation and responsibility, albeit heavily laced with nativist anti-immigrant predilections.

Although the activities of the grievance and judiciary committees could be viewed as indicating the interest of the large-firm, upper-class elite in controlling the behavior of the nonelite, there is little evidence that the ABCNY was ever very successful in either regulating the conduct of nonmembers or influencing the composition of the local and state benches. Indeed, a report of the unethical behavior of New York lawyers in the post–World War II period clearly demonstrates the limited reach of the formal disciplinary apparatus of the organized bar.[72] The average number of lawyers who appeared before the grievance committee in any one year from 1952 to 1961 represented fewer than 2 percent of the number of lawyers who by their own admission violated generally accepted ethical norms in a given year. As the author of this report concludes: "Too few violators are formally charged and punished to suggest that this activity by itself does much to weed out or discipline unethical lawyers."[73] There is no reason to believe that the disciplinary machinery established by the ABCNY was any more efficacious in the earlier period.

Furthermore, the offenses for which lawyers were most likely to be both caught and punished were those that violated the general standards of the community, usually involving the conversion or commingling of clients' funds. Violators of uniquely professional norms, such as those against client solicitation, were much less likely to be apprehended and disciplined.[74] Yet it is for the imposition of these professional norms, allegedly directed at the ethnic underclass of the bar, rather than the enforcement of ordinary standards of honesty, that the

---

72. Carlin, *Lawyers' Ethics*, chap. 9.
73. Ibid., p. 161.
74. Ibid., p. 155.

upper-class elite of the ABCNY is accused of anti-ethnic bias. While the upper-class leadership of the ABCNY constructed and operated the disciplinary machinery of the New York bar, it did not prove to be very effective in actually controlling the conduct of the deviant practitioners, WASP or ethnic, against whom it was directed.

The judiciary committee met with a similar lack of success in determining the quality of the judges elected in New York City. Despite its efforts, political leaders generally went ahead and nominated whom they pleased whether or not the ABCNY could be expected to find their candidates qualified. There is little evidence that the findings of the committee, despite their publication in the major newspapers, influenced the outcomes of elections for local and state judicial positions unless these were closely fought contests. That was rarely the case, because more often than not the slates of judicial candidates nominated by Tammany Hall or local political party organizations stood unopposed as a result of deals made between the parties. Qualified and unqualified candidates from the immigrant, ethnic communities were elected to the bench whatever the reviews they received from the WASPish judiciary committee. Consequently, the quality of the local and state benches remained a serious problem for the ABCNY throughout its history.

The ABCNY may not have been very successful in imposing its view of either acceptable professional conduct or suitable qualifications for the bench upon the rest of the bar or the political parties, but the symbolic significance of its control over lawyer discipline and its citywide screening of judicial candidates was considerable. The development of disciplinary machinery and the institutionalization of a voluntary association's right to investigate complaints and bring charges against all lawyers was fundamentally important to the professionalization process. The pioneer work of the ABCNY grievance committee contributed significantly to the development of professional self-regulation, in particular encouraging the impression that the bar was, and should be, responsible for its own discipline. Critics of the organized bar's performance in lawyer discipline have argued that the appearance of self-regulation was more important than the reality. Jerome Carlin, for instance, contends that the reason the ABCNY was more likely to punish offenders against common standards of public morality than those breaking purely professional norms was to defuse public criticism and forestall the imposition of external controls.[75] While there's no evi-

---

75. Ibid., p. 161. See also F. Raymond Marks and Darlene Cathcart, "Discipline Within the Legal Profession: Is It Self-Regulation?" *University of Illinois Law Forum* (1974): 193.

dence of any disposition on the part of public or governmental agencies to regulate the bar during the period when the ABCNY established its grievance committee, there is no doubt that the development of a self-regulatory apparatus and ideology on the part of the organized bar contributed significantly to the lack of any serious threats of external intervention until the 1970s.

The assumption by the ABCNY of the right and duty to police the profession and screen the judiciary reflected a strong sense of moral superiority on the part of its leaders, implying that it was the repository of professional virtue and ethicality and as such had a responsibility to set the standards for the rest of the bar. This patrician presumption of moral superiority was clearly manifest in the arguments William D. Guthrie, president of the ABCNY at the time, advanced in opposition to the proposal in the mid-1920s to create a "unified" state bar association to which all lawyers would perforce belong. Asserting that the source of the authority of voluntary bar associations such as the ABCNY lay in the fact that they were "representative not so much of the whole Bar as representative of the elite of the bar, of the best part of the bar," Guthrie warned that "democratizing the Bar" would have disastrous consequences for ethical standards.[76] In fact, the ABCNY retained uncontested control over lawyer discipline in New York until the 1970s. Even then, faced with challenges to its control, the elite ABCNY found it very difficult to accept that any other agency could be entrusted with this responsibility.

Furthermore, the functions of lawyer discipline and judicial evaluation came to be identified with the ABCNY, associating it in the public's mind with high standards for the bench and bar and leading to its designation as *the* city bar association. Thus reporting, or threatening to report, a colleague or one's lawyer to *the* bar association meant threatening to invoke the ABCNY's discipline system and make recourse to its superior moral authority. Yet for much of its history the ABCNY was not the only bar association in New York, not even the only one in Manhattan.

AN INCLUSIVE ALTERNATIVE

Notwithstanding its location in the midst of a large and expanding urban bar, the ABCNY grew slowly. It remained an exclusive, minority association with only one out of every nine lawyers in New York in its

---

76. William D. Guthrie in "Discussion of the Report of the Committee on Organization of Entire Bar of the State," *Proceedings of New York State Bar Association* (1926): 272.

membership in 1910.[77] Clearly, the ABCNY scarcely tapped the organizational capacity of the New York bar. In 1908 an alternative inclusive association, the New York County Lawyers Association (NYCLA), was founded by lawyers who disapproved of the clublike atmosphere and exclusive membership policies of the ABCNY. The new association was to be open to all members of the New York bar on the payment of a nominal fee without the necessity of sponsorship by existing members or any further character examination. The lack of restrictive membership requirements reflected a different attitude toward the profession. As one of the original directors of the NYCLA noted:

> If there is an essential difference between the two [organizations] it consists in this, that the policy of the Association of the Bar has been to distrust the profession as a whole while the policy of the Lawyers' Association is to trust it and encourage it to action.[78]

The first president of the NYCLA, John F. Dillon, justified the new organization on the grounds that there were some 14,000 lawyers practicing in New York County who were not members of the ABCNY and therefore had "no authentic voice or organized influence in matters so deeply affecting their vital interests." Dillon's conclusion that "there is an ample and unoccupied field for this new association" was quickly borne out by the rapid growth of the NYCLA.[79] Within a year it had 3,401 members, almost twice the total membership of the ABCNY. As can be seen from Figure 1.1, this was not simply a matter of initial enthusiasm for a new organization. The NYCLA continued to attract a membership considerably larger than the ABCNY until the 1960s.

The rapid growth of this rival organization did not, however, cause any changes in the ABCNY's membership policy. It did not cause it to open its doors to all lawyers without sponsorship or further screening, nor to lower its dues. Despite the direct competition of the NYCLA, and the alternative model of bar organization that it represented, the ABCNY remained an exclusive and elite association.

There were good reasons why the ABCNY was not unduly concerned by the rapid growth of the NYCLA. The admission fee and the higher dues demanded of members by the ABCNY meant it did not require large numbers to underwrite its activities. Furthermore, the ABCNY was able to raise money from its members over and above

---

77. Martin, *Causes and Conflicts,* p. 184.
78. Ibid., p. 185.
79. Ibid.

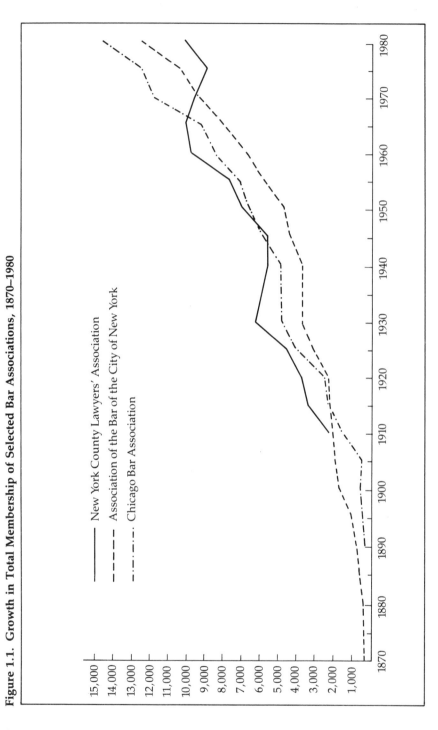

Figure 1.1. Growth in Total Membership of Selected Bar Associations, 1870–1980

New York County Lawyers' Association

Association of the Bar of the City of New York

Chicago Bar Association

dues when required. For example, in the 1870s it established a war chest of $40,000 with contributions from members and friends to finance the investigation and prosecution of the corrupt Tammany Hall judges. In that same decade it also purchased and paid for its first permanent home at a cost of $43,000.[80] It clearly did not need to attract large numbers of members to survive financially.

In addition to possessing more than adequate financial resources, by 1908 the ABCNY had established its role in three major areas of collective professional concern: regulation of lawyers' conduct, judicial screening and evaluation, and legislative review. Although the NYCLA did form its own committees in these areas, it was unable to overcome the ABCNY's advantage of priority and successfully challenge its dominance. In 1910, in an attempt to undermine the ABCNY's monopoly over lawyer discipline, the NYCLA proposed that the state supreme court appoint a "discipline board" independent of the bar associations to oversee the regulation of lawyers.[81] Such a discipline board would have substantially diminished the authority and dominance of the ABCNY. Nothing came of the proposal, however, and the president of the NYCLA subsequently attributed his organization's inability to develop any role in lawyer discipline to the close relationship the ABCNY grievance committee enjoyed with the state supreme court.[82] The ABCNY benefited from being the first in the field; by the time the NYCLA appeared and sought to enter this area, control over the investigation and prosecution of lawyers was firmly lodged in the ABCNY's hands.

The NYCLA did, however, make its own quite distinctive contribution to the development of professional regulation. It established a Committee on Professional Ethics, which in 1912 published the first "ethics opinion."[83] Such opinions were rendered in response to questions from practitioners as to how to proceed in difficult ethical situations, and represented the first attempt by the organized bar to apply the abstract principles of the Canon of Ethics to concrete practice conditions. Other bar associations, including the ABCNY, later formed their own committees on professional ethics after the NYCLA had shown the way. The NYCLA's innovation demonstrated that it was not only the more exclusive, patrician associations that were concerned about ethical issues and professional regulation.

80. Martin, *Causes and Conflicts*, pp. 75, 43.
81. New York County Lawyers Association Annual Report, 1910.
82. New York County Lawyers Association Annual Report, 1913.
83. See Ted Finman and Theodore Schneyer, "The Role of Bar Association Ethics Opinions in Regulating Lawyer Conduct," *University of California Los Angeles Law Review* 29 (1981): 67, 69.

Despite its greater membership, the NYCLA never really threatened the ABCNY's dominant position. The ABCNY remained firmly entrenched as *the* city bar association and the NYCLA always operated in its shadow. Large numbers did not outweigh the resources endowed by upper-class status and the wealth of the large law firms. In addition, there was always considerable overlap in the membership of the two associations, with some of the founders of the NYCLA being at the same time members of the ABCNY.[84] Indeed, its first president was John F. Dillon, a member of the ABCNY of long standing and one of New York's most prominent advocates of the old style. Other prominent corporate lawyers from Wall Street followed Dillon in the presidency, including Joseph H. Choate, who had also served as president of the ABCNY at an earlier date, and Thomas H. Hubbard, Charles E. Hughes, and William Nelson Cromwell, all of whom were founders of large firms. The presence of such Wall Streeters counterbalanced that of the solo and small-firm practitioners so that although the NYCLA did provide an alternative open organization for New York lawyers, it never became a vehicle for the presentation of views that strongly conflicted with the ABCNY. In other words, although opposing the ABCNY on occasion, the NYCLA never developed into a persistent critic of, and countervailing force to, the older patrician organization. On many important professional matters, especially in the interwar years, the NYCLA actually allied itself with the ABCNY.

The establishment of the NYCLA as an inclusive alternative to the ABCNY completed the number of local comprehensive bar associations in New York City and added another voice to the already multiple expressions of the organized bar in the city. Local bar associations had been established in 1872 in Brooklyn and in 1876 in Queens County. Without the convenient transportation links that came later in the nineteenth century connecting Brooklyn and Queens to Manhattan, the legal communities in these counties developed quite separately. Over the decades as communications and transportation facilities improved, the gap between the legal communities did not decline but simply changed to one defined by type of practice and clientele. As the ABCNY became increasingly dominated by corporate lawyers in large firms, most lawyers in Brooklyn and Queens remained general practitioners, representing local small businesses and individuals with legal problems. They practiced in the local courts in these counties and rarely ventured into Manhattan; conversely, the large-firm lawyers of the ABCNY, rep-

---

84. Martin, *Causes and Conflicts*, p. 183. Martin notes that of the thirty officers and directors of the new association, seventeen were members of the ABCNY.

resenting corporate clients, had little reason to cross the East River. Thus the Brooklyn and Queens bar associations represented quite different constituencies from that of the ABCNY and had different interests and concerns from the patrician elite of the Manhattan bar. Although the Bronx County Bar Association was more frequently aligned with the Manhattan associations than were its Brooklyn and Queens counterparts, it also contributed to the diversity of the organized bar in New York City.

Upstate lawyers also formed their own associations and were increasingly influential in the New York State Bar Association. Given the quite different professional context within which upstate lawyers practiced, their views on professional issues were likely to differ from those of the large-firm Wall Street lawyers. An important example of such a difference was the question of the selection of judges. The election of judges was always a major problem for the ABCNY, which consistently sought the institution of an appointive system as a means of decreasing local political influence over the courts and of improving the quality of judges; but it was not such a concern of the upstate bar. The dominant political party upstate was the Republican party, which was more closely connected to the bar elites in upstate communities than were the Tammany Hall Democrats to the ABCNY, and many leaders of the upstate bar benefited from this connection by being nominated for judicial positions. Thus the leaders of the ABCNY found it difficult to convince upstate lawyers of the urgency of the issue and to persuade the state bar association to join its crusades against the election of judges. As most decisions relating to the legal system and the profession were determined in the state legislature, which represented both upstate and city interests, the fact that the state bar association sometimes took a position different from that of the ABCNY, or remained unenthusiastic about ABCNY proposals, directly affected the ability of the Wall Street elite to determine professional and legal policy.

The ABCNY may have been the first of the bar associations founded, and it certainly enjoyed the most munificent resources, but the plural voices of the legal profession in New York City and the state, increasingly buttressed by ethnic and religious differences as the bar became more heterogeneous, meant that the ABCNY did not have a monopoly over the expression of professional interests and positions. Lacking such a monopoly, it frequently had to contend with conflicting viewpoints from within the profession itself. These undermined its capacity to exercise influence over important local and state decision-making arenas.

A HETEROGENEOUS BAR

During the period from 1890 to 1920 a tidal wave of new immigrants from South, Central, and Eastern Europe reached the North American shores. The large urban centers absorbed most of these immigrants; large numbers settled in New York City, the port of entry for so many. By 1920 a staggering 44 percent of the population of New York was foreign born, leading Baltzell in 1960 to declare that New York is "racially and ethnically the most heterogeneous city in the world," including "more Negroes than most cities in Africa, a greater concentration of Jews than at any other time or place in their long history, more Puerto Ricans than any city outside San Juan, more persons of Italian descent than most cities in Italy, and more sons of Ireland than Dublin"—in addition to the old WASP establishment.[85] Such a tremendous influx of foreigners in a relatively short period of time threatened previously dominant WASP groups and resulted in a nativist backlash in the 1920s of which the National Origins Immigration Act of 1924 was a manifestation.

With such an influx of immigrants it was to be expected that the legal profession, especially in large cities such as New York, would become increasingly characterized by ethnic diversity. Lack of serious entry requirements meant that the practice of law presented an opportunity for upward mobility for immigrants and their children. Consequently, the number of new admissions to the bar per year increased substantially in the 1920s, from about 5,000 in 1920 to over 10,000 in 1930, and the number of law schools, especially proprietary schools offering part-time education at night, expanded to service this new source of demand.[86] This influx of newcomers into the bar sharpened the ethnic and functional stratification of the bar, resulting in a profession that was unitary in name only. In 1920, in a highly controversial report on legal education made for the Carnegie Foundation and modeled on the famous Flexner report on medical education published ten years earlier, Alfred Z. Reed demonstrated the extent of this stratification by pointing out that the American bar was split into two quite separate segments each with its own educational and career structures.[87] One segment was populated by graduates of part-time, night law

---

85. Baltzell, *The Protestant Establishment*, p. ix.
86. B. Peter Pashigian, "The Number and Earnings of Lawyers: Some Recent Findings." *American Bar Foundation Research Journal* (Winter 1978): 51–82.
87. Alfred Z. Reed, *Training for the Public Profession of Law* (New York: Carnegie Foundation, 1920). For an extensive discussion of the Reed report, see Auerbach, *Unequal Justice*, pp. 109–114.

schools that provided personal legal services to individuals of low and moderate income frequently in local ethnic neighborhoods; the other was composed of graduates from the established full-time day law schools, who largely practiced business and commercial law or saw to the legal needs of the well-to-do.

The leaders of the ABCNY were well aware of the consequences of open admissions for the standards and heterogeneity of the bar. Indeed, it had been a concern at the time of the ABCNY's founding some fifty years previously. It had not done much in the meantime to raise these standards by making the requirements for admission more demanding. But the especially rapid growth of the bar in the 1920s and frequent complaints about overcrowding in the bar led to a new outcry by the patrician elite in the 1920s and renewed calls for higher entry requirements. That there was genuine concern about the quality of training, or the lack thereof, received by incoming members of the bar and about the standards of practice, is indicated by the outpouring of speeches and articles on professionalism and its meaning in the early decades of the twentieth century.[88] The adoption of codes of ethics and the rendering of ethics opinions by bar associations in these years were part of this general concern with professionalism and reflected the development of a distinctive professional ideology. The concern for higher standards was not just restricted to a patrician elite seeking to exclude members of undesired ethnic groups. How could the professions serve as a means of upward mobility and status definition for the middle and lower-middle classes, as Burton Bledstein argues they did, if there was nothing distinctive about them and if they were open to every person, qualified or not?[89]

While the emerging professional culture of the early twentieth century in a general sense spurred the movement for higher entry standards, the nativist, even anti-Semitic, feelings of the patrician elite of the New York bar were never far below the surface of their complaints about overcrowding in the bar and low standards of practice. George Wickersham, a former president of the ABCNY, attorney general in the Taft administration, and founder of a major Wall Street firm, gave overt expression to these sentiments when he complained that the New York bar was about to be overwhelmed by an influx of foreign-born lawyers who lacked "the faintest comprehension of the nature of our institutions, or their history and development." Guthrie, president

---

88. Robert Stevens, *Law School: Legal Education in America from the 1850s to the 1980s* (Chapel Hill: University of North Carolina Press, 1983). p. 100.
89. Burton J. Bledstein, *The Culture of Professionalism* (New York: Norton, 1976).

during the mid-1920s, was a little more oblique, but the targets of his criticism of "the admission to our bar in recent years of large numbers of undesirable members" were clear enough to both his WASP colleagues in the Wall Street firms and the members of the ethnic underclass of the bar.[90]

In the 1920s, the leaders of the ABCNY played a prominent part in the national movement for higher educational standards. Former secretary of state and president of the ABCNY Elihu Root chaired an important special committee of the ABA on admission to the bar that recommended that two years of college education be required prior to law school, and that three years full-time, or four years part-time, of law school be required.[91] For Root college education was necessary not so much because of the relation it might bear to legal education but to ensure the assimilation of the foreign-born into American institutions and values. College would provide the opportunity for prospective members of the bar to take in "through the pores of [their] skin American life and American thought and feeling."[92] Though the Root report was adopted by the ABA, including its requirement of two years of college education, the ABA was unable to implement it. Changes in admission requirements needed action by state legislatures, decision arenas in which the ABA had little influence. The ball was in the court of local and state bar associations.

In New York State, the Committee on Legal Education of the ABCNY led the crusade to have the state legislature impose more stringent educational requirements for entry to the bar, proposing the adoption of the ABA recommendations.[93] But the state legislature was remarkably resistant to the pressure of the ABCNY and its allies in the state bar association and the NYCLA. It dragged its feet for years, not adopting the two-year college requirement until 1928, and allowing prospective lawyers to train by apprenticeship instead of attendance at law school until the 1970s. New York was not alone in its reluctance to adopt the recommendations of the patrician elite of the bar and limit entry to those who could afford college and legal educations. Auerbach notes that, four years after the ABA adopted its standards, not a single state had enacted them.[94] Here is an important indication that the in-

---

90. Cited in Auerbach, *Unequal Justice*, pp. 121–122.

91. For discussions of Root's role, see Auerbach, *Unequal Justice*, pp. 112–116, and Robert Stevens, *Law School*, pp. 112–130.

92. Cited in Auerbach, *Unequal Justice*, p. 115.

93. See annual reports of the Committee on Legal Education, Association of the Bar of the City of New York, 1922–1926.

94. Auerbach, *Unequal Justice*, p. 118.

fluence of the elite of the bar was not all-encompassing, especially in certain decision-making arenas. The New York state legislature had broader constituencies than the Wall Street bar.

Despite all the attention given by Auerbach to such additional educational requirements as exclusionary devices that were part of a larger anti-ethnic, particularly anti-Jewish, crusade launched by a threatened WASP elite, they were not very effective in blocking the entry of ethnic minorities into the bar even after they were eventually adopted. Certainly, the number of students enrolled at law schools declined during the 1930s and 1940s, but that was due as much to the Great Depression and World War II as to more demanding educational requirements. Two years of prelaw college education did not prove to be an insuperable hurdle, especially for immigrant groups such as the Russian Jews, who greatly valued education; and although legal education came to be largely monopolized by full-time university law schools, there remained schools open to the new immigrants and their children that offered part-time and night classes. In an important study of the achievements of American ethnic groups, Stanley Lieberson documents the quite extraordinary upward educational and occupational mobility of the children of these new immigrant groups. For instance, fully 31 percent of those of Russian origin, chiefly Jews, in the cohort born from 1925 to 1934 were in the professions in 1960 compared to only 17 percent of native-born Americans.[95] Whatever their intention, higher educational requirements did not exclude the children of immigrants from the bar, as is further indicated by Carlin's finding that in 1960 the New York bar was no less than 60 percent Jewish.[96]

From the turn of the century, then, the ABCNY existed in an increasingly diverse ethnic setting, both in terms of the population of New York City and the urban bar. The question was whether the ABCNY could remain an exclusive, WASP-dominated, patrician association in the face of this heterogeneity. Clearly, newly admitted groups of the population would seek access to the organizations of their chosen profession. There would certainly be pressure upon a bar

---

95. Stanley Lieberson, *A Piece of the Pie: Blacks and White Immigrants Since 1880* (Berkeley: University of California, 1980).

96. Carlin, *Unequal Justice*, p. 19. John P. Heinz, Edward O. Laumann, Charles L. Cappell, Terence C. Halliday, and Michael H. Schaalman, "Diversity, Representation, and Leadership in an Urban Bar: A First Report on a Survey of the Chicago Bar," *American Bar Foundation Research Journal* (1976): 725, also found the Chicago bar in the mid-1970s to be very heterogeneous in terms of its ethno-religious composition, reporting that 28 percent were Jewish and a further 29 percent, Catholic.

association that claimed to represent and attempted to regulate all lawyers to become more inclusive of the diversity of the profession.

UPPER-CLASS LAWYERS' CLUB OR PROFESSIONAL ASSOCIATION?

There was clearly an inherent tension between a selective membership policy, especially if that selectivity was tied to the possession of certain ascriptive characteristics, and the claim to standing as a professional association. In theory everyone admitted to the bar was a colleague, and it was not clear what further qualifications the ABCNY could legitimately require of members without undermining its legitimacy as a comprehensive professional association. There was some recognition of this tension among the ABCNY's leadership during the interwar years. Henry W. Taft, president of the ABCNY from 1924 until 1925 and brother of the former United States president, William Howard Taft, presented the question directly to the membership of the ABCNY in his 1925 annual report: Was the ABCNY a private club within the legal profession or was it a professional association open to all lawyers of standing and merit?

> Between the policy adopted by some other associations, which assumes that a lawyer is eligible who has successfully passed the scrutiny of the Examining Board and the Appellate Division, and a policy which applies such tests as are exacted as a condition of admission to a social club, there must be some mean. If the standard deems to accentuate too much race, religion, social environment, or anything other than professional standing and personal character, there is danger lest charges of exclusiveness may be made against the Association, impairing its influence as a civic and professional body; and such charges have not been wanting.[97]

Taft saw that an organization perceived to be too selective would find its authority questioned. Exclusivity could undermine the ABCNY's legitimacy. During his two-year term as president, Taft did attempt to open up the admissions process, actually forming a membership committee with the mandate to seek out and encourage new members instead of simply sitting back and examining the qualifications of those who happened to make application. He also encouraged a spirit of openness and camaraderie among members in place of the heavy formality associated with the conservative, patrician leadership of the past.[98]

---

97. Henry W. Taft, "Annual Report of the President," Association of the Bar of the City of New York, 1924; pp. 140–141.

98. Martin, *Causes and Conflicts*, p. 216.

In welcoming new members, Taft was reflecting a wider movement toward greater inclusiveness among the bar associations of the nation. By the 1920s the major metropolitan bar associations that had been founded just after the ABCNY, and had initially followed similar exclusive membership policies, had generally adopted more open membership stances and, indeed, engaged in membership drives to increase the number of dues-paying members, improve their financial position, and strengthen their claims to representativeness. The Chicago Bar Association (CBA), founded just after the ABCNY in a metropolitan bar much smaller than that of New York, had remained smaller in size than the ABCNY until 1915 (see Figure 1.1). Its rate of growth had sharply exceeded that of the ABCNY since 1905, however, and in the 1920s it surged well ahead of the ABCNY in total membership. As a result, the CBA eventually became fully representative of the bar at large, incorporating the majority of Chicago lawyers in its membership as it moved away from an elite organizational model.[99]

Taft's attempts to move the ABCNY toward a greater openness, however, were short-lived. Guthrie, his successor as president, reversed direction immediately, abandoning the new programs introduced by Taft. In the second year of Guthrie's term, the Special Committee on Membership, created by Taft to seek out new members, reported that its work "during the current year has been selective rather than along 'membership campaign' lines."[100] Thus a movement toward a more open membership policy in the mid-1920s was nipped in the bud despite the fact that this was the direction in which other major metropolitan bar associations, such as the CBA, were moving. Moreover, Guthrie and the ABCNY led the opposition to a proposal for a unified state bar organization in New York and, in so doing, made plain their continued commitment to a selective membership policy and their mistrust of the majority of the bar.

The advocates of unified bars believed that the organizations of the bar would be greatly strengthened by the compulsory membership of all lawyers. Such inclusiveness would increase both their size and their putative influence in political and judicial affairs because the bar would speak with a single representative voice.[101] It was also suggested that unified state bars would improve the regulatory capacity of the profes-

---

99. Terence C. Halliday, *Beyond Monopoly.*

100. Cited in Martin, *Causes and Conflicts,* p. 218.

101. For extended discussion of the integrated or unified bar movement, see Dayton McKean, *The Integrated Bar* (Boston: Houghton Mifflin, 1963), and Theodore J. Schneyer, "The Incoherence of the Unified Bar Concept: Generalizing from the Wisconsin Case," *American Bar Foundation Research Journal* (Winter 1983): 1–108.

sion by bringing all lawyers into the professional organization itself. Originating in the Midwest, and achieving its greatest success in western states with relatively homogeneous bars, the unified bar movement reached New York in the mid-1920s in the form of a proposal to convert the New York State Bar Association into a unified bar by a change in the statutory law requiring all lawyers in the state to join it. Under the unification proposal not only would there be an all-inclusive state bar association but also inclusive county divisions. In New York the debate over its implementation hinged on the relative advantages of inclusive or exclusive membership policies and of elitism versus democratization, with the leadership of the ABCNY strongly and openly defending exclusivity and elitism in professional organization.

The proposal for a unified state bar had considerable support within the state bar association, receiving its endorsement twice in the early 1920s. Indeed, in 1923 a committee of the state bar association unanimously recommended its adoption. Encouraged by this show of support, a bill was introduced into the state legislature in 1925 to effect the unification of the organized bar.[102] The introduction of an actual bill brought the issue wide attention and provoked spirited debate among its supporters and opponents. Not only would the bill establish a compulsory state bar association with local divisions in each judicial district, but local county bar associations could, by a two-third majority vote, choose to become the nucleus of the new divisions. In New York City there was much talk about the NYCLA as the largest bar association in the city following that course, whereupon it would include all lawyers in the city in its membership. In addition, the new county or judicial district divisions of the statewide unified bar would take on the existing "public" functions of the voluntary associations. If the proposal should succeed, then the ABCNY would lose its control over lawyer discipline because that public function would be transferred to the newly constituted county association. Thus, the proposal for the adoption of a unified bar in the state directly threatened the control of the ABCNY and the patrician elite over the regulation of the New York bar.

It was scarcely coincidental that the leading advocate of the unified bar in New York State was Julius Henry Cohen, a prominent Jewish lawyer who, although a member of the ABCNY himself, was only too aware of the implications of the ABCNY's selective membership policy for the city's ethnic minorities. Arguing that a compulsory state bar

---

102. For an outline of the development of the unified bar movement as it affected New York, see Julius H. Cohen, "The National Call for the Organization of an All-Inclusive Bar," *New York Law Review* IV (March 1926): 81–101.

association would avoid invidious distinctions among lawyers on the basis of their backgrounds, Cohen pointed out that in the inclusive NYCLA "no one asks the man's nativity, or where he came from; no one asks whether his father came from Ireland, Russia, or Italy." As long as an applicant could pay the minimal ten dollar dues he was welcome to join.[103] In contrast, Cohen implied, the ABCNY's selective policies encouraged such ascriptive ethnic distinctions to be drawn, distinctions that had no place in a professional body and which kept out good and honorable men and women. Suggesting that Lincoln himself would have been denied admission to many of the city's exclusive clubs, Cohen alleged that the ABCNY, like the clubs, frequently confounded *"fine manners* with *good character"* (italics in original).[104]

Cohen went further, touching on the sensitive matter of the ABCNY's exercise of disciplinary authority over the members of the bar at large, when most of them were not even welcome as members of the ABCNY. Asking what right such a voluntary body had to perform this function, Cohen pointed out that it could only continue to do so in the absence of an all-inclusive organization. When the latter would be formed, it would logically take over regulatory responsibility for the bar, committees on discipline, professional ethics, and unauthorized practice. In doing so, it would have "a real franchise," for the members of those committees "will not be volunteers or chosen only by an elite," but would be selected by the whole bar.[105]

In leading the opposition Guthrie, the abrasive president of the ABCNY, defended the principle of selectivity and elite control by arguing that maintenance of the ethical standards of the profession depended upon the leadership of a moral minority, or elite, of the bar. Here was a clear statement of the upper-class model of professionalism: If you could not exclude the masses from the profession, it was necessary at least to limit leadership to the worthy few. Compulsory membership in a state bar association would open the organized bar to the great mass of "undesirable" lawyers to whom power would naturally pass. The inclusion of all lawyers would allow the weight of numbers to carry the day on matters of professional policy and so dilute the regulatory efforts of the bar associations.[106] Not all the leading

---

103. Julius H. Cohen in "Discussion of the Report of the Committee on Organization of Entire Bar of State," *Proceedings of New York State Bar Association* (1926): 289–290.

104. Cohen, "The National Call for the Organization of an All-Inclusive Bar," p. 91.

105. Ibid., p. 97.

106. For a discussion of Guthrie's role in opposing the integrated bar movement, see Auerbach, *Unequal Justice,* pp. 121–122. See also William D. Guthrie, "Review of the Proposed Compulsory Incorporation of the Bar of the State of New York," pamphlet, Association of the Bar of the City of New York (1926).

members of the ABCNY supported Guthrie in his position; Charles Evans Hughes, for instance, advocated a unified bar as a means of greater social control. But the ABCNY, under Guthrie's leadership, took a position in strong opposition to the unification of the state bar.

Although Guthrie did not openly identify the ethnicity of the undesirable lawyers, it was clear, in this decade of anti-immigrant sentiment, to whom he was referring: lawyers from lower-class, immigrant backgrounds, largely Catholic and Jewish in religion, graduates of night schools, who populated the nether reaches of the New York bar. These were the lawyers he wanted to exclude. And, of course, the moral minority who were fit to lead the bar were upper-class WASPs like Guthrie himself.

The thinly disguised nativism of Guthrie's opposition to integration was plain enough to leaders of the Jewish legal community. Anti-Semitism was rife during this period among the WASP establishment and was manifest in the increasing exclusiveness of the patrician "protective associations" of the time.[107] Jews were excluded from desirable residential communities, prestigious social clubs, and fashionable preparatory schools. Guthrie's statements led Louis Marshall, senior partner in New York's leading Jewish firm and a prominent leader in the Jewish community, to complain to Guthrie of the ABCNY:

> that few Jews were admitted to membership, that men of the highest character and ideals had been ostracized, that others shrank from having their names proposed because of similar indignities . . . that it was only in exceptional cases that men of my faith were appointed on committees of the organization.[108]

A search of the membership roster of the ABCNY reveals that although very prominent Jewish lawyers, such as Marshall himself, Cohen, and the Guggenheimers and Untermyers, were admitted to membership around the turn of the century, and others such as the Greenbaums and Ernsts immediately after World War I, there were very few Jewish members by 1920. Jewish applicants had to have strong sponsorship and not only pass muster with the Committee on Admissions but also receive the favorable vote of the membership. It was not so much that the Committee on Admissions rejected outright Jewish applicants but that the whole process, including the possibility of being turned down finally by the membership at large—which was not such a remote possibility, given the anti-Semitic sentiment of the time—was sufficiently

---

107. See Baltzell, *The Protestant Establishment.*
108. Cited, Auerbach, *Unequal Justice,* p. 122.

frightening that many Jewish lawyers, in Marshall's words, "shrank from having their names proposed."

In his advocacy of a unified bar for New York State, Cohen also raised the issue of the exclusion of female lawyers from the ABCNY. Although women had been eligible for admission to the bar in New York since 1886, and the inclusive NYCLA had welcomed women members from its inception in 1908, the ABCNY continued to exclude all women from membership, whatever their qualifications or interests. Contending that the inclusion of women was an additional reason for a unified state association with similarly inclusive local branches, Cohen noted pointedly that whereas there were forty women members in attendance at the annual dinner of the NYCLA in 1926,

> the daughter of a distinguished lawyer, fired by ambition to follow in his footsteps, might win the highest honors in her college, come out at the head of her class in the law school, be the first in the list of those admitted by the Appellate Division, overwhelmingly demonstrate her character and fitness to the appropriate committee, engage in the practice of law and at once win esteem and confidence, yet she could knock at the doors of the city bar association until the skin fell from her knuckles and the door-keeper would keep her out.[109]

Women eventually gained admission to the ABCNY in 1937, more than ten years after Cohen voiced his criticism, and only then after an extended debate and much controversy. Although women were only a small minority in the New York bar for most of this period, the ABCNY's explicit exclusion of them, in the fashion of the exclusive male social clubs, was a further indication that the ABCNY in many respects resembled an exclusive lawyers' club more than the professional association representing the best elements of the New York bar that it claimed to be.

Guthrie and the ABCNY were successful in their strident opposition to the unified bar proposal, convincing the delegates to the NYSBA to vote it down. The defeat of the unified bar proposal in 1926 ended the last serious challenge to the ABCNY's exclusivity and to its control over lawyer discipline for fifty years. Just as the founding of the NYCLA and its adoption of an open membership policy had not budged the ABCNY from its selective patrician model of organizing, so too did the unified bar movement fail to make any inroads. Reversing Taft's efforts to open up the ABCNY, Guthrie returned the ABCNY to strict adherence to the principle of exclusivity. Consequently, despite the tremen-

---

109. Cohen, "The National Call for the Organization of an All-Inclusive Bar," p. 95.

dous growth in the New York bar during the 1920s, the number of new members joining the ABCNY dropped markedly during Guthrie's two years in office.[110] Succeeding presidents did not attempt to return to Taft's openness. Even during the Great Depression, when declining membership caused financial difficulties for the ABCNY, John W. Davis, president of the ABCNY and perhaps the leading corporate lawyer in the country, expressed the hope that "the day will never come when in the desire for membership enlargement and growth we shall cease to be selective."[111]

By the end of the interwar period, then, the upper-class, male-dominated character of the ABCNY was scarcely dented. True, it had admitted prominent Jewish lawyers since the turn of the century, elected an Irish-Catholic president in the 1920s, and finally declared women eligible for membership in 1937, but there was a deliberate choice by the leadership to remain an exclusive, selective association in the face of inclusive alternatives and pressures toward openness. Even though lawyers from particular ethnic or social backgrounds were not directly excluded from membership in the ABCNY as were women, the forbidding admissions process discouraged applicants who did not share the WASP ascriptive characteristics of the majority of the membership. Furthermore, once the ABCNY had established its reputation and image as the patrician organization of the "Brahmins" of the New York bar, self-selection processes reinforced the selective admissions procedures in keeping it that way. Many ethnic newcomers to the bar simply chose not even to apply for membership, daunted by both the application procedures and the upper-class reputation and culture of the ABCNY.

Thus, throughout the first half of the twentieth century, the ABCNY remained a relatively homogeneous, patrician association in the midst of an increasingly heterogeneous profession. Its membership represented a distinct, albeit substantial, minority of the New York bar, never including more than 20 percent of all lawyers in the city. Yet it presumed to speak for that bar on professional issues, to welcome important guests to New York on its behalf, and even to discipline all its members. In other words, it claimed to be, and acted as, a professional association representing the profession's interests and regulating its conduct while at the same time appearing very much like an exclusive patrician lawyers' club.

110. Martin, *Causes and Conflicts*, p. 217.
111. John W. Davis, Annual Report of the President, *Yearbook*, Association of the Bar of the City of New York, 1932, p. 144.

PART TWO

Environmental Change and Organizational Adaptation

Chapter Two

Broadening the Bases of Membership

When World War II ended, the ABCNY remained an exclusive patrician association including a minority of New York lawyers as members. In the postwar decades, however, there were substantial changes in the ABCNY's professional and normative context that were to result in the relaxation of its membership policy and increased heterogeneity in its composition. In the first place, the demography of the profession itself changed significantly, undergoing a growth spurt in the years immediately after the war and then experiencing sustained and substantial expansion from the mid-1960s. Indeed, between 1960 and 1980 the total number of lawyers in the United States almost doubled, increasing from 285,933 to 542,205.[1] This dramatic growth in admissions to the bar, exceeding even that which might have been expected from the maturation of the postwar baby-boom generation, markedly changed the age structure of the profession, with the median age of lawyers dropping from forty-six years in 1960 to thirty-nine years in 1980.[2] Contributing substantially to the demographic transformation of the bar during this period was an unprecedented influx of women into the profession.[3] Consequently, the bar changed in terms of not only its age structure but also its gender composition. Moreover, it is likely that the rapid growth of the bar further accentuated its internal ethnic heterogeneity even if not its diversity in terms of social-class background.[4]

---

1. Barbara A. Curran, "American Lawyers in the 1980s: A Profession in Transition," *Law and Society Review* 20 (1986): 19.

2. Ibid., p. 23.

3. Ibid., p. 25.

4. Heinz and Laumann actually found in their study of Chicago lawyers that in fact there has been a substantial decline in the proportion of persons from lower socioeconomic origins entering the legal profession in the post–1960 decades. This is a remarkable finding, given the rapid expansion of the bar during these years. See John P. Heinz and Edward O. Laumann, *Chicago Lawyers* (New York: Russell Sage Foundation, 1982), pp. 190–191.

One might expect that such significant demographic changes in the post–World War II decades would result in increased pressure upon the selective ABCNY to open up its admissions policies and include a more diverse representation of the New York bar. But rapid growth of the bar in the 1920s, with a similar change in its age structure, had not led to any long-term change in the ABCNY's membership philosophy. Indeed, it had the opposite effect, with the ABCNY under Guthrie's leadership reaffirming its commitment to an exclusive and elitist organizational model. In the postwar decades, however, the demographic transformation of the bar was accompanied by normative changes in the broader institutional environment of the ABCNY in a way that made its overt exclusivity difficult to maintain. All organizations operate in what Meyer and Scott term "institutional environments" which encompass the larger societal arrangements—political culture, value systems, normative structures—in which an organization is embedded.[5] The immediate salience of the institutional environment varies for different types of organizations. Organizations such as professional associations are likely to be subjected to relatively strong pressures from their institutional environments because an important resource for such membership associations is a generalized legitimacy derived from conformity to wider societal values and norms. When the values and norms of the institutional environment change, then, as they did in the 1960s and 1970s for the ABCNY, one might expect these organizations also to undergo change to enhance their isomorphism with that environment.

Changes in societal values and norms in the post–World War II period made the unabashed aristocratic elitism of the ABCNY no longer tenable. World War II, with the opportunities it provided foreign-born citizens and their sons to participate in the defense of their adopted land, brought a new sense of national identity and pride to ethnic minorities and reinforced their desire to enter the mainstream of U.S. economic and social life. The GI Bill enabled many servicemen from economically disadvantaged backgrounds to attend college and graduate from law school without requiring considerable family support. Ivy League colleges and law schools found it increasingly difficult to limit the admission of Jews and other ethnic minorities, and even opened their doors to women. Jewish and Irish-Catholic law firms joined the traditionally WASP Wall Street firms in offering corporate legal services, and the white-shoe firms themselves, undergoing rapid expan-

---

5. John W. Meyer and W. Richard Scott, *Organizational Environments: Ritual and Rationality* (Beverly Hills, Calif.: Sage Publications, 1983).

sion in the 1960s and needing additional labor, opened their doors to Jewish and Catholic lawyers. Furthermore, the emerging civil rights movement encouraged racial and ethnic minorities to claim their right to participate fully in American institutions from which they had been largely excluded in the past, reaching its acme in the far-reaching antidiscrimination legislation of the 1960s. The feminist movement and the youth rebellion also erupted in the 1960s, making much more difficult the defense of the ABCNY as a male institution controlled by a gerontocracy.

How would the ABCNY respond to these changes in its normative and professional environments? Would they result in the democratization of the ABCNY or would it persist on its course of patrician elitism? The ABCNY did find it difficult to maintain its barriers to entry and, consequently, progressively dismantled them. In 1972 it finally simplified its elaborate admissions procedures so that the process by which a lawyer could become a member was greatly eased. Instead of requiring the sponsorship and recommendation of no fewer than six existing members of the association, the new bylaws required that a prospective member simply be sponsored by one current member. If the applicant did not know a member, then he or she would be introduced to one. There would be no evaluation of the candidate by an admissions committee or vote by the assembled membership. Rather, a list of candidates for membership would be sent to all existing members so as to provide an opportunity for any member who had reason to oppose a candidate's admission to make known the reason for such opposition. Then the Executive Committee, the governing council of the Association, voted on whether to approve the applications of particular candidates.[6] Note that the process still required sponsorship by a member, even if only one, and still allowed for members to express opposition to candidates even if they no longer voted on their admission. Although there still remained these traces of the former philosophy of selectivity whereby it was not assumed that any member of the bar, duly admitted to practice and in good standing, was good enough for membership in the ABCNY, the new process was far simpler and much less daunting to outsiders of the patrician, large-firm elite.

The membership of the ABCNY grew rapidly in the postwar decades, tripling in size from 1946 to 1980, by which time it enrolled more than 10,000 New York members and had a total membership of 12,286, making it one of the largest metropolitan bar associations in the United States. The ABCNY now had substantial size to add to its resources of

---

6. *Yearbook,* The Association of the Bar of the City of New York, 1973.

prestige and income. Indeed, it not only outgrew the inclusive NYCLA during the 1960s and 1970s but even surpassed it in total number of New York members in the early 1970s (see Figure 2.1). The growth of the NYCLA had slowed in the early 1960s, with its membership actually declining after 1965, reaching a trough in 1975 before beginning to recover. Meantime, the ABCNY's membership continued to expand throughout the 1960s, even though its elaborate admissions procedures were not relaxed until 1972 and its dues remained relatively high.

These contrasting growth patterns for the two New York bar associations reflected changes in their demographic and normative environments that worked to the advantage of the ABCNY and disadvantage of the NYCLA. For one thing, the percentage of solo practitioners in the bar as a whole declined substantially over these two decades while, conversely, that of lawyers engaged in firm practice rose.[7] Large law firms underwent particularly rapid growth during this time. The ABCNY, as the association of the large-firm elite of the bar, tended to draw its membership from the increasing pool of firm lawyers, whereas the NYCLA depended more heavily on the declining population of solo practitioners. Furthermore, the 1960s and early 1970s were turbulent times, with the civil rights movement and the Vietnam War leading to controversy and civil disorder. Young people, particularly college graduates, were embroiled in such matters and, of course, these were the very people entering the bar in increasing numbers. Whereas the NYCLA remained largely quiescent on these larger issues, the ABCNY was vocal and highly visible, offering a platform to Martin Luther King, Jr., in the early 1960s and strongly supporting the passage of the Civil Rights Act in 1964. Its leaders were instrumental in having the ABA support the extension of federally funded legal services to the poor through neighborhood clinics. Furthermore, in 1969–1970 the new leadership of the ABCNY became increasingly disenchanted with the Vietnam War and on a personal basis actively supported the antiwar movement within the New York bar. The ABCNY was in the vanguard of change in the profession; if younger lawyers, especially those in large firms, were going to join any association it was likely to be the ABCNY.

Even after its rapid growth in the 1960s and 1970s, however, the ABCNY still included in its membership only a minority of the New York bar as a whole. As a proportion of all New York lawyers in Manhattan and the Bronx, the membership of the ABCNY increased from 20 percent in the early 1950s to 30 percent in 1980, but still represented

---

7. Curran, "American Lawyers in the 1980s," pp. 27–28.

**Figure 2.1. Growth of the New York City Membership
of the Association of the Bar of the City of New York
and of the New York County Lawyers' Association
with Growth of the New York Bar, 1940–1980**

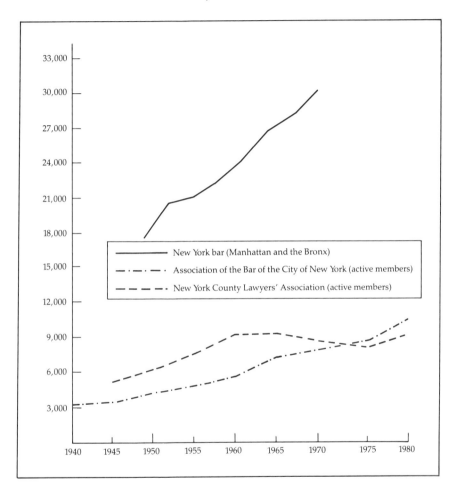

fewer than one out of every three lawyers in its catchment area. In vivid contrast, other major metropolitan bar associations included a majority of the lawyers in their constituencies as early as 1950. Indeed, the Boston Bar Association included 68 percent of the Boston bar in its membership in 1951. Although the Chicago Bar Association moved more slowly toward greater inclusiveness, its membership comprised 69 percent of the Chicago bar in 1970.[8] It is clear, then, that the ABCNY did not become a "mass" association incorporating a majority of the bar despite the simplification of its admissions procedures and its rapid growth in the postwar decades. On the contrary, the ABCNY was the only comprehensive metropolitan association, other than the NYCLA, to include less than 50 percent of the surrounding bar in its membership by 1950.

Although the ABCNY did not come to encompass a majority of the New York bar in its ranks, the question remains as to whether the ABCNY did become more representative of the diversity of the wider bar. Notwithstanding the changes in the professional and institutional environments of the ABCNY, did it remain a relatively homogeneous association in terms of its age, gender, and ethno-religious composition? In the following pages, I examine the changing composition of the ABCNY over the postwar decades, focusing on the admission of previously excluded or underrepresented segments of the bar. Holding that there may well be varying levels of admission and participation in a voluntary membership association, I further examine the differential levels of admission of different subgroups over these decades.

To facilitate such an examination of changes in the composition of the ABCNY, I drew random probability samples of the membership at three points in time—1955, 1965, and 1978. The first two dates were chosen as they occurred in the middle of decades and after periods of considerable membership growth. Although it would have been tidier to select 1975 as the third date, and thus have samples at regular ten-year intervals, 1978 was selected because it permitted sufficient time to elapse after the dismantling of the ABCNY's elaborate admissions process in 1972 to allow lawyers who had joined the Association since that date to show up in the sample. A 1978 sample was more likely to pick up any changes that had occurred in the composition of the Association consequent to the relaxation of the admissions requirements.

Information was coded on those members (N = 900) selected by these samples from the membership cards maintained by the executive

---

8. Terence C. Halliday, *Beyond Monopoly: Lawyers, State Crises and Professional Empowerment* (Chicago: University of Chicago Press, 1987), Table 5.1, pp. 122–123.

secretary's staff, supplemented by information from the Martindale Hubbell legal directories. Members were not interviewed. Data were available on place and date of birth, date of admission to the bar, college and law school education, type of law practice, and participation on committees. Unfortunately, information was not available on members' areas of specialization.

I did not undertake a survey of the New York bar at large and so do not have data on these variables for all New York lawyers with which to compare ABCNY members. This means that I cannot draw definitive conclusions about the representativeness of the ABCNY's membership but only about the extent of compositional change within the ABCNY from one point of time to the next. Some conclusions about the representativeness of the ABCNY can be made, however, based on the findings reported by Jerome Carlin, who did survey the New York bar in 1960, and on the results of John Heinz and Edward Laumann's research on Chicago lawyers.[9] Although New York is not Chicago, there is no reason to believe that its bar is less diverse and segmented.

LEVELS OF ADMISSION

In examining changes in membership and participation in the ABCNY since World War II, we shall observe in some cases a progressive movement from one level of admission or participation to another. Organizations do not merely have the sole option of admission or exclusion when faced with demands for entry from subgroups in their surrounding populations, but have subtle and varied means of accommodation open to them. This is especially so for voluntary occupational associations that occupy a peripheral position in the commitment of most members. Following the models proposed by theorists of ethnic relations who hold that there are several stages or levels of structural assimilation into social groups, I suggest that there are also variable levels of assimilation into organizations.[10] Not all subgroups need be admitted to the same extent or at the same level; furthermore, some subgroups may experience different levels of admission at different points in time.

There are, I suggest, three levels of admission and participation that a voluntary association can use to satisfy demands for entry: (i) *Representation* from subgroups can be invited, (ii) members of the subgroup can be *included*, (iii) or the subgroup and its members can be com-

---

9. Jerome E. Carlin, *Lawyers' Ethics: A Survey of the New York Bar* (New York: Russell Sage Foundation, 1966); Heinz and Laumann, *Chicago Lawyers.*

10. Milton M. Gordon, *Assimilation in American Life* (New York: Oxford, 1964).

pletely *incorporated* into the association in question. While these levels lie on a scale from less to more admission, it is not a simple linear scale. *Representation* is certainly a lower level of admission than *inclusion*, but inclusion involves a different type of admission as well. A large number of individuals from a subgroup may be admitted but then isolated as a separate unit within the host organization. Indeed, *included* subgroups may have less influence on policy-making of the association than subgroups *represented* on leadership boards and committees. Frequently, however, *included* subgroups are also *represented* by one of their members on such boards of directors.

I use the term *representation* to indicate the lowest level of admission to an organization by which a small minority of individuals from a particular subgroup of the population are invited to join as members and thus "represent" their subgroup. Such a minimal presence in an organization may follow external pressure to admit members of various subgroups. Representation readily lends itself to a form of tokenism, in which representatives of different subgroups provide necessary legitimation for the organization's leadership but have little influence on the broader character of the organization.[11] This level of admission has been frequently adopted by organizations with respect to women and racial minorities.

Other subgroups may be *included* in larger numbers but be quarantined once inside the organization. Formal and informal segregation may exist within organizations as well as outside. Members of particular subgroups may be restricted to certain activities, experience little interaction with other members of the organization, and have limited opportunities for advancement. The *inclusion* of these subgroups does not serve to change the character of the host organization to any noticeable degree, as the subgroups are isolated from its mainstream. Organizations frequently include in this way subgroups defined by ascriptive characteristics such as gender and age. Women and young people may be admitted to an organization but their participation effectively limited to certain activities or sections. The common practice of creating separate sections within associations for younger members, or women's auxiliaries, for example, is a way of including these subgroups without necessarily allowing them to influence the overall direction of organizational policies. Occupational and professional associations may also include but isolate subgroups associated with particular types of work settings or areas of specialization.

---

11. See Rosabeth M. Kanter, "Some Effects of Proportions in Group Life: Skewed Sex Ratios and Responses to Token Women," *American Journal of Sociology* 82 (1977): 965–990.

The third level of admission is *incorporation,* where a subgroup admitted to the organization becomes a part of the whole so completely that it does not retain any individuality or separate identity within the organization. The subgroup is not merely *represented* by a token number of its members, nor is it simply *included* and segregated within the organization. Rather the members of the *incorporated* subgroup participate fully in the life of the organization, as leaders as well as members. Furthermore, the character of the host organization changes to reflect the absorption of the newly *incorporated* subgroup. Indicators of a subgroup's full incorporation would include both the presence of members of that subgroup in leadership positions and evidence of its influence on the goals and policies of the association.

Different subgroups within the New York bar experienced different levels of admission into the ABCNY at different points in time. Some subgroups merely gained representation, others were included and segregated, and still others were eventually fully incorporated. Some subgroups moved from one level of admission to another over these decades. There are several criteria that can explain the extent and the timing of the structural penetration of the ABCNY by particular subgroups within the New York bar. These criteria have to do with the characteristics of both the legal positions involved and the incumbents of those positions, including the prestige order of the bar and the social desirability of various ethnic and ascriptively defined categories of lawyers. Combinations of these criteria served to determine the extent and limits of incorporation into the ABCNY.

Some sociologists anticipated that in modern industrial states the importance of social background characteristics, whether ethno-religious or socioeconomic, would decline in favor of performance-related criteria in the recruitment and promotion of persons in hierarchically organized occupational structures. Talcott Parsons, for instance, in his celebrated elaboration of the pattern variables, held that dependence upon achievement criteria would increasingly characterize modern societies.[12] This proposition might be expected to be borne out in the professions where entry and mobility are supposedly determined by meritocratic criteria. In their review of the research on recruitment into different occupations, however, Harold Wilensky and Anne Lawrence noted that "even in the richest countries many, perhaps most, jobs are assigned on the basis of a combination of sex, age, and descent."[13]

---

12. Talcott Parsons and Edward A. Shils, eds., *Toward a General Theory of Action* (Cambridge, Mass.: Harvard University Press, 1951).

13. Harold L. Wilensky and Anne T. Lawrence, "Job Assignment in Modern Societies: A Re-examination of the Ascription-Achievement Hypothesis," in Amos H. Hawley, *Societal Growth; Processes and Implication* (New York: Free Press, 1979), p. 202.

Furthermore, one of the most striking findings of Heinz and Laumann's in-depth analysis of the Chicago bar was the continued "strong influence of ethnoreligious background on the structure of careers in a major metropolitan bar."[14]

Sociologists have long been interested in the progressive assimilation of new immigrant ethnic groups into the mainstream of American society, developing various explanations of the rate and extent of assimilation. One of the earliest researchers in this area, Emory S. Bogardus created a social distance scale in 1925 to measure the proximity of minority ethnic groups to the dominant WASP majority.[15] Despite methodological problems with Bogardus's work, his principal finding that ethnic groups are arrayed along a hierarchical dimension of social desirability and acceptability has held up over time.[16] It seems that minority ethnic groups are differentially ranked by the WASP majority according to the length of time they have been resident in the United States and the degree to which they have adopted the cultural attributes of the dominant group. Studies of residential segregation patterns find a similar ranking of ethnic groups by their degree of segregation from one another.[17]

Confirming the general direction of these findings, then, Erwin Smigel quotes the dean of an Ivy League law school as explaining the discriminatory hiring practices of the Wall Street firms in the 1950s by suggesting, "In almost every case it is not being Jewish that throws a man back but lack of polish that accompanies anyone who is half a generation away from another country."[18] The Jewish lawyers who had gained access to the Wall Street firms by the 1950s, and the founders of the new Jewish firms, were almost all of German origin and of an earlier migration than the East European Jews. Furthermore, many had been educated at the best schools and were well assimilated into upper-class culture. Increased access to the exclusive preparatory schools and colleges of the Northeast during the early decades of this century facilitated such assimilation. According to the Bogardus social distance scale, then, German Jewish lawyers, educated at the best

---

14. Heinz and Laumann, *Chicago Lawyers*, p. 167.

15. Emory S. Bogardus, "A Social Distance Scale," *Sociology and Social Research* 17 (1933): 265–271.

16. Emory S. Bogardus, "Measuring Changes in Ethnic Relations," *American Sociological Review* 16 (1951): 48–53; idem., "Racial Distance Changes in the United States During the Past 30 Years," *Sociology and Social Research* 43 (1958): 127–135.

17. Otis Dudley Duncan and Stanley Lieberson, "Ethnic Segregation and Assimilation," *American Journal of Sociology* 64 (1959): 363–374; Stanley Lieberson, *Ethnic Patterns in American Cities* (New York: Free Press, 1963).

18. Erwin O. Smigel, *The Wall Street Lawyer* (Bloomington: Indiana University Press, 1964), p. 65.

schools and living on the Upper East Side of Manhattan or in West-chester County, would be more likely to be welcomed into the ABCNY than Polish and Russian Jews of recent immigrant stock, with strange names, and who attended local colleges and law schools.

In general, then, I would expect members of the ethnic groups who are closest in culture and appearance to the upper-class WASPs to be most successful in penetrating the ABCNY. Absence of ethnic markers such as "wrong" skin color or complexion, a "foreign" sounding name, or a "different" kind of dress should facilitate assimilation. Compensatory mechanisms also may come into play through a combination of the characteristics of position and person. Educational achievement, practice in respected areas of law, political connectedness, or achievement in the practice of law can serve to compensate for derogated ethnic background. Lawyers without compensatory characteristics, however, who graduated from local law schools and practice in low-prestige areas of the law such as criminal defense, divorce, or personal injury law, can be expected to experience a lower level of admission, if admitted at all.

In addition to ascribed, or social background, factors, the characteristics of the legal positions occupied may well determine the level of admission to the elite ABCNY experienced by different segments of the New York bar. Research on the social differentiation and stratification of the bar suggests that legal positions are stratified along several dimensions. Heinz and Laumann suggest that the most important dimension differentiating and stratifying the bar is that of client type.[19] Legal positions that involve the provision of legal services to powerful corporations are quite distinct from, and enjoy more prestige than, those that involve serving individuals. Client type, then, may serve to predict the extent of incorporation into the ABCNY. By this criterion I would expect previously excluded lawyers occupying legal positions representing corporations to be more readily admitted to the ABCNY than those who largely represent individuals and small businesses.

In addition, the substance of the law and the nature of the legal tasks involved in certain positions vary from those required in others on hierarchical dimensions of intellectual difficulty and "purity/impurity." Heinz and Laumann suggest that different substantive areas of practice can be ranked according to the extent to which they are intellectually demanding, and Andrew Abbott contends, in a provocative essay, that prestige within professions is distributed in an inverse relationship to the messiness and uncertainty of the problems involved

---

19. Heinz and Laumann, *Chicago Lawyers*, Part II.

in different professional tasks.[20] Incumbents of those legal positions having to do with respectable corporate clients and requiring the performance of intellectually demanding tasks, well removed from the impurities of everyday life, will be more likely to be fully incorporated into the ABCNY. Practitioners in less intellectually demanding and more routinized areas of law involving unrespectable clients and considerable unpleasantness might well experience a lower level of admission.

It may also be hypothesized that the incumbents of legal positions having to do with old established areas of the law and wealthy and respectable persons as clients are more likely to be fully incorporated. The law of trusts and estates, for example, serves only individuals, generally wealthy individuals, but it has to do with the transmission of wealth from one generation to another, a traditional concern of lawyers. Despite the fact that they serve individuals, then, we would expect members of the probate bar to be fully incorporated in the ABCNY. Similarly, criminal law is an old established area of practice closely related to important social-control functions, but it has to do with unpleasant, and often poor, clients and with messy fact situations. Because it is a core concern of the legal system, even a patrician association such as the ABCNY could not ignore it. The extent of criminal defense lawyers' involvement in the ABCNY, however, is likely to be more limited than that of probate lawyers because of the inherent unpleasantness of their work and its lower status within the profession.[21]

In the remainder of this chapter, I trace the differential admission into the ABCNY of subgroups defined by age, gender, and ethnicity. We shall see that the process and level of admission for one subgroup has not necessarily been the same as for all. But ascriptive factors should become less important than positional characteristics in determining the level of admission. A simple, unidimensional view of the progressive incorporation of all subgroups, however, is inadequate.

YOUNG LAWYERS AND THE ABCNY

As one observer noted of the ABCNY, "historically, it has not been receptive to young men or new ideas."[22] From the beginning the

---

20. Ibid.; Andrew Abbott, "Status and Status Strain in the Professions," *American Journal of Sociology* 86 (1981): 819.

21. Heinz and Laumann, *Chicago Lawyers*, p. 91.

22. Paul Hoffman, *Lions in the Street: The Inside Story of the Great Wall Street Law Firms* (New York: Saturday Review, 1973), p. 203.

ABCNY was run by a gerontocracy of senior practitioners. During the 1920s there had been a suggestion that power be turned over to responsible younger lawyers, but "nothing was ever done about it, and the same crowd of old gentlemen kept on running the institution."[23] Indicative of the dominance of the senior members of the bar is the fact that the average age of presidents of the ABCNY between 1921 and 1943 was 65.[24] Charles Evans Hughes was appointed a justice of the United States Supreme Court at the age of 48, but not elected president of the ABCNY until he was 65.[25]

The feeling that younger lawyers had no place in the ABCNY was reinforced by the ineligibility of newly admitted members of the bar until they had been in practice three years. Restricting eligibility for membership in this way reflected the notion that lawyers had to achieve standing in the bar before joining the ABCNY. It also indicated the ABCNY's basic distrust of the adequacy of the requirements for admission to the bar in general. Once admitted to the bar, lawyers had to serve a further apprenticeship before they were deemed worthy of consideration for membership in this Association.

Following World War II, with the prospect of the entry of many men into the bar whose professional careers had been delayed by military service, the ABCNY relaxed its requirements and created a new category of associate membership for those newly admitted to the bar. After three years in practice, Associate Members could apply for full membership. Associate Members paid reduced dues and enjoyed privileges of the house and the library but did not have voting rights and could not serve as full members of committees. It was clearly an adjunct status and did not in fact serve to attract a great number of new younger members.[26] Immediately prior to the initiation of the associate membership category, the ABCNY had formed a Committee on Junior Bar Activities "to promote interest in the Association and its activities among its younger members."[27] The model for the new ABCNY committee presumably was the separate sections established for younger lawyers in other bar associations to encourage their membership and participation. The CBA, for instance, created a junior section for younger members in 1932 that was a complete microcosm of the larger association, with parallel committees and its own managing board. A

23. Martin, *Causes and Conflicts: The Centennial History of the Association of the Bar of the City of New York*, (Boston: Houghton Mifflin, 1970), p. 199.

24. Ibid., p. 392.

25. Hoffman, *Lions in the Street*, p. 203.

26. Martin, *Causes and Conflicts*, p. 258.

27. *Yearbook*, Association of the Bar of the City of New York, 1944, p. 133.

completely separate organization within an organization represents a prototypical example of admission by *inclusion*.[28] The ABCNY committee (later the Young Lawyers Committee) provided a focus for younger members but lacked substantive direction or organization-wide authority. Both the formation of this committee and the establishment of a special membership category for newly admitted members of the bar demonstrated the use of *inclusion* as a mechanism for accommodating younger lawyers while the leadership remained firmly in the hands of the senior partners of law firms.

Young lawyers were also given at this time some representation, albeit minimal, in the ABCNY's decision-making councils. Harrison Tweed, an innovative president elected immediately after World War II, initiated the tradition whereby a young lawyer was nominated for the position of secretary of the Association. The incumbent of this position recorded minutes of members' meetings and, as an officer of the Association, attended meetings of the Executive Committee. Thus was effected in the early postwar period the combination of *inclusion* together with minimal *representation* as a means of recognizing and accommodating the younger members of the bar.

The use of inclusion plus token representation on governing boards to accommodate young lawyers was not to survive the 1960s, however. With the rapid influx of young lawyers into the bar in the latter half of the 1960s, and the emergence of age-specific discontents during that time, the disjunction between a substantial portion of the bar and the gerontocracy that governed the profession through the bar associations became increasingly evident. By 1980, fully one quarter of the bar was under 33 years of age, and another quarter between 33 and 40 years.[29] While the average age of the presidents of the ABCNY at the time they took office decreased to 59 years for the postwar period from 1945 to 1970, leadership of the ABCNY, like that of other bar associations, remained in the hands of older practitioners.[30] Feeling that their concerns and voices were not heard in the established bar associations, young lawyers in several metropolitan centers established in 1969–1970 "counter" bar associations either to act as interest groups within the existing framework of the organized bar or to provide alternative

---

28. The CBA in fact quickly progressed beyond *inclusion*, however, to a fuller incorporation of younger members by revising their bylaws in 1936 to allocate 20 percent of all committee positions to them. See Halliday, *Beyond Monopoly*, pp. 92–94.

29. Barbara A. Curran, "The Legal Profession in the 1980s: Selected Statistics from the 1984 Lawyers Statistical Report," paper presented at Law and Society Association Annual Meeting, 1984.

30. Martin, *Causes and Conflicts*, p. 392.

organizations for young lawyers.[31] These groups forcibly brought the concerns of young lawyers, especially elite young lawyers, to the attention of the leadership of the established bar associations.

In New York, associates in large law firms created the New York Council of Law Associates in 1969 to represent their concerns about the distribution of legal services and to organize opportunities for them and their firms to undertake *pro bono publico* work. While the council never became a rival bar association to the ABCNY in the way that the Chicago Council of Lawyers did to the CBA, it served both to organize younger lawyers and to bring pressure on the leadership of the ABCNY to recognize their concerns and to increase the number of opportunities for their participation in the larger association. By 1970 it was clear that the ABCNY could no longer ignore its younger members, nor relegate them to second-class status through the mechanism of inclusion.

The first response of the ABCNY to the increased numbers and visibility of young lawyers was, in 1965, to drop completely the associate membership category, permitting newly admitted members of the bar to join without any "probationary" period at all. Consequently, more young lawyers joined the ABCNY, and sooner after their admission to the bar than had been the case previously. With the admission of more young lawyers, the median age of members of the ABCNY dropped from 47 in 1955 to 42 in 1978. The number of lawyers from 24 to 40 years of age increased from less than a third of the membership in 1955 to almost a half in 1978. By the end of the 1970s, then, the younger members were by far the largest age group within the Association. Table 2.1 convincingly demonstrates the changed age profile of the membership.

It is, of course, one thing for there to be changes in membership composition and quite another for those changes to be reflected in patterns of active participation. This is especially so in an organization such as the ABCNY, where opportunities for participation are limited by small committee size and where the demand for committee appointments exceeds the supply of positions. By examining the age at which members of the three samples were first appointed to committees, we can determine the extent to which the changed-age profile of the membership was reflected in committee appointments. This should indicate the extent to which the new younger lawyers were fully incorporated

---

31. See Raymond F. Marks, *The Lawyer, the Public and Professional Responsibility* (Chicago: American Bar Foundation, 1972); Michael J. Powell, "Anatomy of a Counter-Bar Association: The Chicago Council of Lawyers," *American Bar Foundation Research Journal* (1979): 501–541.

Table 2.1. Age of Members of the ABCNY in 1955, 1965, and 1978

Years Old	1955		1965		1978	
24–40	(76)	30%	(104)	35%	(165)	47%
41–55	(102)	41%	(93)	31%	(111)	32%
56 and over	(72)	29%	(102)	34%	(74)	21%
	(250)	100%	(299)	100%	(350)	100%

SOURCE: Author's survey of ABCNY membership records in 1955, 1965, and 1978.

within the ABCNY. The median age at which members of the 1955 sample received their first committee appointment in the ten years previous to 1955 was 40, whereas for members of the 1978 sample the median had dropped to 34, a marked decrease. Appointing more young lawyers to committees was one way of removing the grounds for the complaint that the ABCNY did not provide opportunities for the participation of young lawyers, and thereby of co-opting younger lawyers who were critical of the dominance of their senior colleagues. Such a policy also helped avert a serious challenge to the ABCNY on the part of the new Council of Law Associates.

Until the 1970s, representation of young lawyers on the Executive Committee had been entirely nominal, instituted through the office of the secretary of the Association. This was to change, however, following the so-called Young Turks revolt in 1971, when three young associates at major law firms successfully ran for Executive Committee positions in opposition to the official nominating committee's slate (see Chapter 4). Suddenly, three young lawyers were members of the Executive Committee, resulting in substantial changes in the nature of its deliberations. Since that time, younger lawyers have been nominated and elected regularly to Executive Committee positions.

The presence of younger lawyers on the Executive Committee in the 1970s, along with their appointment to substantive committees, would suggest that younger lawyers have moved from mere *inclusion* plus *representation* in the 1950s to *incorporation* in the 1970s. The ABCNY has scarcely been taken over by young lawyers, but by the end of the 1970s they participated in many of its activities and in its leadership. Furthermore, new substantive committees of particular interest to younger lawyers were established during the 1970s, and the policies of the ABCNY came to reflect the input of this new constituency, again suggesting its incorporation into the ABCNY.

WOMEN LAWYERS AND THE ABCNY

Although women had been admitted to the bar since the late nineteenth century, they remained a small minority of the legal profession until the 1970s. Women lawyers represented less than 3 percent of the lawyer population during the entire period from 1951 to 1970. Reflecting a social revolution in public attitudes and beliefs about the legitimate occupations available to women, increasing numbers of women entered the profession in the 1970s until by 1980 their proportion in the bar reached 8.1 percent. In the decade of the 1970s, the female lawyer population increased by over 300 percent, compared with only 44 percent for male lawyers.[32] These are quite remarkable figures, indicating significant change in the gender composition of the bar.

Even though the ABCNY voted to admit women in 1937, it was done so grudgingly by the membership at the behest of several of its prominent leaders, and the first woman member did not actually join until 1940. One would not expect women to rush to the ABCNY given its history of exclusion, yet by 1955, 2.8 percent of the membership of the ABCNY were women, about the same percentage as in the national bar at that time. By 1978, the percentage of women members had tripled to 8.9 percent, slightly below their 9.7 percent representation in the New York bar in 1980 but still reflecting a tremendous influx of women. Moreover, the president of the ABCNY reported in 1980 that nearly 25 percent of all the Association's new members that year were women, a proportion not quite so great as that for all new admittees to the bar nationwide but still substantial.[33] It is clear that by 1980 women were almost as likely as men to join the ABCNY.

Women were eligible for membership in the ABCNY since before World War II, but there remained major obstacles to their full incorporation in the life and leadership of the Association—especially in the 1950s and 1960s. For a start, committee positions were highly sought after, and one might anticipate that female lawyers, being few in number and less likely to have connections with the leadership elite of the ABCNY than their male colleagues, would be disadvantaged in competition for the vacant slots.

Furthermore, the meeting arrangements and culture of most ABCNY committees certainly did not encourage the participation of women members. Committee meetings of the ABCNY have always been held in the evening, rather than during the luncheon hour, which makes committee attendance particularly difficult for women who are

---

32. Curran, "American Lawyers in the 1980s," p. 25.
33. Annual Report of the President, ABCNY, 1981.

already working full-time and have families. Many of these evening committee meetings also had the trappings, and much of the atmosphere, of the surrounding male social clubs. Some committees, indeed, met at neighboring clubs, and most commenced with cocktails and dinner, and an opportunity for genteel collegiality, before settling down to business, with cigars lit, at about eight o'clock. Understandably women might hesitate before attempting to penetrate such an all-male institution.

Despite these negative factors, even as early as 1950, women were appointed to committee positions in numbers approximating their representation in the membership at large. In 1950, women occupied 28, or 3 percent, of a total of 977 committee positions. That percentage increased to 4 percent in 1960, and remained at that level through the 1960s until the 1970s, when it began to rise. By 1980, women occupied 7.5 percent of all committee positions, somewhat less than their 8.9 percent in the membership at large. It would seem, then, that whereas in the earlier decades the ABCNY had little difficulty in appointing women to committees in proportion to their presence in the membership, it has experienced difficulty in keeping up with the sudden influx of women members in the 1970s.

However, women members did not have an equal probability of appointment to all committees, by any means. In the 1950s only certain areas of law were considered as suitable for women. Such perceptions resulted in the almost total exclusion of women from the most prestigious, and lucrative, fields of practice.[34] Women were not considered suited to litigation and were thus largely excluded from the courtroom, and most large law firms refused to hire women lawyers, arguing that their corporate clients would not want to be represented by them. The areas regarded as legitimate for women were those either sheltered from client contact or related to what were considered the inherent nurturant capacities of women.

Family law and its related fields of domestic relations, adoption, and juvenile law were regarded as safe areas in which women could practice. These were also, of course, areas of law anchored in the personal hemisphere of legal practice dealing with "personal-plight" types of legal issues, occupying low standing in the bar and receiving relatively low income.[35] It was to committees active in these areas that women

---

34. In general, see Cynthia Fuchs Epstein, *Women in Law* (New York: Basic Books, 1981). The discussion in this section draws heavily upon Epstein.

35. See Heinz and Laumann, *Chicago Lawyers*, for a discussion of the prestige levels of different fields of practice. They develop the notion of two hemispheres of legal practice, one serving corporate clients and the other, individual.

were most often appointed in the 1950s and 1960s. They were certainly the only committees on which women could expect more than token representation. In 1950, for instance, the Committee on the Domestic Relations Court had three women members, and a woman "chairman." Similarly the Committee on Medical Jurisprudence, a rather amorphous committee with an ill-defined domain, had four women members.

This pattern of appointment of women members to a few "suitable" committees was maintained virtually unchanged throughout the 1950s and 1960s. Indeed, in 1970 there were still no women members on the important and prestigious committees on grievances and judiciary, just as there had been none in 1950 and 1960. Consequently, it can be concluded that, although women members were certainly appointed to committees in the 1950s and 1960s in numbers approximating their proportion in the membership at large, they were by no means fully incorporated into the life of the Association. Rather, they were excluded from both the very important professional regulatory committees and the prestigious substantive committees. While there was not a women lawyers' committee as there was a young lawyers' committee, their appointment to certain "suitable" committees was equally an example of the operation of *inclusion* as a mechanism for admitting but not incorporating women lawyers. A further indication of women's inclusion but not incorporation into the ABCNY was, until the 1970s, their absence from leadership positions. During the 1950s and 1960s, no women were nominated for, or elected to, the offices of president or vice president, or to the Executive Committee.

Changes in the level of women's participation in the ABCNY followed changes in the recruitment patterns of the large law firms in the 1970s. As more and more women gained entry to the major national law schools, so they gained the qualifications necessary for admission to the large firms. Beginning in the late 1960s, some of New York's large firms, generally the more progressive Jewish firms—such as Stroock, Stroock & Lavan and Proskauer, Rose, Mendlesohn & Goetz—willingly recruited and promoted women lawyers; others, especially the older, more traditional Wall Street firms, dragged their feet.[36]

The willingness of these large firms to hire women lawyers was sharply increased by two Title VII lawsuits in the early 1970s filed by female law-school graduates against two Wall Street firms, Rogers & Wells and Sullivan & Cromwell, claiming discriminatory recruitment

---

36. Epstein, *Women in Law*, chap. 11.

practices.[37] The terms of the settlements of these suits accepted by the law firms required them to offer at least 25 percent of their associate positions each year to female graduates and not to hold firm-sponsored events in clubs that barred women. The symbolic significance of these suits, and the 'settlements entered into, were considerable. Women began to gain access to the large law firms in greater numbers. Cynthia Epstein notes that in the 1970s, in fact, Wall Street "became a preferred place for [women] to seek and find employment." She reports that by 1977 women represented 12 percent of the lawyers in the thirty-two largest New York City law firms.[38] Indeed, women were more likely to find opportunities for employment in the large firms of New York City than in the hundreds of small firms where the older partners found it difficult to adjust to women as colleagues at such close quarters.

As we have seen with the ABCNY, however, admission does not necessarily mean full incorporation. Historically, the pioneer women in Wall Street law firms were disproportionately located in backwater areas removed from both client contact and high-risk types of practice,[39] such as trusts and estates and legal research. Women were noticeably absent from the higher prestige areas of corporation law, which involved close interaction with the management of client corporations, and from the litigation department, which demanded a high level of time and energy commitment during the course of a trial. In these areas of large firm practice where the demands are diffuse and unbounded, "professional life can spill over into all parts of private life," making it very difficult for women to manage both career and family.[40] Epstein, however, reports that by the end of the 1970s women lawyers had begun to break out of their stereotyped roles in the large firms. Of the forty-one women partners on Wall Street in 1980, five were in litigation and thirteen in corporate work, compared to only six in the traditional trusts and estates area.[41] Did women members, then, manage to penetrate the core substantive and professional committees of the ABCNY during the 1970s as a consequence of their changed position in the large law firms? Or were women members still subject to processes of inclusion and restricted to a few "suitable" committees?

In the first place, examination of committee listings in 1980 shows that women were appointed to committees in areas of traditional con-

---

37. Ibid., p. 179.
38. Ibid., p. 180.
39. Ibid., pp. 196–200.
40. Rosabeth M. Kanter, "Reflections on Women and the Legal Profession: A Sociological Perspective," *Harvard Women's Law Journal* 1 (1978): 8.
41. Epstein, *Women in Law*, pp. 197–200.

cern for women lawyers in even larger numbers than previously. In 1980 there were six women members of the Committee on Legal Assistance and four on Surrogates Court (Trusts and Estates), and eleven women members (including the chairman) on the Committee on Family Court and Family Law. Women lawyers were also to be found on committees in lower prestige, "local" areas of practice in which they had not been represented before, such as the Municipal Affairs and City Court committees, and, reflecting their recent expansion in numbers, on the Young Lawyers Committee.

In the second place, the ABCNY established two new committees in the early 1970s on which women have been very active. These were the Committee on Consumer Affairs, an area in which women have been active working for various legal-aid and non-profit organizations, and the Committee on Sex and Law, which dealt with the legal issues relating to gender and sexuality. In 1980 both of these committees had women chairs and more than half their members were women. While the disproportionate concentration of women on these committees suggests the continuation of processes of inclusion, their establishment in the first place reflects the growing influence of women on Association policy. This is especially the case for the Committee on Sex and Law, which was established in response to feminist concerns and was to be instrumental in shaping ABCNY policy on gender issues. The influence of women through these committees indicated their greater incorporation into the Association in the 1970s.

In the third place, by 1980 women lawyers sat on almost all the major substantive and professional committees, including core corporate committees such as Corporation Law (four women), Securities Regulation (three), and Taxation (three), and the important federal committees such as Federal Legislation (six) and Federal Courts (two). Generally, the proportion of women on these committees was below or at about the 20 percent level that Rosabeth Kanter posits is necessary to avoid the dynamics of tokenism.[42] Yet Kanter's 20 percent is an arbitrary level, and substantially in excess of women's representation in the Association as a whole or in the wider bar. The presence of women on these core committees reflects a significant change in their gender composition.

A further indicator of the increased incorporation of women in the 1970s is that whereas, in both 1950 and 1960 there was only one committee chaired by a woman, in 1980 nine committees were so chaired,

---

42. Kanter, "Some Effects of Proportions in Group Life."

including the Committees on Courts of Superior Jurisdiction, State Legislation, Copyright, and Corporation Law.

For many women, as for men, appointment to ABCNY committees in core substantive areas was an important form of status conferral and recognition. It is not coincidental that the first two women appointed commissioners of the Securities and Exchange Commission (SEC) were plucked directly from service on prestigious corporate committees in the ABCNY. Roberta Karmel was the first, appointed to the SEC in 1976 for a three-year term. She was a partner at Rogers & Wells at the time, but also an active member of the ABCNY's Committee on Securities Regulation, which gave her wide visibility within the securities bar. Karmel was followed at the SEC by Barbara K. Thomas, partner at Kaye, Scholar & Handler, who was at the time chair of the Committee on Corporation Law. ABCNY committees are small and selective, and appointment to the major substantive committees is a sign of having "arrived" in your specialty.[43] Committee membership not only conferred status but also provided the opportunity to interact with other prominent attorneys. In this way, committee service helped younger and mid-career attorneys to build the professional networks so necessary to successful practice. Positions on the Committees of Securities Regulation and Corporation Law were particularly sought after for this reason. For members of rising groups within the New York bar, then, committee appointments were of considerable importance in confirming, and improving, their professional standing.

Although women have been appointed to a wide variety of committees, full incorporation could only come with their active participation in the leadership of the Association. As of 1980, no woman had been elected president, or even nominated for the presidency, and only one woman had been elected to an officer's position. However, since 1971 there has always been a woman elected to the Executive Committee. One of the three young lawyers elected to the Executive Committee in the "Young Turks' Revolt" of that year was a woman—Sheila Avril McLean—who was at the time an associate at Cravath, Swaine & Moore. McLean served for two years as the only woman on the Executive Committee, but then was joined by other female lawyers in each of the two succeeding years of her four-year tenure. From 1973 there was at least one female member in each new "class" of four persons elected to the Executive Committee, so that in 1980 there were four women on the committee out of a total of sixteen members. In a scant

---

43. This is true not only for women but for all lawyers. Epstein cites a young lawyer as observing that committee membership was invaluable as it marked the lawyer's "arrival." Epstein, supra note 22, p. 254.

ten years, then, female members had moved from no representation at all on the policy-making council of the ABCNY to comprising a full 25 percent of its membership. It took the aggressive action of the "Young Turks" to break the barrier against women, but once broken, female members were represented on the Executive Committee in numbers exceeding their presence in the Association at large.

The penetration of women into the core substantive committees and the Executive Committee in just one decade has been quite remarkable. Clearly, the ABCNY was under pressure in the 1970s to demonstrate its acceptance of female lawyers after such a long history of exclusion. In addition, women lawyers increasingly have professional statuses similar to those of male members of the ABCNY. Thus, the first female officer of the ABCNY and the first woman on the Executive Committee both were from Cravath, Swaine & Moore and bore the Cravath stamp of acceptability. By 1980 women had moved from inclusion to incorporation in the ABCNY to the point where the election of the first female president is by no means out of the question. Indeed, in 1982, the ABCNY hired a woman lawyer as its executive secretary, a key administrative position, the incumbent of which works closely with the president and the committees. Following our earlier predictions, as women increasingly earned the achieved statuses of the dominant group in the ABCNY—graduation from national law schools, employment by large law firms, and practice in corporate law—they have been more fully incorporated into the ABCNY.

ETHNIC MINORITIES AND THE ABCNY

Over the one hundred years or so since the foundation of the ABCNY, the New York bar has become increasingly differentiated in terms of its ethnic composition. There was a steady process of admission into the bar of new immigrant groups in the nineteenth century, especially the Irish-Catholic and German-Jewish progeny of earlier migrations. The scale of admission of diverse ethnic groups changed dramatically, however, subsequent to the massive immigration from South, Central, and Eastern Europe that occurred from 1890 to 1920. Whereas the New York bar in the early years of life of the ABCNY was relatively homogeneous in ethnic composition, by the post–World War II period it was almost as diverse as the neighborhoods of the city. The question, then, is to what extent did lawyers from diverse ethno-religious backgrounds gain entry into the patrician ABCNY as it relaxed its admissions policies and expanded in size in the postwar decades?

In his study of the Wall Street law firms, Erwin Smigel found in the early 1960s that Catholicism *per se* was no longer an important factor in their recruitment of new lawyers, suggesting rather that "discrimination against Catholics is based more on their 'lower-class' origins, their foreign-born parents, and their lack of 'proper' education."[44] Indeed, Catholicism in and of itself was not a major obstacle to membership and even leadership in the ABCNY as far back as 1890. In that year Frederic R. Coudert, a strong supporter of Catholic causes and frequently a spokesman for the Catholic Archdiocese of New York, was elected president. But Coudert was of French extraction, a prominent Democrat, trustee of Columbia University, and was listed in the Social Register in 1900. Furthermore, he was an authority on international law and a founder of the noted international law firm, Coudert Brothers. Coudert had the right social class and professional credentials to offset his Catholicism.

Following Emory Bogardus's proposition that ethnic groups are hierarchically valued according to their length of time in the United States and their similarity to the dominant group, we would expect to find that Irish-Catholic lawyers have been more fully integrated into the ABCNY in the postwar period than other, more recent, ethnic minorities, particularly if they graduated from Ivy League colleges and law schools and practiced corporation law.[45] After all, Irish Catholics were early immigrants to the United States and were indistinguishable in appearance and language from Anglo-Saxon Protestants.

The first Irish Catholic elected to the presidency of the ABCNY in 1921, James Byrne, demonstrates the progress Irish Catholics had made since the days of Charles O'Conor, fifty years earlier. Although from an immigrant family, Byrne graduated from both Harvard College and Harvard Law School and went on to become one of the lions of Wall Street.[46] He was founder of a large law firm and a leading New York corporation lawyer. His listing in the Social Register in 1913 indicated that he had been accepted into the patrician elite of New York; his high social standing was further demonstrated by his election in 1920 to the Harvard Corporation, the governing body of the university, the first Catholic to be so honored.

Byrne was by no means a typical representative of the Irish-Catholic bar, but his elevation to the president's office reflected the acceptance in the ABCNY of Irish-Catholic lawyers who had certain achieved characteristics—elite college and law-school education, membership in a respectable firm, and assimilation into the dominant WASP culture. From the 1920s, then, Irish Catholics with these credentials were to be

44. Smigel, *The Wall Street Lawyer*, p. 45.
45. Bogardus, "A Social Distance Scale."
46. For a brief outline of Byrne's career, see Martin, *Causes and Conflicts*, pp. 202–206.

found on the Executive Committee and on other core committees of the ABCNY.

Lawyers from other Catholic ethnic groups of more recent immigrant status, such as Italian and Polish Catholics, have not been so commonly found in the ABCNY, however. The percentage of members with Italian last names did double from 1955 to 1978 but remained a paltry 4 percent of the membership. Similarly, while Irish names were to be found on the partnership rosters of leading law firms by the 1950s, and two "Irish firms"—Cahill, Gordon & Reindel and Donovan, Leisure, Newton & Irvine—had emerged to take their place among New York's large firms, few lawyers of Italian or Polish origin were to be found in the Wall Street firms in the 1970s. Following the same logic one would expect the most recent Catholic immigrants, those from Latin America, to be even less represented within the large law firms and among the membership of the ABCNY.[47]

The full incorporation of Jewish lawyers into the ABCNY was to take longer than that of the Irish Catholics. Given the strength of anti-Semitic feeling among the Northeastern, Protestant establishment during the first decades of this century, such delayed integration of Jewish lawyers is perhaps to be expected.[48] Yet the dramatically increasing numbers of Jewish lawyers in the New York bar made the openness of the ABCNY to their membership of critical importance. As a professional association claiming to represent the bar at large, and exercising control over it, the ABCNY could not continue to ignore, or only partially admit, such a large proportion of the bar. In Baltzell's terms, the willingness of the ABCNY to admit Jewish lawyers to full membership and participation in the postwar decades was a test of its ability to move beyond the "caste-like" exclusionary mind-set that had been dominant in the American upper class during the interwar years with its explicit anti-Semitism.[49] Was the ABCNY in the postwar years able to transform itself into an open professional elite and welcome to full membership lawyers of achievement whatever their ethnicity?

Not having interviewed the lawyers included in my samples, I use last names as an indicator of ethnicity in order to determine the representation of Jewish lawyers in the ABCNY. Clearly, dependence upon names as ethnic markers is risky as names are frequently changed for the very purpose of avoiding ethnic identification. Use of such a meth-

---

47. There are so few members with Spanish last names that none appeared in my random surveys, even in that of 1978.

48. On upper-class anti-Semitism see E. Digby Baltzell, *The Protestant Establishment: Aristocracy and Class in America* (New York: Vintage Books, 1964).

49. Ibid.

odology to identify Jewish members will certainly result in an under-count because Jewish names have frequently been shortened or other-wise changed to Anglicize them. Yet, last names do provide some indication of the presence of Jewish lawyers, especially of those not afraid to be identified as Jews and therefore more likely to contribute to the ethnic diversity of the ABCNY.[50] Furthermore, there should at least be some internal consistency, as the same method was applied to all three samples, allowing comparison from one point of time to an-other.

Confirming the earlier argument that the ABCNY entered the post-war period overwhelmingly a WASP organization, only 14 percent of the membership in 1955 were identified as Jewish, a very small pres-ence in the ABCNY, given that by 1960 Jewish lawyers accounted for 60 percent of the New York bar. In addition to the continued percep-tion of the ABCNY as an upper-class, Protestant association in which Jews were not welcome, the overrepresentation of Jewish lawyers among solo and small firms, practitioners in personal-plight fields of practice, and their underrepresentation in large firms contributed to their absence. Jerome Carlin found in 1960 that 61 percent of New York lawyers in large firms were members of the ABCNY compared to only 13 percent of those from small firms and 10 percent of the solo practi-tioners.[51] He further notes that "most individual practitioners and small firm lawyers are first- or second-generation Americans, of eastern European Jewish origin. The large-firm lawyers are predominantly Old Americans of British, Irish, or northwestern European origin." The identification of the ABCNY with large-firm, corporate practice made it likely that Jewish lawyers who were significantly underrepresented in the large law firms in the 1950s would also be seriously underrepre-sented in the ABCNY.

To what extent were those Jewish lawyers who were members of the ABCNY in the 1950s, although a small proportion of the member-ship, involved in its life? At what level were Jewish lawyers admitted to the ABCNY? Recall that in the 1920s a leading member of the Jewish community, Louis Marshall, had complained that Jewish members were infrequently appointed to committees of the ABCNY. By the 1950s, however, it does appear that Jewish members were being ap-pointed to the committees at a level commensurate with their represen-tation in the membership. In the 1946 to 1955 period, 34 percent of

---

50. Coding accuracy was facilitated by the employment as coders of native New Yorkers who were very familiar with ethnic names.
51. Carlin, *Lawyers' Ethics*, p. 36.

those members of the 1955 sample identified as Jewish were appointed to at least one committee position compared to 32 percent for the membership at large. In other words, in the ten-year period preceding 1955, Jewish members of the ABCNY stood as good a chance of gaining a committee appointment as other members.

We noted in the previous section that women lawyers had tended to be appointed only to committees in low-status fields of law in which women had traditionally been very active. The appointment of Jewish lawyers to committees might be expected to follow a similar pattern. In 1955, there were few Jewish lawyers on committees in high-prestige corporate fields of law; in contrast, there were relatively large numbers on committees with a local orientation or in areas in which Jewish lawyers have been traditionally overrepresented. Thus, in 1955, Jewish lawyers composed half the membership of the Committees on Arbitration, Domestic Relations, Labor and Social Security Legislation, and Real Property Law. Jewish lawyers were also well represented on committees dealing with the local courts, the Committee on Bankruptcy and Reorganization, and the Committee on Criminal Courts, Law and Procedure, frequently serving as chairs of committees in these areas. Such a concentration of Jewish lawyers in committees in the lower-prestige areas of law does indeed suggest a pattern of inclusion similar to that experienced by female lawyers in the 1950s and 1960s.

While the ABCNY did not have any women in its leadership during the 1950s or 1960s, Louis Loeb was elected as its first Jewish president in 1956. While he was scarcely typical of Jewish lawyers in New York City, his nomination and election presaged significant changes in their position in the ABCNY. Descended from an old established German-Jewish banking family, Loeb was educated at Phillips Exeter and Yale, was a Republican, and a senior partner in Lord, Day & Lord, one of the oldest and most traditional of the New York firms. Like James Byrne thirty years earlier, then, Loeb was every bit as establishmentarian as any WASP: His academic and legal credentials were impeccable, and his style was indistinguishable from that of the WASP leaders of the Wall Street bar.

Although Jewish lawyers have remained underrepresented in large-firm practice into the 1980s,[52] their situation began to improve in the 1960s as the large firms adopted less discriminatory hiring practices. A detailed analysis of the placement of graduates of the Yale Law School from 1952 to 1962 undertaken by the *Yale Law Review* found remnants

---

52. Heinz and Laumann, *Chicago Lawyers* (pp. 203–205), found Jewish lawyers significantly underrepresented in the large firms in the mid-1970s.

of discriminatory practices and attitudes that detrimentally affected Jewish students, but concluded that overall overt discrimination by the large New York firms was declining.[53] Indeed, it does appear that in the 1960s, the large New York firms hired larger numbers of Jewish graduates of top law schools than before and were more willing to promote them to partner. Smigel reported, for instance, in 1969 that in one large firm 25 percent of its partners were Jewish in 1968 compared to none at all in 1957, and confidently asserted that "for Jews discrimination as indicated by hiring practices is essentially gone."[54]

The reasons for this noticeable change in hiring practices are several. There were increased disincentives to continuing discriminatory practices as embodied in federal fair employment practices legislation and the decreased public acceptability of blatant anti-Semitic sentiments. As the *Yale Law Review* suggested, "the changing standards of our society . . . have rendered unacceptable once 'respectable prejudices.' "[55] Furthermore, the high level of achievement of many Jewish students at Ivy League schools made it difficult for the large law firms, increasingly involved in a competition for talent, to ignore them. The rapid growth of the large firms in the 1960s meant that they had to expand the pool from which they recruited new lawyers. Continuing to bypass bright Jewish students at the top law schools meant restricting their hiring at a time when the large firms were desperate for legal talent. Thus, the rapid growth of the large firms in the 1960s and 1970s meant a much-expanded opportunity structure for members of ethnic minorities.[56]

Not only were Jewish lawyers increasingly present in the Wall Street firms, but Jewish firms founded in the interwar years experienced rapid growth in the postwar decades until they rivaled the Wall Street firms in the provision of corporate legal services. Table 2.2 presents a listing of the twenty largest law firms in New York City in 1957 and 1980. The changes in this listing over the twenty-three-year period are considerable, demonstrating the rapid growth and increased market importance of the relatively new Jewish and mixed ethnic firms.

Note that the Irish-Catholic firms—Donovan, Leisure and Cahill, Gordon—were already well established in the 1950s. They retained their

53. Note, "The Jewish Law Student and New York Jobs: Discriminatory Effects in Law Firm Hiring Practice," *Yale Law Journal* 73 (1964): 625–660.

54. Smigel, *The Wall Street Lawyer*, p. 370.

55. Note, "The Jewish Law Student and New York Jobs," *Yale Law Journal* 73 (1964): 653. See also Charles E. Silberman, *A Certain People: American Jews and Their Lives Today* (New York: Summit, 1985).

56. For data on and a discussion of the growth of large law firms, see Robert L. Nelson, "Practice and Privilege: Social Change and the Structure of Large Law Firms," *American Bar Foundation Research Journal* (Winter 1981): 95–140.

Table 2.2. Twenty Largest Law Firms in New York City in 1957 and 1980

1957 Name	Total Lawyers	1980 Name	Total Lawyers
1. Shearman & Sterling	125	1. Shearman & Sterling	312
2. Cravath, Swaine & Moore	116	★2. Fried, Frank, Harris, Shriver & Jacobsen	207
3. White & Case	109	3. Sullivan & Cromwell	206
4. Dewey, Ballantine, Bushby, Palmer & Wood	105	★4. Skadden, Arps, Slate, Meagher & Flom	205
5. Simpson, Thatcher & Bartlett	97	5. Davis, Polk & Wardwell	203
6. Davis, Polk & Wardwell	97	6. Simpson, Thatcher & Bartlett	201
7. Milbank, Tweed, Hadley & McCloy	94	7. Dewey, Ballantine, Bushby, Palmer & Wood	199
8. Cahill, Gordon, Reindel & Ohl	84	★8. Cleary, Gottlieb, Steen & Hamilton	191
9. Sullivan & Cromwell	84	★8. Weil, Gotschal & Manges	191
†10. Chadbourne, Parke, Whiteside & Wolff	70	10. Milbank, Tweed, Hadley & McCloy	190
†11. Breed, Abbott & Morgan	66	11. Cravath, Swaine & Moore	187
†12. Winthrop, Stimson, Putnam & Roberts	63	11. Paul, Weiss, Rifkind, Wharton & Garrison	187
13. Cadwalader, Wickersham & Taft	61	13. Cahill, Gordon & Reindel	185
†14. Willkie, Farr & Gallagher	60	13. Donovan, Leisure, Newton & Irvine	185
15. Donovan, Leisure, Newton & Irvine	58	★15. Coudert Brothers	183
†16. Lord, Day & Lord	56	16. White & Case	179
17. Royall, Koegel & Rogers	55	‡17. Rogers & Wells	172
†18. Mudge, Rose, Guthrie & Alexander	55	★18. Kaye, Scholer, Fierman, Hays & Handler	164
†19. Kelley, Drye & Warren	50	19. Cadwalader, Wickersham & Taft	151
20. Paul, Weiss, Rifkind, Wharton & Garrison	50	★20. Stroock, Stroock & Lavan	150

Sources: 1957 figures come from Smigel (1969, p. 34n); 1980 figures come from *National Law Journal,* 13 October 1980, pp. 32–37.
† Not in twenty largest firms in 1980.
★ Not in twenty largest firms in 1957.
‡ Listed as Royall, Koegel & Rogers in 1957.

position in 1980 but were joined in the largest twenty firms by several Jewish and combined Jewish/Gentile firms. Whereas in 1957 Cahill, Gordon was the only non-WASP firm to break into the top ten largest firms, by 1980 four Jewish or composite ethnic firms were among the ten largest law firms in New York, and nine out of the twenty largest were non-Protestant firms. Equally noticeable is the number of noted older Wall Street firms that had dropped out of the twenty largest firms by 1980, including such traditional WASP firms as Breed, Abbott and Morgan, Winthrop, Stimson, Putnam & Roberts, and Lord, Day & Lord. Though size is certainly not the only, or even the best, criterion by which to judge the success of a law firm,[57] such a turnover in the largest firms in little more than twenty years reflects an increasingly open and competitive market for legal services. In general, the new non-Protestant firms grew because they had special skills at the cutting edge of the legal market or because they had developed expertise in derogated corporate work such as litigation, bankruptcy, mergers, and real estate, which became increasingly central to the interests of large corporations in the 1960s and 1970s.

As a result of the emergence of the large Jewish and Irish firms, high-status corporate legal work was no longer restricted to the established Protestant firms. Jewish and Irish lawyers could become corporate lawyers without needing to gain access to the old Wall Street firms. Such a development, along with the increased willingness of the Protestant firms themselves to hire non-WASPs, resulted in a much more heterogeneous large-firm elite in New York.

As the penetration of the corporate hemisphere of legal practice by Jewish lawyers proceeded, their participation in the ABCNY also increased markedly. In 1978, 25 percent of the membership were identified as Jewish by their last names, a percentage still substantially lower than their presence in the New York bar as a whole but almost double that of 1955. Jewish lawyers were also present on a much wider array of committees than in 1955, being much in evidence on the core Committees on Grievances, Judiciary, and Federal Legislation in 1978. Furthermore, by 1978, Jewish lawyers were well represented on the substantive committees dealing with corporation and banking law, for which there was keen competition for positions. Indeed, the chairman of the prestigious Committee on Securities Regulation in 1978 was Jewish, as were four other members of that committee. Such broad participation in committee work suggests movement from the earlier level of inclusion where Jewish lawyers were concentrated in low-status committees toward the full incorporation of Jewish lawyers into the life of the ABCNY.

---

57. James Stewart's recent book on the elite large law firms—crème de la crème—does not include any of the arrivistes, suggesting that the prestige rankings are still topped by the old WASP firms. See James A. Stewart, *The Partners: Inside America's Most Powerful Law Firms* (New York: Simon and Schuster, 1983).

Furthermore, Jewish lawyers have been increasingly nominated for and elected to leadership positions since World War II. Since Loeb in 1956 there have been more Jewish presidents—Samuel Rosenman in 1964, Bernard Botein in 1970, and Adrian DeWind in 1976 followed in quick succession. All were Democrats and closely identified with the Jewish community. The selections of Rosenman and Botein are particularly interesting as the two men achieved their standing in the bar through careers quite different from those of previous ABCNY presidents.

Rosenman, the son of an immigrant, was born in the South and educated at Columbia College and Law School, a path well trodden by many aspiring Jewish lawyers for whom Columbia was as close as they could get to Harvard. On graduation, Rosenman became active in Democratic politics and developed a close friendship with Franklin Delano Roosevelt, leading to an appointment to a vacancy on the New York Supreme Court when Roosevelt was governor of New York. Rosenman joined Roosevelt in Washington, D.C., in the mid-1930s as an advisor and speech writer. Upon returning to New York he was again appointed to the bench, and after retirement he established his own law firm, Rosenman, Colin, Kaye & Freund, putting to use his substantial Democratic political capital. His standing was considerable in New York, where he was a frequent figure on committees and commissions established by Mayors Wagner and Lindsay. His selection as the official nominee for the president of the ABCNY in 1964 indicated that the Republican old guard in the ABCNY had come to terms with the legacy of the New Deal, which it had once bitterly opposed. Rosenman's election was a portent of things to come, as he was followed as president by Russell Niles, dean of New York University Law School and the first academic to be elected president, and by an unbroken succession of Democrats into the 1970s.

Bernard Botein did not have even the compensatory achievement credential of a Columbia legal education. The son of a rabbi, Botein was a typical product of a New York Jewish ethnic and immigrant background. Educated locally, he graduated from Brooklyn Law School and worked as a prosecutor in the Manhattan district attorney's office before being elected a judge. Having developed a strong record for his probity and legal acuity, Botein reached the highest local judicial position, that of presiding justice of the First Department of the Appellate Division of the New York Supreme Court. Following his retirement from the bench, he joined an established Jewish firm as a name partner, at which point he was elected president of the ABCNY.

Although Botein had worked with the ABCNY in the 1960s in court reform, he was very much a local figure by ethnicity, background, education, and career. His nomination and election as president in 1970 were significant in that he was the first such local figure to gain the position. It does not mean, however, that the ABCNY was willing to consider as presidents leading local ethnic lawyers. Botein was unusual, given his outstanding career on the bench. Since Botein there have been no other local legal or judicial figures elected president, although the office no longer appears to be narrowly restricted to successful corporate lawyers. The third Jewish president of the ABCNY, Adrian DeWind, elected in the mid-1970s, was a Democrat like the others and actively involved in the Jewish community, but was a partner in a large law firm, having followed a more orthodox career path.

In addition to the election of Jewish presidents, the number of Jewish members elected to the Executive Committee also increased steadily after World War II. Whereas one-fifth of the members of the Executive Committee were Jewish during the 1950s, and one quarter during the 1960s, more than a third were Jewish during the 1970s. It is clear, then, that by the 1970s Jewish lawyers were well represented in the leadership of the ABCNY at all levels.

Though Jewish ethnicity *per se* was no longer grounds for exclusion from leadership positions in the ABCNY, not all Jewish lawyers have benefited equally from the increased openness. Of the Jewish lawyers who served on the Executive Committee from 1959 to 1980, only two had strictly local educational backgrounds—that is, attended local New York colleges and law schools other than Columbia and New York University, as have so many Jewish lawyers. In other words, the increased presence of Jewish lawyers in the leadership of the ABCNY does not represent the incorporation of local Jewish lawyers practicing in personal-plight areas of law. Such local lawyers remain included in isolated personal-plight or local court committees to the extent that they are present at all. The increased presence of Jewish lawyers in the leadership of the ABCNY reflects rather the increased number of Jewish lawyers with the "right" credentials, that is, graduation from an Ivy League college and an elite law school and engagement in large-firm or corporate practice. These Jewish lawyers, part of a more heterogeneous large-firm elite, have been fully incorporated into the ABCNY.

FROM ASCRIBED TO ACHIEVED CHARACTERISTICS: TOWARD A LARGE-FIRM MERITOCRACY

While the presence of Jewish lawyers in the ABCNY almost doubled in the twenty-three years from 1955 to 1978, it remained at a much lower level than in the New York bar in general. Given the progressive in-

Table 2.3. Law Practice Characteristics of Members

	1955		1965		1978	
Solo	(37)	15%	(36)	12%	(24)	7%
Small Firm	(59)	24%	(70)	23%	(74)	21%
(2–10 Members)						
Medium Firm	(28)	11%	(44)	15%	(49)	14%
(11–20 Members)						
Large Firm	(27)	11%	(71)	24%	(116)	33%
(21 or more)						
Not in Private	(57)	23%	(76)	25%	(78)	22%
Practice						
No Information	(42)	17%	(3)	1%	(9)	3%
	(250)	101%	(300)	100%	(350)	100%

SOURCE: Author's survey of ABCNY membership records in 1955, 1965, and 1978.
NOTE: Total percent may not add up to 100 because of rounding.

corporation of Jewish lawyers into the mainstream of the ABCNY over this period, however, it is unlikely that the reason for their continued underrepresentation in the membership lies in their ethnic and religious distinctiveness, that is, in their ascribed characteristics. Rather, it is their continued overrepresentation in solo and small-firm practice and underrepresentation in large-firm corporate practice that limits the presence of Jewish lawyers in the ABCNY. Examination of the practice situation of ABCNY members in 1955, 1965, and 1978 shows that the representation of large-firm lawyers in the Association increased rather than declined over the twenty-three-year period, whereas that of solo practitioners halved, and that of small-firm lawyers declined marginally (see Table 2.3). The presence of lawyers from large firms—defined very conservatively as those firms with twenty-one or more partners—actually tripled from 1955 to 1978.

The increased presence of lawyers from large firms is, in large part, simply an artifact of the tremendous growth both in size and numbers of large law firms during this twenty-three-year period. Similarly, the decline in solo practitioners reflects a profession-wide decrease in the proportion of lawyers practicing alone.[58] Yet the growth in the percent of large-firm lawyers and the decline in the percent of solo practitioners are so substantial as to suggest that these trends in the ABCNY's membership more than simply reflect wider patterns. For example, Barbara Curran reports that the percentage of solo practitioners in New York State declined from 56 percent in 1970 to 48 percent in 1980, a signifi-

---

58. Curran, "American Lawyers in the 1980s," p. 23.

**Table 2.4. Law Schools Most Frequently Represented
by Members of the ABCNY in 1955 and 1978**

	1955		*1978*	
Columbia	(77)	31%	(70)	20%
Harvard	(43)	17%	(61)	17%
Yale	(21)	8%	(27)	8%
NYU	(22)	9%	(58)	16%
Fordham	(20)	8%	(19)	5%
NY Law School	(14)	6%	(9)	3%

SOURCE: Author's survey of ABCNY membership periods in 1955 and 1978.

cant decline but not of the order of the decline of solos in the ABCNY's membership.[59] The figures presented in Table 2.3 suggest that the ABCNY, far from becoming more representative of the diversity of the New York bar, has in fact become more closely identified with large-firm practice. Analysis of new members included in the random samples, those who had joined the ABCNY in the six years preceding 1978, confirms this prognosis. Thirty-five percent of the new members in 1978 were from large law firms, compared to only 14 percent of the new members in 1955.

Furthermore, comparison of the law schools from which members of the ABCNY in 1955 and 1978 graduated demonstrates that the relative position of graduates of local law schools has not improved at all; indeed, if anything, it has worsened. Graduates of local law schools are unlikely to practice in the elite large firms or to represent corporations but are much more likely to practice in small firms or alone and to represent individuals on personal-plight matters. Table 2.4 shows that whereas the percentage of members who graduated from Columbia declined markedly over this period, the percentage from Harvard and Yale remained constant. The increased percentage of members who graduated from New York University School of Law, a law school approaching Columbia in reputation, almost makes up for the decline in Columbia graduates.[60] The percentage of graduates from the local schools, Fordham and New York Law School, has in fact decreased. The recruitment base of the ABCNY has become wider, but not to encompass those lawyers who graduated from local law schools.

A further indication of the extent to which the ABCNY has broadened its recruitment is its recognition of lawyers practicing before dif-

59. Barbara A. Curran, *Lawyers' Statistical Report* (Chicago: American Bar Foundation, 1985).

60. See "How New York University Caught Columbia," *The American Lawyer* 5 (November 1983): 92–95.

ferent courts and in various substantive areas of law by the formation of committees in these areas. The creation of such committees enables the Association to contribute to, and influence, developments in particular areas of legal practice. Thus, the formation of new substantive law and court committees indicates the emergent areas of practice the bar association regards as legitimate and wishes to encourage. Once established and functioning, committees provide a focus within the Association for members who practice in their jurisdictions and serve to attract new members who wish to become professionally active in their specialties. Committee formation, then, acts as a barometer of the openness of a bar association to different practice subgroups within the bar.

The ABCNY was generally slow to form substantive law committees, slower than both the NYCLA and the CBA, as can be seen from Table 2.5, but it was particularly dilatory in establishing committees in the personal-plight areas of law in which solo practitioners and small-firm lawyers predominated. Whereas by 1945 the CBA had no fewer than five standing committees that dealt with the legal problems of individuals (Industrial Commission, Civil Rights, Juvenile, Personal Injury, Matrimonial), the ABCNY had only two (Criminal Courts, Law, and Procedure, and Bill of Rights). It did not establish a committee on matrimonial law until 1964, although it did have a committee on the Domestic Relations Court from 1934. Furthermore, though by 1945 the CBA had four separate committees dealing with aspects of the criminal law and courts, the ABCNY had only one, reflecting the fact that the criminal justice system had not been a major concern of the ABCNY for much of its history. Not only were these areas of practice—criminal, divorce, and personal injury law—held in relatively low esteem within the profession because they involved the messy, unpleasant problems of individuals, but, in addition, lawyers from lower-class, recent immigrant ethnic backgrounds were heavily overrepresented among their practitioners. Accordingly, the patrician leadership of the ABCNY was slow to recognize them and to encourage their participation by the formation of committees.

The ABCNY established more committees in the personal-plight realm in the 1960s and 1970s, including several new committees in the criminal justice area,[61] demonstrating its greater openness to more diverse elements of the bar and a new willingness to encourage the par-

---

61. In 1980 the ABCNY expanded the number of committees working in the area of criminal law and institutions to five. These committees were organized under an umbrella Council on Criminal Justice and greatly expanded the presence of the criminal law bar in the ABCNY.

Table 2.5. Formation of Substantive Law Committees in the Association of the Bar of the City of New York, the New York County Lawyers Association, and the Chicago Bar Association

	ABCNY	NYCLA	CBA
	International Law (1920) Trade Regulation and Trademarks (1925) Admiralty (1925) Copyright (1925) Patents (1925) Criminal Courts, Law and Procedure (1925)	Patents and Trademarks (1912) American Citizenship (1925) Bankruptcy (1925) Art (1930) Aeronautical (1932) Communications (1932) Copyrights (1932) Bankruptcy Receivership (1933)	Industrial Commission Board (1923) Administration of Banking (1924) Corporation (1930) Taxation (1934) Insurance (1935) Securities (1937) Administrative (1938)
INTERWAR YEARS	Taxation (1929) Aeronautics (1939) Insurance Law (1939) Bill of Rights (1939)	Commerce (1933) Taxation (1935) Admiralty (1935) Foreign Law (1935) International Law (1935) Workmen's Comp (1935) Civil Rights (1938) Administrative Law (1938)	Civil Rights (1938) Public Utility (1938) Juvenile (1939) Labor (1939) Personal Injury (1939) Patents (1940) Real Property, Probate and Trust (1940) Matrimonial (1940)
IMMEDIATE POSTWAR PERIOD	Administrative Law (1944) Arbitration (1944) Labor and Social Security Legislation (1944) Bankruptcy and Reorganization (1944) Medical Jurisprudence (1944) Corporate Law (1944) Art (1944) Real Property Law (1946) Military Justice (1947) Municipal Affairs (1948) Atomic Energy (1949)	Labor Relations (1947) Military Justice (1947) Socio-Legal Jurisprudence (1948) Real Property Law (1949) Securities and Exchanges (1949)	Criminal (1943) Adoption (1944) Aviation (1944) Constitutional Revision (1940) Antitrust (1949)

	ABCNY	NYCLA	CBA
1950–1965	Foreign Law (1959) Banking Law (1959) Corporate Law Depts (1960) Housing and Urban Development (1960) Securities Regulation (1962) Matrimonial Law (1964)	Psychology, Psychiatry and the Law (1959) Atomic Energy and Nuclear Law (1960) Customs Law (1960) Law of Space (1960) Medical Jurisprudence (1960) Municipal Affairs (1960) Corporate Law (1961) Criminology and Criminal Justice (1965) Matrimonial Law (1965)	Antitrust (1950) Federal Civil Procedure (1954) Admiralty (1958) Commercial Code (1958) Consumer Credit (1962)
1966–1980	Civil Rights (1966) Medicine and Law (1966) Trusts, Estates & Surrogates Crts (1966) Transportation (1968) Immigration & Naturalization Law (1968) Penology (1969) Consumer Affairs (1970) Energy (1971) Environmental (1971) Sex and Law (1971) Inter-American Affairs (1971) Inter-National Human Rights (1973) Communications (1973) Philanthropic Organizations (1973)	Trade Regulation (1967) Women's Rights (1973) Consumer Agreements (1978) Communications and Entertainment Law (1978)	Mental Health (1966) Food and Drug (1969) Science & Technology (1969) Environmental (1971) Narcotics (1971) *From 1972:* Agri-Business Law Arbitration Bankruptcies & Reorganizations Civil Practice Commodities Law Corporate Law Depts Employee Benefits (ERISA) Financial Institutions Immigration and Naturalization Customs Law International and Foreign Land Trusts Local Government Military

Sources: ABCNY and NYCLA committees and dates come from the annual yearbooks of these associations. CBA committees and dates come from Terence C. Halliday, *Beyond Monopoly: Lawyers, State Crises and Professional Empowerment* (Chicago: University of Chicago Press, 1987), pp. 70–71.

ticipation of lawyers from these areas of practice. Of course, the formation of a substantive or a practice committee in itself does not
necessarily mean the full incorporation of its constituency, as the committee can be isolated without any influence over the policies of the
host organization and without opportunities for its members to participate in its leadership. This had long been the fate of the criminal defense bar, which had been included in the ABCNY since 1925 in the
form of the Committee on Criminal Courts, Law, and Procedure, but
largely ignored ever since. Service on this committee did not result in
opportunities for wider leadership in the Association as the nominating
committee kept on putting up slates of large-firm, corporate lawyers
for organization-wide positions. Frustrated by such lack of opportunity
and recognition, criminal defense attorneys from this committee attempted a coup in 1970, running a rival slate of their own candidates
for vacant positions on the Executive Committee. Although defeated,
their action spurred the ABCNY nominating committee into regularly
including on its slates members from this segment of the bar.

Most areas of specialization within the personal-plight sphere were
progressively recognized by the ABCNY during the 1960s and 1970s,
but one substantial area of practice was not acknowledged at all. By
1980 the ABCNY still had not established a committee on tort or personal injury law despite its prominence within the profession generally
and within the New York bar in particular. The absence of a committee
that could serve as an attraction and organizing focus for personal injury plaintiffs' attorneys is highly significant, especially given that 15
percent of the New York bar in 1960 specialized in this sort of legal
work.[62] In sharp contrast, the CBA established a committee on personal injury law as far back as 1939. Lawyers from that committee came
to play a very active role in the leadership of the CBA in the 1960s and
1970s, with several leading personal injury attorneys serving as president during this period. The work of the personal injury plaintiff's attorney was perhaps the most repugnant to the old patrician leadership
of the bar, based as it was on the contingency-fee system and popularly associated with ambulance-chasing. Furthermore, it was an area
of practice in which lawyers from newer ethnic groups and graduates
from nonelite law schools predominated. Thus personal injury lawyers
were at a disadvantage in terms of both ascriptive and occupational
criteria. The continued lack of recognition and legitimation afforded
personal injury lawyers by the ABCNY indicates the maintenance of its
elitist, large-firm character even as it became more inclusive in the
1970s.

---

62. Carlin, *Lawyers' Ethics*, p. 12.

The rapid growth of the ABCNY in the postwar decades and the eventual abandonment of its elaborate admissions requirements in 1972 indicate a broadening of the bases of recruitment into the ABCNY. Changes in the demography of the bar, and in its institutional environment, made it much more difficult for the ABCNY to maintain overt or covert barriers to the admission of lawyers distinguished by their ascribed characteristics, whether age and gender or ethnic and religious background. During these decades, then, women, younger lawyers, Jewish lawyers, and Catholic lawyers were progressively incorporated within the organization, coming to participate fully in its committees and leadership to the extent that they shared the achieved characteristics of graduation from an elite law school and engagement in large-firm, corporate practice. In addition, practice subgroups within the personal-plight hemisphere of legal practice were also increasingly present within the ABCNY, as indicated by the formation of substantive committees in these areas, although they were more likely to be included than incorporated, with perhaps nominal representation in the leadership. The exception was the personal injury plaintiffs' bar, which remained beyond the pale. By 1980, then, the ABCNY was certainly a much more heterogeneous association than in the past, with a broader range of subgroups from with the bar.

The ABCNY did not, however, undergo radical democratization during this time and become fully representative of the New York bar in terms either of the ethnic composition or practice characteristics of its membership. Still including only a minority of the New York bar, the ABCNY remained different from the other comprehensive metropolitan associations that had long since included a majority of their surrounding bars. The CBA by the mid-1970s, for instance, not only encompassed a majority of the Chicago bar but also was fully representative of its ethnic and practice diversity.[63] Jewish and Catholic lawyers were as likely to be members of the CBA as were Protestant lawyers. Although lawyers from large firms and elite law schools were overrepresented in the leadership of the CBA, compared to solo and small-firm lawyers and graduates of local law schools, the sheer numerical presence of lawyers from these latter categories was substantially greater. Furthermore, throughout the 1970s, ethnic Jewish and Irish-Catholic lawyers, engaged in the personal-plight practice of law as solo practitioners or in small firms, dominated the presidency of the CBA.

---

63. Heinz et al., "Diversity, Representation and Leadership in an Urban Bar," *American Bar Foundation Research Journal* (1976): 717–785; Terence C. Halliday and Charles L. Cappell, "Indicators of Democracy in Professional Associations; Elite Recruitment, Turnover, and Decision Making in a Metropolitan Bar Association," *American Bar Foundation Research Journal* (Fall 1979).

The leadership of the ABCNY, however, has remained firmly lodged in the hands of the large-firm elite of the New York bar. The composition of this elite has changed since 1960, becoming less exclusively WASP in its character. Consequently, the ABCNY leadership has also become more heterogeneous and less characterized by the possession of previously important patrician attributes. For instance, the percentage of its leaders (officers and members of the Executive Committee) who were listed in the *Social Register* or belonged to one or more of New York's exclusive social clubs at the time of their occupancy of a leadership position has decreased since the early 1960s.[64] The ABCNY, then, is no longer so evidently a WASP association representing patrician professionalism within the New York bar; but it remains very clearly the organization of the legal elite of the city.

---

64. From 1968 to 1977, only 21 percent of the ABCNY's leaders belonged to an exclusive club and 23 percent were listed in the *Social Register* compared to 33 and 37 percent respectively in the preceding ten-year period.

Chapter Three

The Politics of Organizational Change

Although the ABCNY did not become a mass-based professional association in the postwar decades, it did experience rapid growth with an influx of members with more diverse ascribed characteristics than in the past. An organizational structure designed for a homogeneous membership, assuming substantial value consensus and behavioral congruence, may not serve so well once the membership has become more heterogeneous. Greater heterogeneity brings with it the potential of increased intraorganizational conflict as members with different social backgrounds and values cannot be expected to share the same policy positions. Furthermore, segments of the population that had been historically excluded from male WASP associations such as the ABCNY were unlikely to be enamored of their upper-class culture and organizational peculiarities and thus could be expected to seek to change them once they gained entry.

After outlining the formal organizational structure of the patrician ABCNY, this chapter examines the changes in this structure that were implemented in the postwar decades to accommodate and control a larger and more diverse membership with increasingly plural interests.

HOMOGENEOUS MEMBERSHIP, PRESIDENTIAL AUTHORITY, AND DECENTRALIZED DECISION MAKING

As it entered the troublesome 1960s, the ABCNY was rather similar to an upper-class club in its culture and organizational structure. It was relatively small in size and homogeneous in composition, stuffy in atmosphere and conservative in politics, and informal in administration and decision making. Depending upon the voluntary contribution of members' time—the amateur spirit—it lacked even an executive secretary to oversee its administration. Committees were few in number and small in size, with little turnover in membership from year to year.

Its organizational structure was characterized by apparently inconsistent features. On the one hand, it was a "president-run organization," with considerable authority and discretion vested in the office of
the president. On the other hand, the committees enjoyed considerable
autonomy, and members' meetings (called "Stated Meetings") were
used to determine important matters of policy. Committee autonomy
and collective decision making appear contrary to the centralized authority of the president's office. As we shall see, the apparent contra-
diction was largely resolved by two factors, (1) the president made all
committee appointments, thereby determining the composition of the
committees, and (2) the relative homogeneity of the membership
meant that members could be relied upon to act like gentlemen and
make the "right" decisions at members' meetings.

Whereas in most professional associations, such as the ABA or the
CBA, the president serves a one-year term, in the ABCNY all presidents hold office for two years. Although elected for only one year
initially, the practice was for the president to stand for a second term
of office to which he was always reelected unopposed. Remaining in
office for two years, the president had the opportunity to place his
stamp on the organization.

The most important authority vested in the president was the power
to make committee appointments. The president of the ABCNY was
solely responsible for making all appointments to committee positions
that came vacant during his two-year term of office, including committee chairs. This was an important source of patronage for presidents
because there were few committee positions and they were much
sought after; it is only to be expected that many of his appointments
reflected his professional and friendship networks. More importantly,
the president could influence the work of the committees by his appointments. Power over committee appointments, then, enabled the
president to exert indirectly his influence over the development of association policy.

The president also enjoyed considerable discretion in his actions.
Although there was a managing committee of members, the Executive
Committee, it did not limit in any significant way the president's authority. Its limited schedule indicated its restricted role in the Association's policy-making structure. Unless there were occasions calling for
emergency meetings, the Executive Committee met only once a month
for ten months of the year. In fact, much of the Executive Committee's
time was taken up with budgetary oversight, membership questions,
and discipline recommendations from the grievance committee. Such a
limited schedule and restricted agenda left little time for the consider-

ation of weighty substantive matters or for the development of policy initiatives, leaving the president free to develop his own programs and policies.

In associations with a more heterogeneous membership, and consequently a more centralized decision-making structure, the governing board usually plays a more active role. The board of managers of the CBA, for instance, has scheduled lunch meetings every two weeks and often meets weekly. These meetings frequently continue for two or more hours and involve the consideration of substantial issues. Almost all committee reports come before it, and it has shown little compunction about becoming involved in the substantive and procedural issues raised by these reports.[1] In these organizations, in contrast to the ABCNY, the governing board exercises considerable countervailing power to the president.

In addition, prior to 1945 the president of the ABCNY was not constrained by the presence of an executive secretary or director who administered the day-to-day operation of the Association's affairs. As the elected officers of most professional associations come and go, the administrative staffs generally exercise considerable power as they provide continuity and coordinate the running of the association. Indeed, an executive secretary who has been in office a long time may become a dominant force in a voluntary association, one to whose knowledge and experience even presidents must defer.[2] The president of the ABCNY suffered no such constraint on his discretion because the only staff positions until after World War II were those of building manager and librarian.

The president's freedom to create his own programs was further enhanced by the process by which he was chosen. There were no defined succession stages through which presidential candidates moved prior to their elevation to the presidency. Vice presidents in the ABCNY, unlike in many other associations, served a largely ornamental purpose, contributing to the standing of the organization by their association with it, but were not stepping-stones to higher office. Nor did the president serve a year as "president-elect" before taking on higher office. Rather, the president was plucked from the membership

---

1. For a discussion of the organizational structure of the CBA, see Terence C. Halliday and Charles L. Cappell, "Indicators of Democracy in Professional Associations: Elite Recruitment, Turnover, and Decision Making in a Metropolitan Bar Association," *American Bar Foundation Research Journal* (Fall 1979): 697–767.

2. For a discussion of the great influence of the executive director of the AMA in the years prior to World War II, see Oliver Garceau, *The Political Life of the American Medical Association* (Cambridge: Harvard University, 1941).

at large by a nominating committee, a rather mysterious body elected by the members annually but whose names were never listed in the yearbook. Traditionally, a small group of former presidents and older ABCNY leaders were particularly influential in the choice of the nominee for the presidency, whether or not they officially constituted the nominating committee. In practice, of course, the individual chosen as the presidential candidate was usually a prominent member of the New York bar, almost always a senior partner of a major law firm who had been particularly active in the Association. The absence of a defined line of succession did provide the nominating committee, however, with freedom to select a relative outsider as the nominee should they decide the Association needed fresh impetus, or new direction. It also meant that a new president who was not embedded in the politics of the ABCNY was likely to feel a greater degree of freedom to make changes than he might otherwise feel. Such a succession process encouraged the operation of strong presidential leadership.

In apparent contrast to the authority centralized in the hands of the president, the committees enjoyed considerable autonomy in the preparation and publication of reports. Committees had to meet only minimal requirements prior to issuing their reports: They were required to present their reports for the perusal of the president before they published them. This requirement was intended not to enforce centralized authority but to prevent the issuance of conflicting reports from different committees, or of reports that contradicted previously enunciated ABCNY policy. Generally, the reports were given a perfunctory review before they were allowed to proceed, with the president and Executive Committee accepting the superior substantive expertise of the committees.

As late as 1972, the Special Committee on the Second Century in its report on the Association's decision-making structure recommended the continuation of committee autonomy, suggesting that the Executive Committee avoid overturning committee positions on substantive issues, provided those positions have been arrived at fairly:

> The Executive Committee should never, in a matter where reasonable men can differ, substitute its judgment for that of the substantive committee merely on the basis that a majority of the Executive Committee disagrees with a majority of the substantive committee on the merits of the question.[3]

---

3. "The Decision-Making Structure of the Association," Report of the Special Committee on the Second Century, *Record of the Association of the Bar of the City of New York* 28 (1973): 103.

Having appointed to vacant committee positions those members he knew and trusted, however, the president could rest secure in the expectation that they would not upset the applecart. Given the homogeneity of the ABCNY prior to the 1960s, the risks involved in allowing committees considerable latitude were minimal. Furthermore, the importance of the reports published by the committees was lessened by the fact that they went out under the name of that committee. Strictly speaking, they were not reports of the Association as a whole, but of the committee, although that frequently was a fine distinction lost on the audiences who received the reports. If a committee wanted its report to have the Association's endorsement, then it went for approval to a "Stated Meeting" of the members. One or two committees that operated in highly controversial areas of the law, such as the Committee on Labor and Social Security Legislation, were required to present all their reports to the members for approval. In this way the autonomy granted committees to issue their own reports was complemented by substantial decision-making authority being placed in the hands of the members.

Relative committee autonomy was not the only manifestation of the homogeneity and assumed value consensus of the members. The use of members' meetings, so-called Stated Meetings, held quarterly, as the venue for decision making was introduced in the 1940s and reflected a similar confidence in the good judgment of the members. Such a decision-making process resembled the town meeting much beloved by New Englanders as allowing for the operation of republican virtue. Concerned and active citizens would come to these meetings and express their opinions. Decision making by town meetings or members' meetings was a form of direct democracy, but was to be clearly distinguished from the mass democracy of referenda and plebiscites. It was democracy of a certain type, reflecting strongly held values about the importance of active participation. The ABCNY historically spurned the use of referenda and plebiscites as permitting the authority of numbers to prevail not only over the expertise of the committees but also, perhaps more importantly, over those active members concerned enough to turn out to meetings of the Association.

The range of matters determined at members' meetings was not restricted to matters of association policy. Not only did the members at the Stated Meetings have the authority to admit or reject candidates for membership, but also the members assembled at the annual meeting ultimately controlled the succession process. Executive committee members and association officers were elected at the annual meeting. There was no mail ballot. So members who were not present at the annual meeting could not vote. Usually the slate of candidates put up by the nominating committee was voted into office unopposed, but if there was a contested election supporters of particular candidates could pack the annual meeting and determine the outcome.

The town-meeting style of decision making reflected not only certain values relating to participation but also the belief that the members were colleagues and gentlemen and shared certain values as to both procedures and outcomes. Otherwise the town meeting could readily degenerate into a debating forum where partisan views competed and the larger purposes of the Association were defeated. In expanding the decision-making authority of the members at Stated Meetings in 1946 to include passing on the evaluations of judicial candidates by the judiciary committee, the president expressed confidence that members would put "conscience and pride above politics and profit."[4] Members would not stoop so low as to "pack" a meeting to ensure that their point of view won or that an unfavorable recommendation of the judiciary committee was overturned. Decision making at members' meetings left itself open to that eventuality, however, as usually only a small proportion of the total membership ever attended such meetings, permitting an organized and vocal minority to determine the outcome. In this case the president was to be proved wrong even during his own administration when the supporters of a particular judicial candidate "packed" a Stated Meeting to reverse the recommendation of the judiciary committee as to the candidate's qualifications for the bench.[5] It happened but once, however, and the Stated Meeting survived as an important decision-making venue until the onslaught of young lawyers in the 1970s.

Thus the members, not all the members but those who attended association meetings, held ultimate authority over the admission of new members, the succession process, and the direction of ABCNY public policy, constituting a decision-making system unusual among large professional associations. Such associations had generally moved in the direction of highly centralized and representative decision-making structures, with committees reporting to governing boards and leadership elections generally by mail ballot.[6] The successful functioning of a system that placed so much trust in the members' collective

---

4. George Martin, *Causes and Conflicts: The Centennial History of the Association of the Bar of the City of New York* (Boston: Houghton Mifflin, 1970), p. 263.

5. Ibid., p. 262.

6. See, for example, Halliday and Cappell's "Indicators of Democracy" for the organizational structure of the CBA, and Garceau, *The Political Life of the American Medical Association*.

decision-making capabilities depended upon a high degree of homogeneity and value consensus among the members. With greater diversity among members, more conflict over both procedures and substance could be expected, rendering the town-meeting system of decision making less workable.

As the ABCNY entered the postwar period, then, its organizational structure was characterized by a strong presidency, small, select committees with considerable autonomy, and a town-meeting style of decision making. The question is, to what extent could this structure, predicated as it was on membership homogeneity and face-to-face, collegial forms of control, accommodate rapid growth in size and a more heterogeneous membership with the inevitable attenuation of collegial control that these developments entailed? In the following sections, I examine the sources and consequences of change in the ABCNY's formal structures and organizational culture in the postwar period.

NEW LEADERSHIP AND ORGANIZATIONAL CHANGE

The consequence of permitting the president so much discretion was that a new president could quickly alter the whole complexion of the organization. Furthermore, the open succession process, whereby the nominating committee was free to espouse the candidacy of a relative outsider should it choose to do so, permitted it to select a president who could introduce changes at critical points in the Association's history. This occurred twice in the postwar period, when outsiders were nominated and elected as presidents. Both succeeded in bringing about changes in organization and culture that facilitated the ABCNY's adaptation to the new age and demonstrated the significant role that strong leadership can play in voluntary associations.

The first was Harrison Tweed, elected president in 1946 although a comparative outsider to ABCNY politics.[7] Not having a big investment in the status quo, Tweed was able to sweep with a clean brush and introduce major changes. Creating several new committees in significant substantive areas of law, Tweed both broadened the reach and influence of the ABCNY and increased the opportunities for members to participate in its life. During his time in office the bylaws were changed to limit continuous committee service to three years and to reorganize committee members into three annual "classes," with one class being appointed each year. Recognizing that the late 1940s would

---

7. For an outline of Tweed's contributions to the ABCNY, see Martin, *Causes and Conflicts*, pp. 248–265.

see an influx into the bar of new lawyers, many of whom had deferred law school to serve in the military, Tweed established the status of associate member to permit at least a minimal degree of participation in the Association for newly admitted and younger lawyers.

But, perhaps, his innovation that had the most enduring effect was the establishment in 1945 of the office of executive secretary. Previous to this time the president and officers of the Association handled the administrative demands of their positions through their law firms, but as the Association grew in size and complexity dependence upon voluntarism became increasingly problematic. Managing membership records, implementing committee appointments, coordinating committee activities, and handling relations with external agencies required considerable time and energy. The amateur spirit was no longer enough to ensure efficient management and control, as Tweed himself recognized when he noted that, although the amateur may be a fine fellow, he "lacks the time, the experience and the absolute devotion necessary to achieve maximum results."[8]

The new executive secretary's office was responsible not only for maintaining the membership files and records of the Association, but also for providing support to the president and the committees and editing a new journal introduced during Tweed's reign, the *Record of the Association of The Bar of the City of New York*. These activities made the executive secretary a key figure in the organization through whom a great deal of information flowed, allowing him to become a power broker within the ABCNY. The first executive secretary, Paul DeWitt, remained in the position for thirty-five years, accumulating considerable knowledge and experience. Presidents came and went but DeWitt stayed, and consequently came to exercise extensive influence over association policy, committee appointments, and nominations for elected positions.

Tweed expanded the ABCNY's horizons by appointing new committees and rationalized the administration by creating the office of executive secretary, but he also sought to lighten the heavy atmosphere associated with the ABCNY since Guthrie's austere days. Believing that the members ought not just work together on committees but socialize, he organized entertainments, smokers, debates, and concerts. These enlivened the Association and did much to encourage informality among members, but they did little to modify its patrician culture. After all, Tweed himself was the very epitome of a successful WASP large-firm lawyer. Well known in the New York establishment as a

---

8. Ibid., p. 251.

clubman, painter, and yachtsman, Tweed was a senior partner in a major Wall Street firm who represented members of the Rockefeller family. While concerned to encourage a more relaxed and convivial atmosphere, Tweed was scarcely the one to democratize the Association.

Two decades later, in the late 1960s, the nominating committee again went outside the inner circles of the ABCNY to find a president who would be attractive to younger lawyers disenchanted with established institutions like the ABCNY. They nominated Francis T. P. Plimpton, a successful debentures and bonds lawyer and a name partner at one of New York's leading firms. A graduate of Amherst and Harvard Law School, a member of the city's most exclusive clubs and listed in the Social Register, Plimpton was, like Tweed two decades earlier, a quintessential WASP member of the upper class.[9] But he was a Democrat, a "dove" on Vietnam, and held views that appealed to many of the younger members of the New York bar.

The times were different than when Tweed reigned, with greater external pressures on the Association, and Plimpton went much farther in involving the ABCNY in national politics and controversy. He led the ABCNY into virgin territory in opposing President Nixon's nomination of G. Harrold Carswell when traditionally it had not commented on nominations for seats on the United States Supreme Court, and then orchestrated the opposition of the Northeastern legal establishment to the nomination. He allowed the meeting hall to be used for a rally of lawyers opposed to the Vietnam War, and then personally, albeit in his private capacity, led a march of twelve hundred New York lawyers on Washington, D.C., to protest the invasion of Cambodia. Bernard Botein, presiding justice of the Appellate Division of the New York Supreme Court, First Department, and Plimpton's successor as president, commented that Plimpton "turned the corner on identification with burning issues which a lot of members thought were no business of the Bar Association."[10] Plimpton's involvement of the ABCNY in these matters provoked considerable consternation among more conservative members, causing several resignations from among those who thought the ABCNY should restrict its activities to more traditional professional concerns, but made him "something of a hero" to young lawyers.[11] Plimpton forcefully expanded the purview of the ABCNY to include a broad range of social and political issues.

---

9. Geoffrey Hellman, "Periodpiece Fellow," *New Yorker*, December 4, 1971.

10. Ibid., p. 214. Hellman presents a fascinating account of Plimpton's adventures while president of the ABCNY.

11. Ibid., p. 74.

The spectacular excursions of the ABCNY into the national political arena did not end with the leadership of Plimpton. His immediate successors, Bernard Botein and Orville H. Schell, both had participated in the antiwar march on Washington and so enjoyed similar credentials in that respect to Plimpton. Under Botein and Schell, the Association continued to take controversial public stands. In 1970, the younger members called a special membership meeting to consider a resolution denouncing the invasion of Cambodia. Botein, as president, chaired the stormy meeting at which the original motion decrying the Cambodian invasion was amended from the floor into a much stronger resolution opposing in general the continued American involvement in Indo-China and urging the immediate withdrawal of all American forces therefrom. The resolution was passed overwhelmingly and the ABCNY was committed to an antiwar position.[12] The old guard Republicans, led by Whitney North Seymour (president in the early 1950s), vainly tried to stem the tide. The break between the old and the new leadership of the ABCNY was demonstrated vividly in the debate, with Plimpton, immediate past president, presenting the case for the antiwar resolution and Seymour leading the opposition. Seymour opposed the resolution on the grounds that opposition to the war was something an organization of lawyers should not get into. This was in the tradition of a more conservative definition of the role of a bar association such as the ABCNY: It should restrict itself to involvement in matters clearly to do with the legal profession and the legal system. Overstepping those boundaries, it was suggested, would lead to the dilution of the organization's legitimacy and authority. The ABCNY was going in another direction, however, as Cyrus Vance, chairman of the Special Committee on the Second Century and soon to be president, later noted: "We're moving toward the direction of involvement in many issues which are not strictly legal . . . and I think that's a very good direction to move in."[13]

Plimpton's legacy to the ABCNY, then, was considerable. The door he had opened to greater activism on controversial issues was not to be easily closed. His immediate successors were not "bar association regulars" either—neither Botein nor Schell had been particularly active in the leadership of the ABCNY previous to their election—and they shared his activist stance. Perhaps more important in the long run than the controversial positions the ABCNY took while under their guidance, however, were the formation of new committees in areas of law

---

12. Ibid., pp. 220–222.
13. Paul Hoffman, *Lions in the Street* (New York: Saturday Review Press, 1973), p. 222.

infused with ideology and the appointment of younger members bringing new perspectives both to these new committees and to other established committees. Plimpton formed a Special Committee on Consumer Affairs, which brought a strong pro-consumer perspective into the ABCNY for the first time, and Botein established a Special Committee on Sex and Law, which gave women lawyers a voice in the ABCNY and tackled controversial issues such as abortion, homosexual rights, and the Equal Rights Amendment. Both committees have tended to swathe the ABCNY in controversy, as they presented viewpoints not previously heard in its august halls.

Like Tweed's presidency in the late 1940s, Plimpton's term in office resulted in a redirection of the ABCNY, introducing into the Association new elements and new issues that disturbed its tradition of consensual politics. It is not coincidental that both presidents, who were responsible for introducing substantial changes to a relatively conservative organization, had impeccable upper-class credentials. These undoubtedly enhanced their influence with the legal establishment and facilitated the adoption of change. It is also clear, as their nomination for the presidency while relative outsiders demonstrates, that there was recognition of the need for change among the inner circle of ABCNY regulars. Both Tweed and Plimpton utilized the considerable powers of the presidency to initiate significant changes in the Association. And both moved to accommodate the increasing numbers of younger lawyers in the bar, Tweed by introducing a new category of membership for them, and Plimpton by creating new committees for them and responding to their substantive policy concerns.

GENERATIONAL CONFLICT AND THE ABCNY

The fifteen-year period from 1965 to 1980 was the time during which not only more young people entered the bar than ever before but also age-specific social movements emerged, two of which directly affected the bar. The first of these was the civil rights movement, which in the early 1960s was transformed under the leadership of Martin Luther King, Jr., into a national movement receiving widespread support, particularly from the Northeast. With civil disobedience by blacks aflame throughout the South, there was considerable need for legal representation. A number of young law school graduates volunteered their assistance to programs such as the Mississippi Project and moved to the South to defend blacks.[14] Others, caught up in the enthusiasm of the

---

14. See F. Raymond Marks, *The Lawyer, the Public and Professional Responsibility* (Chicago: American Bar Foundation, 1972).

Kennedy administration, joined the Department of Justice, which was increasingly active in defending blacks' civil rights. This was a social movement appealing to the idealist concerns of young lawyers and it eventually led to the formation of committees on civil rights law in major bar associations.

The second social movement of this period, not only directly relevant to but also led by lawyers, was the legal-services movement. An outgrowth of the "rediscovery of poverty" in the mid-1960s, the legal-services movement sought to correct the evident imbalance in the distribution of legal services by making lawyers more available to the poor and to persons of limited means. Institutionalized in the Office of Equal Opportunity, the legal-services movement had at once strong ideological overtones, which led to attempts to organize the poor as a class and engage in advocacy litigation, and practical concerns manifested in the representation of poor clients by lawyers in legal-aid offices located in poor neighborhoods and rural areas.[15] Again, this movement appealed directly to young lawyers, many of whom contracted to serve in legal-aid offices upon graduation. Indeed, for some, legal aid offered an alternative to more traditional career paths. The legal-services movement was similar to the civil rights movement in that in both movements lawyers sought to extend the protection of the law to segments of the population largely unprotected in the past. Therefore the two movements appealed to similar groups within the bar, generally elite younger lawyers who were secure in their own status and unlikely to be materially affected by fair housing acts and legal-aid offices.

The third social movement directly involving young lawyers was the anti–Vietnam War movement, which grew in strength and intensity in the late 1960s. Broader than the legal-services movement, the antiwar movement was even more age-specific in its appeal. It affected young lawyers not so much as lawyers, in the way that both the civil rights and the legal-services movements did, but as young men subject to the draft. Young lawyers, especially those of middle- and upper-class background, shared the strong antiwar sentiment that inflamed college and university campuses across the nation until President Nixon finally extricated the United States from Vietnam. Encouraging the expression of other antiestablishment discontents, the antiwar movement resulted in a substantial disenchantment with the established institutions of American society on the part of the young. Subsidiary youth move-

---

15. Earl Johnson, *Justice and Reform: The Formative Years of the OEO Legal Services Program* (New York: Russell Sage Foundation, 1974).

ments sought to make societal institutions, including legal institutions, more responsive to the demands of people whose lives were affected by those institutions.

These age-specific discontents heightened awareness of other age differences in the bar and increased the potential for intergenerational conflict in the bar associations. In the legal profession, age and cohort divisions serve as important means of role allocation and division of labor. Theoretically a young lawyer can do anything an older lawyer can do, but in fact there frequently are significant role distinctions according to age. These distinctions are seen most clearly in the large law firms, where young lawyers typically serve a lengthy apprenticeship as associates on salary before a small number are elevated to full membership in the partnership that constitutes the firm. Age is also an important qualification, or disqualification, for serving other roles in the legal system and profession. Young lawyers are generally not appointed or elected to the bench on the ground that they lack experience. It is presumed that as an individual lawyer progresses through various age levels, he accumulates the knowledge and experience that enable him to perform certain social and professional roles. In voluntary associations, such as the ABCNY, age may not be an explicit criterion for the allocation of role, but nevertheless informal norms of seniority frequently apply. Certainly, leadership in these associations is assumed to require professional experience and standing, both of which take time to acquire.

As a consequence, there was a certain asymmetry in age relations in the bar whereby the older lawyers acted from positions of authority toward the younger. This characteristic is by no means peculiar to the legal profession. Eisenstadt notes that this "basic asymmetry of power and authority" is characteristic of the interaction between differing age grades in many institutions in many societies.[16] But in such asymmetry lies the potential of hostile age relations unless the authority relations are regarded as legitimate and are based on shared values. The asymmetry may become particularly poignant if it is underlined by sharp differences in value orientations according to age. The effect of the three social movements affecting lawyers in the 1960s, together with the rapid increase in the number of younger lawyers during this period, was to encourage such differences within the bar. Participation in various protest movements confirmed the sense of age solidarity among younger members of the society and emphasized discontinuity with older age groups.

16. Schmuel N. Eisenstadt, *From Generation to Generation: Age Groups and Social Structure* (Glencoe: Free Press, 1956), p. 29.

Demonstrating an awareness that age differences had become sharper during the 1960s, a leader of the CBA observed in 1969 that "young lawyers nowadays have an entirely different philosophy of the legal profession."[17] For many younger lawyers, the organized bar was too hesitant and conservative, too likely to place the profession's self-interest before the public interest, and not responsive enough to the widespread need for legal services. Not only were young lawyers disappointed with the performance of bar associations, but they had strikingly different views as to the relative importance of the various functions bar associations might serve. In their 1974 survey of the Chicago bar, Heinz et al. asked lawyers to rate the importance of thirteen possible objectives for bar associations in general and the CBA in particular. On seven of the thirteen proposed objectives, young lawyers (under thirty-five) differed significantly from older cohorts over the level of importance assigned to these objectives. Whereas older lawyers in Chicago rated as important objectives such as "improving the status of the profession," "disciplining lawyers," and "unauthorized practice," younger lawyers gave significantly higher ratings to objectives such as "improving the lot of the disadvantaged" and "taking stands on controversial issues."[18] Although age is not necessarily a predictor of political values, it is clear that younger lawyers during this period of turmoil wanted their bar associations to adopt a more activist stance than did their older colleagues.

The "counter" bar associations formed in 1969 and 1970 in major metropolitan centers served to express the reformist agenda of elite young lawyers. In Chicago, the Chicago Council of Lawyers, with a membership largely composed of younger lawyers from large firms and legal-aid offices, aggressively pushed for a higher quality bench, improved access to justice, and reforms in the legal system. Despairing of achieving these ends through the inclusive CBA, where competing interests within the bar all too often seemed to stymie reform initiatives, the Chicago Council of Lawyers presented itself as an alternative voice within the Chicago Bar. For its part, the CBA was hostile to the Chicago Council from the outset, denying it access to CBA facilities and refusing to accord it any recognition, thereby encouraging the council's independent, competitive stance.[19]

---

17. Cited in Michael J. Powell, "Anatomy of a Counter-Bar Association: The Chicago Council of Lawyers," _American Bar Foundation Research Journal_ (Summer 1979): 506.

18. John P. Heinz, Edward O. Laumann, et al., "Diversity, Representation and Leadership in an Urban Bar," _American Bar Foundation Research Journal_ (Summer 1976): 744–766.

19. Powell, "Anatomy of a Counter-Bar Association."

In other cities young lawyers who formed similar "councils" satisfied themselves with more modest goals. They did not attempt to become alternative organizations competing with the established bar associations to represent the legal profession. Rather, they sought to operate as pressure groups within the metropolitan bars, encouraging them toward serving the public interest. Formed in the same year as the Chicago Council of Lawyers, the New York Council of Law Associates took this more limited path. It sought to provide opportunities for public-interest law activities and to serve as a meeting place for associates in large law firms. Although it eschewed direct involvement in politics, even in the antiwar movement, which was popular among young professionals in New York City, its leadership was active in liberal political and social causes, including the antiwar movement, reflecting its reformist predilection.

In large part, the reason for the New York Council's more modest agenda can be found in its perception of the ABCNY as an organization relatively sympathetic to its concerns. Heinz and Laumann found that the sort of lawyers who led the ABCNY, elite corporate practitioners, were much more liberal on civil libertarian and social issues than their colleagues practicing in the personal hemisphere.[20] There was also a basic similarity of interest and style between the large-firm leadership of the ABCNY and the founders of the Council, predominantly associates at the large firms, graduates of elite law schools, who also practiced in the corporate hemisphere.

Furthermore, the ABCNY had already demonstrated considerable sensitivity on issues of civil rights by providing Martin Luther King, Jr., with a platform in New York City, endorsing the Civil Rights Act early and vigorously, and supporting the Mississippi Project. In these respects it contrasted sharply with the CBA, which oscillated and procrastinated on civil rights matters, not coming out in support of the Civil Rights Act until it was too late to matter.[21] The ABCNY in the late 1960s also supported neighborhood legal clinics and, in general, the wider provision of legal services, with its leaders pressing the ABA to endorse federal expenditures in legal aid. And, of course, under the leadership of Plimpton, the ABCNY had become increasingly identified with the antiwar movement. Proving themselves to be quite progressive on these matters, perhaps because their practices and life-styles

---

20. John P. Heinz and Edward O. Laumann, *Chicago Lawyers* (New York: Russell Sage Foundation, 1982).

21. See Terence C. Halliday, "The Idiom of Legalism in Bar Politics: Lawyers, McCarthyism and the Civil Rights Era," *American Bar Foundation Research Journal* (Fall 1982): 911–989.

were not threatened by them, the leaders of the ABCNY were not viewed as impossible obstructionists by the young lawyers of the New York Council.

In contrast again to the CBA, the ABCNY sought to accommodate the New York Council, providing it with free space in its building and generally seeking to cooperate with it rather than to oppose it. Such accommodation followed the classic strategy of co-optation, whether conscious or not, and further undermined any tendency on the part of the New York Council to become more oppositional.[22] Yet that is not to say that the young lawyers who formed the New York Council did not want change in the ABCNY, or did not pose a challenge to its leadership. They did. They sought more support for public-interest law, including the sponsorship of "public interest law firms," and wanted greater opportunities for the active participation of young lawyers in the affairs of the ABCNY. Despite its modest pretensions, the Council was an age-specific organization that encouraged a form of age solidarity among younger members of the bar with potentially unpredictable consequences. After all, the ABCNY, notwithstanding its support of civil rights and civil libertarian issues, was still controlled by a gerontocracy. Young lawyers now had an organizational forum from which to challenge this basic asymmetry.

REVOLT OF THE YOUNG TURKS

The challenge to the control of the older lawyers of the ABCNY was not long in coming. In 1971, the year following the criminal defense bar's unsuccessful challenge to the dominance of the large-firm elite, young lawyers ran as an insurgent slate for three of the four vacancies on the Executive Committee in direct oppostion to the official candidates of the nominating committee. With the New York Council as an organizational base from which to work, the young insurgents were able to gain the support of younger members and consequently to pack the annual meeting with enough young lawyers to win easily.

Journalist Paul Hoffman observed of the "Young Turks' Revolt," as the incident came to be dubbed, that:

> Other than the generation gap, there were no issues in the contest. Other than gaining a vote in its management, the Young Turks evinced no desire to take over the Bar Association and were content with presidents like Plimpton and Botein.[23]

22. See Philip Selznick, *TVA and the Grassroots* (Berkeley: University of California, 1949).
23. Hoffman, *Lions in the Street*, pp. 223–224.

Hoffman's observation is pertinent: The Young Turks had no reason not to approve of Plimpton and Botein, who had followed a course entirely satisfactory to the elite young reformers. It was certainly not a coup d'état: There were only three young lawyers on a committee of sixteen, and the presidency remained secure in the hands of the official nominee, Judge Botein.

Their purpose was to gain representation for younger lawyers at the highest level in the ABCNY. Yet it would be wrong to dismiss the so-called revolt as without significant consequences for the ABCNY. It severely tested the whole succession process, resulting in changes in that process the following year; it jolted the nominating committee, three of whose candidates were defeated by lawyers still in their twenties; and it resulted in the first election of a woman lawyer to the Executive Committee. Though there may not have been substantial policy differences between the Young Turks and their seniors in leadership positions in the ABCNY at that time, the newcomers brought a wholly different atmosphere to the meetings of the Executive Committee. They were also able to form coalitions with other more liberal members of the Executive Committee on certain policy issues and thus influence policy decisions.

The sudden introduction of youthful lawyers, including a woman, into the rather clubbish, all-male enclave of the Executive Committee was a considerable shock. Generally, the members of the Executive Committee were older lawyers, partners at the large firms or in established legal positions, who knew one another well prior to their election. Consequently, they interacted with a considerable degree of informality. The Young Turks, however, were mere associates just out of law school, and one of them was a woman! They could not interact easily and informally with their much senior colleagues, who included such well-known figures as future Secretary of State Cyrus Vance and Whitman Knapp of the "Knapp Commission." The election of a woman in itself made for changes in the clublike culture of the Executive Committee: no more dinners at the neighboring, exclusive all-male social clubs, and distinct limits on the all-male camaraderie that tended to develop at such meetings. On top of that, the Young Turks proclaimed they could not afford the expensive dinners that traditionally preceded the Executive Committee meetings; subsequently, apart from one annual dinner at the end of the year, the Executive Committee met after dinner. Thus the effect of the election of the Young Turks was to change the culture of the Executive Committee from one reflecting the aristocratic tendencies and private club experiences of many of its members to something more closely approximating that of a governing board of a comprehensive professional association on which differing, and sometimes conflicting, constituencies were represented.

Not so respectful of inherited tradition as their elders, the Young Turks challenged accepted ways of doing things. For example, the chairman of the Executive Committee each year had always been a member of the senior "class" of the committee, chosen consensually by his other classmates although nominally elected by the committee as a whole. In 1971 the Young Turks nominated their own candidate for the important chairman's position in opposition to the senior "class" candidate. The Young Turks' nominee lost, but it was the first election for the position in living memory. Such actions, naturally enough, disturbed the highly consensual atmosphere that had previously prevailed on the committee. Proceedings became much more contentious, even though the Young Turks were similar to their older colleagues in many respects.

The revolt of the Young Turks brought in its train changes not only in the culture of the Executive Committee but also in its future composition. Thenceforth, the nominating committee deliberately endeavored to make it more broadly representative by nominating lawyers with more diverse ascriptive backgrounds. Since 1973, for example, women and blacks have been regularly nominated for and elected to Executive Committee positions. Indeed, since the mid-1970s, the Executive Committee has been more representative of the bar at large than has the membership. Moreover, these newcomers to the committee were not content for it to remain a relatively powerless entity within the ABCNY. As a consequence, there was a significant increase in the number of policy issues considered by the Executive Committee in the 1970s.

THE DEMISE OF THE MEMBERS' MEETING

Further changes in the organizational and decision-making structures of the ABCNY followed the election of the Young Turks and the turbulent events of 1970–1971. These changes moved decision-making authority in apparently opposite directions at the same time: In certain areas, decision making was diffused from the members' meeting to all the members, while in other areas the authority to make binding decisions was centralized in the Executive Committee. Although the simultaneous diffusion and centralization of decision-making authority appear inconsistent, both processes had the same effect—the diminution of the role of the members' meeting and the consequent demise of the town-meeting style of decision making.

The election of the three Young Turks to the Executive Committee in 1971 triggered an almost immediate change in the ABCNY's electoral process. Up until this point officers of the Association and members of the Executive Committee were elected at the annual meeting by those members in attendance. As we have seen, such a process left open the possibility that a discontented group of members could pack the meeting and elect its own candidates, as did the young lawyers. To ensure that this did not happen again, mail ballots were instituted, thereby extending voting rights to all members, not just to those who attended the annual meeting. As mail ballots permitted the participation of a greater number of ABCNY members in the elective process than had been the case before, the democratic Young Turks could hardly oppose the change, even though, ironically, its effect was to make it much more difficult for such an insurgency to succeed in the future. Whereas it is relatively easy to pack a meeting with one or two hundred supporters and win an election that way, it is much more difficult to mobilize enough support to win a mail vote in which two or three thousand members, or more, participate. Election by mail ballot diffused the electoral process and made successful challenges to the slates of candidates proposed by the nominating committee less likely in the future.

The controversy caused by the special members' meeting called by young lawyers to protest the United States invasion of Cambodia in 1970 also resulted in further diffusion of decision-making authority and in clear limits being placed on members' discretion at these meetings. Once again, the dangers of town meeting decision making had been demonstrated: One segment of the ABCNY's membership was able to commit the Association to a position on a matter of public controversy simply by being in a majority at a meeting of the members even though it is not at all clear that their position reflected the views of a majority of the entire membership. Thus a minority of the members could determine the policy positions adopted by the Association. To minimize that possibility, former leaders of the ABCNY suggested that there should be a provision for referenda of all the members on matters of general public interest before the Association could be committed to a position. The suggestion was somewhat ironic, in that in the past the leadership of the ABCNY had vigorously opposed the whole notion of referenda and plebiscites as catering to the uninformed opinion of the mass of members. Even after the special meeting on Cambodia there was still considerable skepticism about referenda. The Special Committee on the Second Century (1972) observed with reference to internal decision making:

We therefore believe that a referendum approach to the decision of public questions should be used only in the exceptional case, because we do not believe that a head count of the membership is the best way to ensure a competent result.[24]

Nevertheless, in 1975 the bylaws were amended to provide that in matters of "general public interest" a resolution introduced at a members' meeting can be submitted to the entire membership in referendum, should 45 percent of those present at the meeting so desire. Thus provision was finally made for decision making by referenda on matters of public policy in case it was necessary, a step that represented the further diffusion of decision-making authority to the members at large.

The controversial 1970 special meeting of members also resulted in limits being placed on the ability of members at such meetings to amend from the floor resolutions proposed in advance. This change decreased the likelihood of unpredictable outcomes. To ensure against "unexpected results," stringent limitations were placed on what could be done at stated or other membership meetings. The full text of any resolution to be voted on at a meeting of members had to be published well in advance so that all members would be fully informed and able to plan to attend if they so desired. Furthermore, resolutions could only be amended from the floor if the proposed amendment did not substantially depart from the terms of the original resolution. The argument was that members had come to the meeting prepared to vote only on the published resolution; any significant divergence from the substance of that resolution was unfair to the members, both to those who were in attendance and those who were not. Consequently, the members' meeting could approve or disapprove a resolution, take no position or action, or refer it to a committee of the Association, but not substantially amend it.

Other changes in the role of the members' meeting during this time led to the further diminution of its decision-making authority and increased the importance of the Executive Committee. As part of the transformation of the admissions' requirements in 1972, the locus of final authority over whom to admit to membership was transferred from the members' meeting to the Executive Committee. In addition, the decision was made to abolish the requirement that certain committees, especially the Committee on the Judiciary, report to the member-

---

24. "The Decision-Making Structure of the Association," Report of the Special Committee on the Second Century, *Record of the Association of the Bar of the City of New York* 28 (1973): 101.

ship for the approval and adoption of their reports. Instead, the committees were either authorized to publish their own reports without further approval, as in the case of the judiciary committee, and so given greater autonomy, or required to report to the Executive Committee. While some matters of policy, especially very controversial matters, would still be submitted to the membership for approval, on most matters the Executive Committee was increasingly vested with the authority to speak for the ABCNY as a whole.

Perceived as having become too unpredictable to serve any longer as a reliable decision-making device, members' meetings were used less and less to determine the policies of the Association. From 1950 to 1959 the position of the ABCNY on fifty-eight policy issues, that is, issues other than those to do with internal governance, membership, or judicial evaluations, was determined at stated meetings; in the decade from 1960 to 1969 that number declined to twenty, and in the most recent decade of the 1970s to only six. If you add to these figures the loss of final authority over the electoral and admissions processes, and over judicial evaluations, the decline in the role of membership meetings becomes startling indeed.

CONTINUITIES IN COMMITTEE STRUCTURE

There was some tightening of centralized authority over committees with an extension of the length of time committee reports were to be lodged with the executive secretary prior to publication (from three to five days). The purpose of this requirement was to allow time for the executive secretary and the president to peruse the reports to ensure that the positions taken did not conflict with previous policies adopted by the ABCNY or with positions taken by other committees. With a greater number of committees, some of which had overlapping jurisdictions, it was clear that a mechanism was needed to decrease the possibility of inconsistent reports emanating from the ABCNY. Furthermore, if committees wished to publish their reports as representing the position of the ABCNY as a whole, then they had first to receive the approval of the Executive Committee rather than the members assembled at a stated meeting.

These, however, were relatively minor restrictions on committee autonomy as they were still permitted to publish their own reports without first going through any central authority, provided those reports were presented as reports of the committee and not of the Association. How was the organization able to permit its committees so much latitude when it was becoming more heterogeneous and experiencing considerable internal conflict? It was possible because committees remained small in size, and therefore relatively exclusive, and because the committee-appointment process remained centralized in the hands of the president.

The committees of the ABCNY have always been small and select. In 1955 each standing committee was to include fifteen members plus a chairman, unless the bylaws explicitly decreed otherwise. As many of the committees were exempt from the fifteen-member size limitation, the average size of standing committees in 1955 was, in fact, eighteen members. Subsequently, the bylaws were amended to permit the president to appoint additional members to all committees, in increments of three, up to a total of twenty-seven members. This relaxation of the requirements for committee size, however, did not increase greatly the average size of committees. By 1978 the average number of persons on a standing committee numbered only twenty, and half of the committees still had only fifteen to eighteen members. Few committees had reached the maximum size of twenty-seven members. ABCNY committees, then, remained relatively small and, as a consequence, selective.

Although there were many new committees established in the three decades after the end of World War II, and thus a substantial increase in the total number of committee positions, the ratio of committee positions to members actually decreased. In 1955 there were 824 committee positions on both standing and special committees; by 1978 that number had increased to 1,460, a 77 percent increase. Over the same period of time, however, the active membership of the ABCNY virtually doubled in size. Thus the 77 percent increase in committee positions, impressive when viewed alone, failed to keep pace with membership growth as a whole. Consequently, there was less likelihood that a new member in 1978 would receive a committee appointment than had been the case in 1955.

Examination of the actual committee participation rates of ABCNY members in 1955 and 1978 demonstrates such a decreased likelihood. In 1955, 48 percent of the active membership of the Association had served on at least one committee up to and including that year, whereas in 1978, the proportion dropped to 38 percent. Consequently, the percentage of members who had never served on a committee increased between 1955 and 1978. These changes in participation rates occurred despite stricter enforcement since the 1950s of requirements for turnover of committee membership and despite a decline of 9 percent in the number of members appointed to more than one committee simultaneously. Committee positions, then, were even scarcer at the end of the 1970s than they had been in the mid-1950s and, as a consequence, demand for these positions remained very high. Many members who wished to serve on a committee in the 1970s, as in the 1950s, were unable to do so.

In direct contrast, many comprehensive bar associations opened their committees to all members who wished to serve on them, no longer selecting among those interested or actively recruiting elite practitioners as members. In the case of the CBA this led to large, open committees, in some cases with more than two hundred members. The advantage of such large committees was that members who wanted to serve were not frustrated by the lack of openings, and therefore presumably were less likely to be dissatisfied with the organization. A significant disadvantage, other than their obvious unwieldiness, was that by being fully inclusive the large committees diminished the incentive for more established practitioners to participate. While the exchanges on a mass committee like many of those of the CBA might benefit a neophyte lawyer, they were hardly likely to reward the participation of a senior partner in a large law firm or an established practitioner who no longer needed to develop referral networks. In contrast, an invitation to participate on a small, select committee such as those of the ABCNY was in itself an indication of standing in the bar, a form of status conferral. Furthermore, the quality of interchanges was likely to be higher and therefore more rewarding to experienced members of the bar. The "elite" model of a committee, then, which the ABCNY retained, would be more likely to garner the active participation of leading members of the bar than would the mass committee.

Similarly, whereas in the CBA and other associations, a "Committee on Committees" was established to oversee the process of committee appointments, in the ABCNY this process remained centralized in the office of the president. Of course, a president could not possibly know personally sufficient lawyers in all the various fields of law to make the appointments unassisted. The president depended on the assistance of the executive secretary, who attended many committee meetings and was likely to know the more active members, and the committee chairs who might be expected to know those lawyers who had achieved a degree of prominence in their fields. In general, selection of committee members was an informal process. A member gained a committee appointment in the ABCNY either through personal networks and ties, or by having a strong reputation in a particular field of law and thereby becoming known to the leadership of the committee.

In 1977 a limited step was taken toward opening up the process of committee appointment. By means of a survey of the membership, asking those who wanted to serve on committees to list their preferences, a pool of candidates for committee positions was developed. The president and committee chairmen had access to this pool in making new appointments that year and in succeeding years. Examination of committee appointments in 1978, however, indicates that the new procedure made little difference to the outcome of the allocation process other than by giving it the appearance of openness. Positions on committees that were highly sought after, such as those in the corporate law field, were generally filled by lawyers with established reputations, many of whom did not formally request such placement. Few members who requested placement on these committees through the survey were so placed. The president, with the assistance of committee chairs, continued to appoint to the prestigious substantive committees members with established reputations.

The committee-appointment process had changed since the 1950s, however, in one respect. An effort was made to appoint to committee positions members from the ascribed groups that in the past had been denied recognition: young lawyers, women, and members of ethnic minorities. But there were no changes in the essential elements of the appointment process and in the limited opportunities for committee service.

CENTRALIZATION OF DECISION-MAKING AUTHORITY

As a direct consequence of the diminution in the role of the members' meeting, the decision-making authority of the Executive Committee was expanded. By the end of the 1970s it had the final authority to admit new members, and was authorized to pass on committee reports that sought the endorsement of the Association as a whole. At the same time, it broadened its agenda to include wider policy matters. In large part this reflected the assertiveness of its new members, who were less willing to accept a passive or secondary role in the development of the Association's policies. While it was taking upon itself a larger and more active role in policy-making, the Executive Committee at the same time became much more diverse in composition as the nominating committee deliberately sought to ensure representation from a wide range of groups within the bar. Consequently, meetings became more contentious, with the influence of the younger and newer members evident in the positions it took during the 1970s.

The increased unpredictability of a more representative Executive Committee, however, was counterbalanced by the undiminished authority of the president and the addition of the vice presidents as voting members. As the Special Committee on the Second Century noted in 1972, "The Association is a president-run organization; we believe it should remain so."[25] Presidents continued to serve for two-year terms, and with the increased size of the Association and its expanded programs, the position required almost a full-time commitment. As the president was unpaid, the time demands of the job effectively restricted the pool of potential incumbents to those in large law firms or to those who had some other means of financial support that would allow them to spend more than half their time on association affairs. Consequently, the presidents continued to be overwhelmingly senior partners from large firms. Indeed, all the presidents in the 1970s were males, and from large firms, despite the Association's increased diversity.

Moreover, the office of vice president was vested with new authority within the organization. Previously honorary officers without any specific responsibilities, vice presidents were given the right not only to attend but also to vote at meetings of the Executive Committee. As vice presidents typically were recruited from the same status group within the bar as the presidents, prominent lawyers who were frequently senior partners of large law firms, their participation in Executive Committee deliberations and votes on policy decisions served to dilute the effect of a more representative Executive Committee.

Of the three major elements of an upper-class organizational structure that characterized the ABCNY in the 1950s—town-meeting style of decision making, committee autonomy, and presidential discretion—only the first underwent significant change in the decade of the 1970s. Committees remained relatively small and selective in their membership and retained a considerable degree of autonomy. The changes in the conduct and role of the members' meeting were considerable, resulting in the simultaneous diffusion and centralization of decision-making authority. Even those changes, however, that resulted in the diffusion of decision-making authority in particular instances to the membership at large were not intended to encourage participatory democracy as much as to shield the ABCNY from minority takeovers and unpredictable outcomes. Indeed, these changes made it more difficult for disaffected members to challenge successfully the leadership or established policy. Diffusion of decision-making authority was really a means of maintaining control. Members' meetings still determine constitutional and bylaw changes and still debate matters of policy, but their role in decision making has been considerably lessened.

25. "Administration of the Association," Report of the Special Committee on the Second Century, *Record of the Association of the Bar of the City of New York* 28 (1973): 714.

What can we say, then, in summary, about the direction of organizational changes affecting the ABCNY over this period? Just as the changes in the membership composition of the ABCNY, on examination, turned out to be less sweeping than anticipated, and certainly not to lead to the democratization of the membership, so too the changes in decision-making processes and organizational structure were less than revolutionary. Continuities outweighed, or at least balanced, changes. That is not to decry the significance of the changes in the composition of the Executive Committee and in the culture of the Association that did occur, but only to suggest that they did not entail the fundamental democratization of the ABCNY. Furthermore, by the simultaneous diffusion and centralization of decision-making authority, the leadership was able to manage the unpredictability introduced by the influx of disenchanted younger lawyers in the 1970s. These were successful adaptive strategies that enabled the ABCNY to accommodate a more diverse membership and yet retain its overall elite organizational structure.

The general direction, then, of the changes and continuities in the organizational and decision-making structures of the ABCNY in the postwar years was the increased centralization of authority and control in the leadership. The growth in the size and complexity of the ABCNY required some rationalization of its administration and management. Amateurism and voluntarism were no longer enough. The establishment of the executive secretary's office in 1945 led eventually to the development of a differentiated administrative staff with three separate departments and a total of twenty-eight employees by 1980. Clearly, the emergence of such a substantial administrative capacity made possible the more efficient handling of membership records, budgetary matters, and association activities, and permitted greater bureaucratic control.

In centralizing decision-making authority, the ABCNY has followed the same path other associations took much earlier as they grew in size and diversity and could no longer rely on personal interconnections and homogeneity as means of organizational control. The CBA removed virtually all authority from its members' meetings prior to World War I and extended the control of its managing board over the committees in the 1940s. All committee reports within the CBA were submitted to the board of managers and none could be published without its prior approval.[26] Such centralization was clearly a means of maintaining intraorganizational control and stability.

26. Terence C. Halliday, *Beyond Monopoly: Lawyers, State Crises and Professional Empowerment* (Chicago: University of Chicago Press, 1987), pp. 94–100.

We have discussed changes and continuities in the ABCNY's organizational and decision-making structures as if these were disembodied forms, but they are not without important substantive consequences. Organizational structures can be used as both a means of control and a means of implementing change. The considerable extent of presidential discretion meant that a new president could implement dramatic changes in short order, as did both Tweed and Plimpton. The structure encouraged strong leadership on the part of the president. New committees were created and new people appointed to old committees, especially during Plimpton's presidency. In that way new perspectives and ideas could be, and were, introduced readily into the organization.

The introduction of new people and new ideas, however, enhanced the likelihood of conflict within the Association, especially given differences in age, gender, and professional values. Indeed, the politics of consensus collapsed in the face of the new diversity of interests and ideologies in the 1970s, and the patrician organizational culture, based upon similarities in social background, was displaced by a new professional elitism. Previously committees were not only exclusive but had little membership turnover, and their meetings were as much occasions for social intercourse as for undertaking the work of the profession. With enforced membership turnover they became working committees, the members of which were selected more for their professional accomplishments than for their gentlemanly manners and ascribed characteristics. As Parsons noted, the "cultural superiority" associated with achievement in an occupational role is quite different from the "cultural refinement" of the aristocrat.[27]

With increased numbers of committees, and new perspectives represented within the ABCNY, jurisdictional disputes and conflicting policy recommendations were increasingly likely. In the next chapter I examine the heightened dissensus that followed the introduction of new people and ideas and demonstrate how the organizational structure of this elite professional association affected its policy positions and effectiveness.

---

27. Talcott Parsons, "Equality and Inequality in Modern Society, or Social Stratification Revisited," in *Social Stratification: Research and Theory for the 1970s*, ed. by Edward O. Laumann (New York: Bobbs-Merrill, 1970), p. 13.

Chapter Four

Managing Diversity and Dissensus

Increased membership diversity resulted in a higher level of dissensus in the ABCNY than in the past. In particular, the existence of generational differences in values and expectations as to the functions of bar associations became particularly pertinent in the late 1960s and early 1970s with age-specific social movements heightening intergenerational conflicts. Similarly, the belated admission to the ABCNY of previously excluded elements of the bar, such as women and ethnic minorities, also increased the diversity of viewpoints and ideologies represented. Jews have traditionally been Democrats and strong supporters of the extension of civil rights to all members of the society,[1] whereas educated career women were more likely to be supporters of feminist causes and wish to see the removal of the vestiges of sex discrimination.

In addition to adding to the diversity of the social backgrounds and ideological positions represented in the ABCNY, some of the new entrants brought with them client loyalties different from those of the dominant large-firm elite. Although large-firm lawyers serving a predominantly corporate clientele were overrepresented in the new cohorts joining the ABCNY in the 1970s, some of the newcomers were engaged in legal-aid work, consumer law, or government practice. Indeed, the presidents during this period of transition in the ABCNY went out of their way to appoint lawyers from diverse backgrounds to many committees. By 1980 even the Executive Committee itself included lawyers from highly diverse practice settings with quite different clienteles. Taken together, this new diversity of backgrounds, ideologies, and client loyalties was likely to disturb the highly consensual politics of the ABCNY and result in a new level of internal conflict.

---

1. See Angus Campbell, Philip E. Converse, Warren E. Miller, and Donald Stokes, *The American Voter* (New York: Wiley, 1960).

The relevance of these bundles of background, ideology, and clientele that new members brought with them into the ABCNY can be expected to vary across different types of issues. Whereas feminist ideology will be particularly apposite to debates over gender issues, it will bear little relevance to discussions of antitrust legislation or securities regulation. In contrast, the nature of a lawyer's clientele is unlikely to determine the position that that lawyer takes on gender issues, unless perchance the gender issues directly affect the interests of a set of clients.

In this chapter, I examine how the ABCNY responded to the substantive and ideological demands of newly admitted members and managed the subsequent higher levels of internal conflict. It followed, I suggest, two strategies. The first, a co-optive and accommodative strategy, sought to meet the new demands by co-opting the newcomers and providing them with opportunities to participate in policymaking at the committee level. This was achieved through the creation of committees in areas of special concern to the young reform-oriented newcomers and the broadening of representation on existing standing committees to incorporate the new perspectives. This accommodative strategy resulted in increased inter- and intracommittee dissensus and, at the same time, involved the ABCNY in new policy issues.

The second strategy involved avoidance rather than accommodation. Certain core substantive areas of central concern to the corporate, large-firm leadership were handled by committees that maintained a low profile and hid behind a facade of specialization and esoteric knowledge, thereby avoiding the disruption introduced by the diverse new elements of the ABCNY. These "enclave" committees retained their relative homogeneity and stability. In addition, ad hoc, special-purpose committees were appointed by the president from time to time to deal with particularly important and controversial issues. In this way these issues could be kept out of the hands of the standing committees with their more diversified composition. In the following sections we shall see examples of both the accommodative and avoidance strategies, and consider how they either encouraged dissensus or facilitated the management of conflict and the maintenance of the status quo.

NEW COMMITTEES AND INTERCOMMITTEE CONFLICTS

It has been through the work of its various substantive and court committees that the ABCNY generally has arrived at policy positions on legal issues and sought to influence the direction of legal change.

Although the positions taken by committees do not commit the organization as a whole unless approved by the Executive Committee or by the membership at large, committees advocate and promote their reports with legislators and other decision makers. Frequently, the distinction between the committee making a report and the host association of which it is part is forgotten and so the committee position is taken as the association position. The common identification of the committee with the organization means that the leadership cannot ignore what the committees are doing even though it can deny that committee statements reflect association policy. Committees served to extend the Association's influence into particular substantive or practice areas as well as to provide an opportunity for different groups in the bar to express their interests. The president has the discretion to create special committees from time to time to respond to critical issues or to contribute to newly emerging areas of law. In time some of these special committees are institutionalized as standing committees of the ABCNY and thereby become permanent parts of the ABCNY's structure. The standing committees generally have a mandate to monitor developments in their areas of competence, especially to review pending legislation at either the state or federal level. Occasionally, standing or special committees may draft and propose new legislation.

There were three new committees formed during the late 1960s and early 1970s around areas of law defined as much by ideological position as by doctrinal substance. The first of these was the Special Committee on Natural Resources and Conservation (later renamed the Committee on Environmental Law), formed in 1969. It was quickly followed, in 1970, by the Special Committee on Consumer Affairs and, in 1971, by the Special Committee on Sex and Law. These three new committees served to bring new groups of lawyers and new perspectives on legal change into the ABCNY.

The first two of these committees were established by Plimpton, and the lawyers he selected to lead them determined the direction they took. The first chairman of the Committee on Natural Resources was a pioneer environmental lawyer in New York City, one of the few members of the bar who had staked out a practice in this area prior to its sudden growth in the 1970s. The committee he put together reflected the interests of that time in environmental protection, and although Plimpton placed one or two older corporate lawyers from the large firms on the committee as a moderating influence, they were easily outvoted by the younger, pro-conservation forces.

Similarly, the Special Committee on Consumer Affairs attracted those lawyers with an ideological commitment to the protection and extension of consumer rights. Plimpton chose for the first chairman of this committee Stephen L. Kass, a young lawyer educated at Yale and Harvard who had been an associate at Plimpton's own firm before leaving to join a community legal-services organization, where he gained experience in consumer law. Kass agreed to chair the committee provided he could recruit several pro-consumer lawyers who were not even members of the Association at this time. Plimpton agreed to this condition, and so Kass's committee in its early years included a number of consumer activists, academics, and a government lawyer working for the Federal Trade Commission (FTC) in New York. Lawyers from large firms that generally represent manufacturers and retailers were also present on the committee, but they tended to be outnumbered by the pro-consumer forces.

Initially, the Special Committee on Sex and Law was a little different from the other two new committees. Perhaps because the issues it would deal with were highly controversial and affected strongly held social values, the first two chairmen were older members of Wall Street firms. The committee was composed of both female and older male corporate lawyers who tended to take liberal positions on matters affecting sex and discrimination. The older lawyers did not serve to obstruct the committee from taking strong positions on controversial social issues, although they had undoubtedly been placed on the committee to be a moderating influence. As time passed, however, the Special Committee on Sex and Law became increasingly dominated by its female members, with decreasing representation from the older members of the large firms. Whereas in its first year the committee had been chaired by Orville Schell from Hughes, Hubbard & Reed and had an equal number of male and female members, by 1978 it was chaired by a woman, and twelve out of the nineteen members were women. The female members were associates in large firms, lawyer wives of established practitioners, or law professors. Although they were not radical feminists, they certainly favored positions advocating women's rights and the elimination of sex discrimination. Furthermore, the committee always had one or two women members who were active in the feminist movement. Indeed, the first committee included as "public" or adjunct members two active feminists who were not lawyers.

Each of these three new committees, then, included newcomers to the ABCNY who brought with them distinctive ideological viewpoints on environmental, consumer, and gender issues. In this way the ideological battles raging in the larger society penetrated the boundaries of the ABCNY and contributed to increased internal conflict. Reflecting the ideological commitments of their members, these new committees invaded the domains of existing standing committees and produced reports that conflicted with them. Indeed, the new committees were criticized by members of the older substantive committees for advocating positions based more on ideological than on legal grounds.

For example, in the early 1970s, the Committee on Environmental Law supported environmental considerations over energy needs in disputes over power-plant sites, urged mandatory environmental impact studies prior to approval of major construction projects, and advocated the expansion of access of citizens' groups to decision-making processes relating to major construction proposals. Furthermore, in 1972, the committee drafted a model "citizen's suit" act that would allow for the first time citizens concerned about environmental pollution to file suit against offending companies without first having to demonstrate that they were specifically harmed by the pollution, an affirmative requirement that was very difficult to meet.[2] Conservation and environmental organizations supported both environmental impact legislation and the expansion of citizens' rights in these matters, but they were strongly opposed by the utilities and the construction industry.

The adoption of positions such as these brought the Committee on Environmental Law into conflict with other older ABCNY committees. It was not the only committee interested in the issue of the siting of power plants, and its strong stance that environmental considerations should be given priority in decisions on siting met with the opposition of the Committee on Atomic Energy, which advocated a position more in line with the power industry itself—that considerations of energy need should prevail over concern for the environment.[3] Unable to reconcile the differences on this key policy issue, the president of the ABCNY allowed both committees to publish their positions and to present them to the state legislature. Similarly, the Committee on Environment ran up against the Committee on Housing and Urban Development in its advocacy of environmental impact studies.[4] Again the two committees could not agree, and both views were presented to the legislative leaders and the governor.

In the mid-1970s, the Securities Exchange Commission (SEC) requested opinions of the best means by which it could assist corporations to meet the requirements of the 1969 Environmental Policy Act. It suggested the use of disclosure to encourage compliance; corporations would have to disclose if any of their ventures involved substantial environmental risks that might give rise to expensive litigation. The ABCNY Committee on Securities Regulation strongly opposed any such rule as too uncertain and difficult to enforce whereas, predictably, the Committee on Environmental Law supported the SEC proposal.[5]

---

2. See Annual Reports, Special Committee on Environmental Law, 1970–1975.

3. For reference to this conflict, see Annual Report of Special Committee on Environmental Law, 1971.

4. Annual Report of Special Committee on Environmental Law, 1975.

5. Ibid.

Once again, two committees presented conflicting perspectives to the relevant decision-making authorities—in this case, the commissioners of the SEC. Representing a viewpoint not previously expressed within the ABCNY, the establishment of the Committee on Environmental Law led to increased dissensus, as its ideological commitment to the protection of the environment conflicted with the interests manifested in other substantive committees.

The Committee on Consumer Affairs was no less active or controversial. Consistently advocating policies that would protect and extend consumer rights at both the state and federal levels, it also experienced the opposition of other ABCNY committees. Initially controversial was the committee's advocacy of liberal consumer class-action remedies at both the state and federal levels. Even though other committees endorsed the principle of consumer class-action remedies, they balked at proposing specific pieces of legislation in the legislature. At one time, the Executive Committee was called upon to resolve a dispute between the Committees on Consumer Affairs and State Legislation over a class-action bill pending in the state legislature. Assisted in no small part by the advocacy of Stephen Kass, formerly chairman of the Committee on Consumer Affairs and by this time a member of the Executive Committee, Consumer Affairs was able to win the endorsement by the ABCNY of its pro-class-action position.[6]

Class-action legislation was not the only substantive issue on which the Committee on Consumer Affairs affected the shape of policies emanating from the ABCNY. In the early 1970s the extent of the jurisdiction and authority of the Federal Trade Commission (FTC) was under discussion in Congress. As the FTC regulated interstate commerce and trade, issues related to it usually came under the auspices of the Committee on Trade Regulation, which had in the past stridently opposed any expansion of the regulatory powers of the FTC. This time, under pressure from consumer advocates and with a changing membership composition itself, the Committee on Trade Regulation issued a joint report with the Committee on Consumer Affairs, endorsing the extension of the FTC's rule-making and remedial powers.[7] This action, taken in 1972, came at the outset of the considerable expansion of FTC activities in the remainder of the decade. The presence of a committee vociferously advocating the interests of the consumer had important implications for the policy positions adopted by other ABCNY committees.

---

6. Annual Report of Special Committee on Consumer Affairs, 1973; Minutes of Executive Committee, June 10, 1975.

7. Report of Special Committee on Consumer Affairs and Committee on Trade Regulation, 1972.

The third of the new committees, the Special Committee on Sex and Law, also advocated controversial policies that resulted in internal disagreement. The major issue affecting women in the 1970s was, of course, the Equal Rights Amendment (ERA), which the ABCNY addressed prior to the formation of this new committee. In 1970, the Committee on Federal Legislation issued a report on behalf of the ABCNY opposing the Equal Rights Amendment as unnecessary tinkering with the Constitution.[8] One of the first acts of the new Special Committee on Sex and Law was to seek the reversal of that earlier position. In 1973 it presented a joint report with the Committee on Civil Rights strongly supporting the ERA.[9] Henceforth, the special committee was active in support of the amendment at both the state and the national levels and was successful in gaining the ABCNY's endorsement of the ERA.

In addition to its predictable support for ERA, and for legislation intended to eliminate discrimination based on gender differences, the Committee on Sex and Law tackled a number of other controversial issues. In 1972, together with the Committee on Civil Rights, it opposed efforts to repeal the liberal abortion laws of New York State and proposed that the laws prohibiting sodomy between consenting adults be erased from the statute books. It also proposed that discrimination based on sexual orientation should be explicitly prohibited by state legislation. During the course of the 1970s, then, the Special Committee on Sex and Law took positions supporting ERA, liberal abortion laws, the decriminalization of homosexuality, and the prohibition of discrimination based on sexual preference.[10]

By the formation of these three new committees, the ABCNY provided an expression for viewpoints articulated by younger reformist lawyers and feminists within the profession. With the dissensus between committees brought about by the new committees' advocacy of controversial positions, the ABCNY leadership was forced to support either one committee position or the other, or to avoid the issue altogether by permitting both committees to publish their reports. On several occasions the Executive Committee took the former path, endorsing the position of the Committee on Consumer Affairs on class-action legislation and eventually on lawyer advertising (see Chapter 6) and of the Committee on Sex and Law on the ERA. On other occasions, however, it avoided making any decision at all and allowed conflicting re-

---

8. Report of Committee on Federal Legislation, 1970.

9. Report of Committee on Civil Rights and the Special Committee on Sex and Law, *Record of the Association of the Bar of the City of New York* 28 (1973): 172–182.

10. See Annual Reports, Committee on Sex and Law, 1971–1980.

ports on proposed legal changes to proceed from the ABCNY. An increasing tendency toward this alternative was of concern to some leaders of the ABCNY who saw it as an abdication of leadership responsibility on the part of the Executive Committee. With two opposing reports from committees of the ABCNY, either side to a policy dispute could claim its support and thereby effectively nullify the influence any one committee might exercise. The inclusion of the new groups and interests within the ABCNY by means of the formation of new committees, then, resulted in increased intercommittee conflict that threatened the ability of the ABCNY to exercise decisive leadership.

NEW PEOPLE ON OLD COMMITTEES

The second way in which the ABCNY accommodated claims for participation in decision making on policy issues was to make the substantive committees more broadly representative. Not only were younger and female lawyers and Jewish practitioners increasingly incorporated on these committees, but also there were attempts to ensure the representation of a broader range of practice settings in addition to the large law firms. Those committees that acceded to such compositional diversification risked substantially increased internal conflict and changes in policy outcomes.

Even though members of bar association committees are assumed to leave the particular interests of their clients outside the committee door, and most probably try to do so, it should not be surprising that committees frequently arrive at positions similar to those held by the clients of the majority of their members.[11] After all, in a detailed examination of the social and economic values of Chicago lawyers, Heinz and Laumann find that "lawyers' positions on economic and civil libertarian issues appear to be determined in substantial measure by the kinds of law they practice and by the kinds of clients they serve."[12] It is not that all lawyers consciously adopt their clients' views, although

---

11. See, for example, Melone's study of the positions adopted by the ABA on legislative developments where he demonstrates a close linkage between the interests of clients of ABA committee members and committee recommendations. Albert P. Melone, *Lawyers, Public Policy and Interest Group Politics* (Washington, D.C.: University Press of America, 1977). Cappell and Halliday also suggest that client type and practice setting were linked to the professional policies of the CBA in the 1950s and 1960s. See Charles L. Cappell and Terence C. Halliday, "Professional Projects of Elite Chicago Lawyers, 1950–1974," *American Bar Foundation Research Journal* (1983): 291–340.

12. John P. Heinz and Edward O. Laumann, *Chicago Lawyers* (New York: Russell Sage Foundation, 1982), p. 166.

some may do so, but that their socialization and work experiences frequently lead them to share their clients' positions. Consequently, committee positions can be expected to vary according to the types of practice and clients represented on the committee. When substantive
committees are overwhelmingly dominated by large-firm, corporate
lawyers who usually defend large corporations, as the committees of
the ABCNY were until this point, we would expect the committee decisions to reflect the interests of that segment of the bar and its clientele. As we would anticipate lawyers who represent plaintiffs, consumers, or the government to hold views different from those of members
of the corporate defense bar, their addition to ABCNY committees in
the 1970s could be expected to accentuate intracommittee conflict and
to lead to changes in policy recommendations.

In this section I use the experience of the Committee on Trade
Regulation during the 1970s to demonstrate the effect on committee
decision making and policy outcomes of the participation of a much
more diverse range of lawyers. This committee dealt with antitrust law,
a major area of concern to corporations and their legal advisors since
the Sherman and Clayton acts of the 1890s. Antitrust work represented
a substantial portion of the legal services provided to corporations by
the large law firms. Maintaining a watching brief in this area, the Committee on Trade Regulation was clearly an important substantive committee for the large-firm elite of the New York bar.

In addition to the large-firm lawyers, there were other segments of
the bar interested in developments in this area: government lawyers in
the Justice Department and the FTC who investigated alleged violations, academic lawyers who taught the subject in law schools and
wrote about it in law reviews, and, more recently, a plaintiffs' antitrust
and class-action bar whose members brought civil suits against corporations. Although these segments of the antitrust bar grew in size in
the 1950s and 1960s, the Committee on Trade Regulation remained
firmly under the control of the defense-oriented large-firm lawyers.
Consequently, throughout this period the committee consistently
adopted positions opposing any extension of the antitrust laws or any
strengthening of the enforcement powers of the federal government.

The conservative bent of the committee was demonstrated by the
positions it adopted on three proposals for substantial changes in the
antitrust laws in the 1961–1962 Congress.[13] It opposed bills to increase
the financial penalties assessable against violators of the antitrust laws
and to extend the powers of the FTC by enabling it to issue temporary

---

13. Annual Report of Committee on Trade Regulation, 1962.

"cease and desist" orders pending completion of FTC proceedings. Without such authority, the FTC had no means available to it to stop the alleged violations until the agency was eventually successful in litigation, an outcome that could take several years. The committee also strongly opposed a bill to amend the Clayton Act to permit civil actions to be brought under it by private parties for treble damages for violations of Section 3 of the Robinson-Patman Act. This amendment would have greatly broadened private rights of action, strengthened the plaintiffs' bar, and indirectly aided antitrust enforcement. It would also, of course, have increased the vulnerability of corporations likely to be targets of private actions, and was naturally opposed by business interests. These proposals for change surfaced throughout the 1960s with the ABCNY committee remaining constant in its opposition to them.[14]

Another recurring legislative proposal in the 1960s, which also did not achieve enactment, was a proposal to remove the tax deduction available for companies forced to pay damage awards to private parties for violations of the antitrust laws. The fact that civil damage awards were tax deductible in their entirety diminished considerably their sanctioning effect on corporate offenders; it was argued that these penal awards should not be deductible as business expenses and therefore partly paid by the United States Treasury. Business organizations vigorously opposed such a change, as did the antitrust committee of the ABCNY, which sent copies of its report opposing the proposal to all members of the United States Senate.[15]

The Committee on Trade Regulation, then, established a definite track record of opposing any expansion in antitrust enforcement. Its positions consistently reflected the interests of the large-firm defense lawyers who predominated in its membership. The positions it adopted began to change, however, toward the end of the 1960s, with new leadership and changes in its composition. In 1968, Plimpton appointed George D. Reycraft, a partner at Cadwalader, Wickersham & Taft, as chairman of the committee. Reycraft had been for many years in the antitrust division of the Justice Department before entering private practice, and consequently had more understanding of the government position on antitrust than most members of the private bar. He was not so dogmatically opposed to strengthening the antitrust laws, and he attempted to bring more balance to the committee by introducing as members academics and practitioners who had some government experience.

---

14. See Annual Reports, Committee on Trade Regulation, 1960–1969.
15. Annual Report of Committee on Trade Regulation, 1966.

In 1969–1970, the final year of Reycraft's chairmanship, the effects of the changes in the committee's membership upon its deliberations were vividly demonstrated when the committee found itself too divided to take a position on increased criminal sanctions for antitrust violations.[16] The committee had not experienced any difficulty in opposing increased criminal sanctions for violations of the antitrust laws in the past, but now was stymied over the issue because of its more diverse membership.

Reycraft was followed as chairman by Harvey J. Goldschmid, a Columbia law professor who continued to broaden representation on the committee. He added to its membership another law professor (who was a consumer advocate) and representatives of both the plaintiffs' bar and the FTC. As a consequence, the committee continued its movement away from its earlier consistent pro-business responses to legislative developments and undertook projects that would have been inconceivable a few years earlier. At the end of Goldschmid's first year as chairman, he described the committee's legislative activities in the following manner:

> Responding to growing public sensitivity and increasing legislative initiative, the Committee on Trade Regulation spent a substantial part of its time this year on projects and legislation aimed at assisting and protecting aggrieved consumers.[17]

Consequently, the committee joined the newly created Special Committee on Consumer Affairs in 1972 in endorsing a senate bill that "strengthens and supplements the authority of the Federal Trade Commission."[18] Subsequently, the committee played a major role in the passage of important antitrust legislation that included stiffer penalties for violators.

During the period of 1972 to 1974, the Democratic leadership in the United States Senate pressed several measures intended to strengthen antitrust enforcement and break up large economic concentrations. The committee's response to two of these measures demonstrated clearly its changed composition. The first of these was the Senate bill known as The Antitrust Procedures and Penalties Act, sponsored by John V. Tunney of California.[19] The Tunney bill had several provisions not welcomed by big business, including changes in consent-decree proce-

---

16. Annual Report of Committee on Trade Regulation, 1970.
17. Annual Report of Committee on Trade Regulation, 1972.
18. Ibid.
19. See Antitrust Procedures and Penalties Act, House Report No. 93-1463, 1974.

dures, requirements for the disclosure of corporate lobbying with government officials concerning the terms of such decrees, and increased monetary penalties for antitrust violations. Notwithstanding widespread opposition within the business community, the ABCNY's Committee on Trade Regulation supported the bill. Faced with the opposition of business groups and much of the organized bar, including the ABA, Senator Tunney was so pleased to receive the endorsement of the ABCNY committee that he made its chairman, Professor Goldschmid, the leadoff witness at hearings before the Senate Subcommittee on Antitrust and Monopoly. Following the adoption of some minor modifications that had been recommended by the ABCNY's committee, Tunney's bill was eventually passed. Tunney paid tribute to the Committee on Trade Regulation for its assistance; it had been the only major bar association committee to support the bill.[20]

In supporting the Tunney bill, the committee reversed the consistent position it had maintained throughout the 1960s in opposition to increased penalties for antitrust violations. Over the course of a decade, then, the Committee on Trade Regulation had moved from unqualified opposition to increased penalties, to being split on the issue and unable to take a position, and finally to supporting Tunney's bill with its heavier sanctions. The changed composition of the committee had clearly resulted in changes in its policy outcomes.

The second major piece of antitrust legislation in Congress in the early 1970s was Senator Hart's Industrial Reorganization Act, a bill containing much more radical implications than had the Tunney bill.[21] Hart's bill was designed to break into smaller units large corporations operating in concentrated markets, thus encouraging competition and the redistribution of economic wealth and power. As such it was very controversial and violently opposed by the leaders of big business. After lengthy consideration, the ABCNY committee found itself once again too divided to take a position, and so restricted itself to providing Congress with "a careful and comprehensive critique" of the drafting of the bill.[22] The fact that it took no position further demonstrated the diversity of views represented on the committee and the consequent high level of intracommittee dissensus. The Hart bill drew the wrath of pro-business groups and the vigorous opposition of other bar associations, including the ABA.[23] In the past, such a radical proposal

---

20. Annual Report of Committee on Trade Regulation, 1974.

21. For a discussion of Hart's Industrial Reorganization Act, see *Digest of Public General Bills*, 1975, pp. A-191–192.

22. Annual Report of Committee on Trade Regulation, 1973.

23. Sharon Tisher, Lyn Bernabei, and Mark Green, *Bringing the Bar to Justice* (Washington, D.C.: Public Citizen, 1977), p. 157.

would have been equally strongly opposed by the ABCNY committee, but with large-firm lawyers constituting only one segment of the anti-trust bar represented in the 1970s, it was no longer so easy for them to carry the committee.

Important to this process of change was the selection by Presidents Plimpton and Botein of lawyers who had some independence from the antitrust defense bar to be chairmen of this committee. While the leadership of bar association committees continues to hold that their committees seek to find and present "the disinterested legal view,"[24] the fact is that policy positions taken by substantive committees on legal change frequently reflect the interests and types of practice represented on the committees. The changed composition of the Committee on Trade Regulation in the 1970s resulted in pro-consumer and antitrust enforcement measures being supported, a marked change from the 1950s and 1960s. Greater diversity in committee membership also resulted in increased internal dissensus, to the point where the committee was unable to endorse or oppose significant pieces of legislation and therefore unable to influence their passage.

ENCLAVE COMMITTEES
AND THE PROTECTION OF EXPERTISE

Not all committees of the ABCNY underwent significant changes in composition or in policy direction. A small number of core substantive committees, closely identified with central concerns of the large-law-firm elite, and representing a cohesive community of lawyers, were largely able to exclude those elements of the bar that held perspectives conflicting with those of the large-firm elite. They were particularly able to do this if they dealt with highly technical areas of law, occupied insulated positions in the Association, and maintained low profiles. Although not excluded from full participation in the ABCNY, as were the lower status committees discussed in Chapter 3, these "enclave" committees largely kept to themselves, making few demands of the Association's leadership. As Terence Halliday observes, for members of enclave committees the organization "merely provides a convenient organizational niche for their activities rather than being the focus of their attention."[25] Whereas isolation within the Association had been imposed on one set of interests to their detriment, it was a positive advantage for another.

---

24. Ibid, p. 158.
25. Terence C. Halliday, *Beyond Monopoly: Lawyers, State Crises and Professional Empowerment* (Chicago: University of Chicago Press, 1987), p. 327.

One such enclave committee was the Committee on Securities Regulation. Until 1962 the Committee on Corporation Law had maintained a watching brief over developments in the securities area, intervening from time to time as it saw fit. There was not a great need for a consistently active committee in this area because the Securities and Exchange Commission had settled down to minimal intervention in the stock markets once the first flush of New Deal enthusiasm had dissipated.[26] The 1960s were a different story, however, with greatly increased trading volume and a new, activist chairman at the SEC who instituted a "special study" of the operation of the markets and regulatory functions of the SEC. Consequent to the special study there were numerous proposals for rule changes emanating from the SEC and the probability of greater regulatory intervention in the markets.[27] Naturally, the "securities bar," which was largely located in New York City, was concerned, and so in 1962 the ABCNY formed a special committee to monitor developments in this area. It eventually became a standing committee on securities regulation.

As New York City was the dominant financial center in the United States, and the New York Stock Exchange the oldest and largest marketplace for the selling and buying of shares, the securities bar in New York enjoyed a natural preeminence. Not only was it prominent nationally, but its members also enjoyed high prestige within the New York bar. Traditionally, a small number of old, WASP Wall Street firms, such as Sullivan & Cromwell, Cravath Swaine & Moore, Rogers & Wells, Davis, Polk & Wardwell, Simpson, Thatcher & Bartlett, dominated the New York securities bar. Each of these firms had several senior partners who specialized in securities work, and they all knew one another well. In the 1950s, the securities bar was a tightly knit and clubbish group of lawyers with a distinctly conservative political coloration. By the 1970s, this group of highly skilled practitioners had become a little more diversified following the entrance into the field of the Irish and Jewish firms and the gradual changes in the composition of the large-firm rosters. But even in 1980, a successful female member of this professional elite described the securities bar as a very "close" bar that remained a little clubbish.[28]

The Committee on Securities Regulation represented this conservative and exclusive segment of the New York bar. Its first chairman was W. Ward Foshay, a senior partner at Sullivan & Cromwell and one of

---

26. Joel Seligman, *The SEC and the Future of Finance* (New York: Praeger, 1985).

27. For the history and consequences of the "Special Study," see Seligman, ibid.

28. Roberta H. Karmel, of the firm of Rogers & Wells, personal interview by author, May 22, 1980.

the doyens of the securities bar, and its membership included only lawyers from the major Wall Street firms. Quickly establishing itself as a major feature on the national securities landscape with its prominent leadership and highly qualified members, the Committee on Securities Regulation became one of the most prestigious in the ABCNY. Gaining a position on it was not only recognition that a practitioner had achieved a certain standing within this elite segment of the bar, but it was also possibly a stepping-stone to greater opportunities.

The Committee on Securities Regulation regularly commented on proposals for rule changes made by the SEC, and, because of its members' high level of competence and considerable experience, its comments were treated very seriously by the staff of the SEC and frequently resulted in the modification of these proposals.[29] Furthermore, the committee had sufficient stature for the commissioners and senior staff of the SEC to attend committee dinners from time to time and present reports on current SEC policies and likely future developments. The committee also served as a place where information could be informally exchanged among practitioner members as to ongoing interactions with the SEC in nonroutine matters. Given the informal character of much securities work, information about other lawyers' interactions with the SEC on particular matters could be very useful. Membership on the committee, then, provided opportunities for informal exchanges with the staff of the SEC and fellow practitioners. Consequently, positions on this committee were very highly sought after.[30]

The cohesiveness of the securities bar, its prestige within the profession, and the highly specialized nature of its work enabled the Committee on Securities Regulation to carve out for itself a relatively autonomous niche within the ABCNY. Preferring to get on with its business in a low-key manner, the committee rarely invoked the authority of the Association as a whole and so did not need to channel its comments through the Executive Committee. Indeed, it avoided controversial legislative debates, which might have resulted in internal disagreements, and concentrated on the more technical realm of administrative rule changes. For instance, in the mid-1970s it refused to get drawn into the legislative debates over the dismantling of fixed commission rates and the creation of a national securities market. Rather, it went about quietly and efficiently preparing its "comment letters" to the SEC on pro-

---

29. Arthur J. Brown, Securities Exchange Commission, personal interview by author, November 19, 1980.

30. The major Wall Street firms like to keep a member on this committee, leading to suggestions that there are "firm seats." Chairmen have to resist this pressure when making committee appointments.

posed rule changes. By limiting itself to this less visible arena, the committee avoided drawing undue attention to its actions.

Following the model of an enclave committee, the Committee on Securities Regulation preferred to be left to its own devices, and it was successful in maintaining a considerable degree of autonomy. As we have seen, the president is responsible for committee appointments, usually in consultation with the chairs of the committees in question. But in the case of the securities committee, and one or two other equally specialized substantive committees, it was really the chairs who selected new committee members, making recommendations to the president that were generally followed. As a rule, the president liked to appoint one or two generalists to the substantive committees to encourage them to take a broad view, and from 1970 onward he was under pressure to diversify representation on all committees. The Committee on Securities Regulation refused to go along with these tendencies, however, emphasizing the esoteric and technical nature of its work and, therefore, the need for expertise on the part of members. Generalists were not welcome, nor were young associates without sufficient knowledge or experience to enable them to undertake projects in the area.[31] The heavy demand from large-firm lawyers for places on the committee, and its traditional autonomy and enclave status, were built-in counters to the pressures to open it up to a more diverse cross section of the bar.

With de facto control over appointments to the committee in the hands of its chairs, the Committee on Securities Regulation remained relatively homogeneous even in the 1970s, with the vast majority of its members still from Wall Street firms. Membership did become a little more diverse in the late 1970s, with the appointment, to the committee, of women, albeit women from large firms, and law professors. The academics were a small minority, however, on a committee still overwhelmingly composed of large-firm lawyers. Such moderate shifts in the composition of the committee did not result in the incorporation of widely divergent viewpoints. The sources from which alternative voices might have been heard—the public-interest lawyers who were demanding the SEC to take steps to make corporations more accountable to the public, and the so-called derivative bar, which brought stockholder class-action suits against management—were not represented at all on the committee.

---

31. Interviews with both presidents of the ABCNY and chairmen of the Committee on Securities Regulation made clear the committee's insistence on experience and expertise and its opposition to having generalists on board.

The continued exclusion of these interests within the bar from the Committee on Securities Regulation is especially noteworthy given the activism of the derivative bar based in New York City in the postwar decades and the emergence of questions of corporate governance and responsibility as prominent issues during the 1970s. The SEC was at the center of these debates. Its enforcement division played a major role in raising questions of corporate responsibility by producing evidence of substantial corporate wrongdoing, including the bribery of public officials and undisclosed campaign contributions. As the SEC regulated relations between corporate management and stockholders, proposals to modify the structure of corporate governance were made to it. There were proposals to make management more accountable to stockholders, to include representatives of the public on boards of directors, and to provide boards of directors with broader powers vis-à-vis management.[32] So-called public-interest groups were in the forefront of those calling for the increased regulation of corporate activity, but the Committee on Securities Regulation continued to use requirements of expertise and experience to exclude lawyers from these groups from its membership.

Although the leadership of the committee could legitimately exclude public-interest lawyers on the grounds that they lacked substantive expertise, it was more difficult to sustain that argument for members of the derivative bar. Their continued exclusion was based more on the distaste of the elite securities bar for practitioners whom they regarded as stirrers of litigation and little better than "ambulance chasers" in their solicitation of clients.[33] These lawyers clearly knew the securities and corporate law, but they received the same exclusionary treatment as the personal injury lawyers.

As might be expected, given the lack of any significant changes in its composition during the 1960s and 1970s, the committee evidenced little change in the overall direction of its comments on proposed rule changes by the SEC. The two predominant concerns of the committee in the 1960s remained very much its concerns in the 1970s.[34] First, it

---

32. For a discussion of these proposals to modify corporate governance, see Leonard M. Leiman, "Corporate Governance: The United States Debate," in *Journal of Comparative Corporate Law and Securities Regulation* 2 (1972): 89–98.

33. Members of the plaintiffs' "derivative bar" are generally held in low esteem by securities and corporate lawyers. They are accused of stirring up litigation needlessly, of soliciting clients, and of various other unethical tactics. Most are Jewish and take delight in challenging the traditionally conservative, WASPish, securities bar. Abraham L. Pomerantz, leading member of the derivative bar, personal interview, June 23, 1980.

34. Annual Reports, Committee on Securities Regulation, 1962–1979.

had a consistent interest in limiting the extent of SEC regulation. Time after time, the committee sought, through its comment letters and conferences with SEC staff, to push the SEC back from more interventionist positions advocated in its proposals for rule changes. Second, the committee sought increased predictability and certainty in securities regulation. Many of its comments were attempts to get the SEC to specify the applicability of it rules and to remove the vagueness of the language in proposed rules. Committee members wanted to be able to advise their clients with some degree of certainty as to whether a particular course of action would run afoul of the SEC and so wanted specific and clear language; the SEC, for its part, wanted to maximize its discretionary authority.

That the Committee on Securities Regulation has remained relatively unaffected by changes in the composition of the ABCNY during these years, and by the consequent pressure to adopt stances more favorable to the so-called public interest, is evident from the positions it took on two matters of particular concern at the time. We have already noted that in the mid-1970s the Committee on Securities Regulation opposed "the disclosure of environmental and other socially related issues of doubtful economic significance on the part of publicly held companies."[35] Similarly, in the late 1970s, the securities committee evinced little enthusiasm for the movement led by Ralph Nader and his supporters in Congress to make boards of directors more accountable to the public by placing public members on them. SEC proposals for changes in corporate governance along these lines were consistently opposed by the Committee on Securities Regulation on the grounds that the SEC was overstepping its congressional mandate.[36] The environmental and "public-interest" lobby among younger members of the ABCNY, which had influenced other committees, apparently had not penetrated the Committee on Securities Regulation.

Unlike the Committee on Trade Regulation, the Committee on Securities Regulation was not forced by the representation of alternative viewpoints in its midst to consider seriously any major expansion or modification in the role of the SEC or to endorse radical changes in corporate governance. Eschewing participation in the broader political debates over corporate responsibility and the regulatory functions of the SEC, the Committee on Securities Regulation generally restricted itself to the more technical role of commenting on actual proposals for rule changes on the part of the SEC. In contrast, the Committee on

---

35. Annual Report of Committee on Securities Regulation, 1975.
36. Annual Reports, Committee on Securities Regulation, 1975–1976.

Trade Regulation was caught up in debating the merits of highly controversial antitrust legislation, and so attracted the attention of a variety of interests within the bar. By keeping to writing "comment letters," and emphasizing the technical and esoteric nature of its work, the Committee on Securities Regulation was able to remain relatively isolated and immune to the wider changes going on elsewhere in the ABCNY.

AD HOC OR SPECIAL-PURPOSE COMMITTEES

If certain core professional interests of the large-firm elite of the ABCNY were protected from the turbulence of the period by their treatment as technical legal issues in enclave committees, other more controversial and public matters could likewise be removed from internal association debate by establishing ad hoc or special-purpose committees to handle them. These committees were specially appointed by the president to do a specified, limited task and thus were less unpredictable than the standing committees, many of which had diversified memberships and broad mandates. Furthermore, generally these special ad hoc committees were not required to submit their reports to the membership as a whole, or even the Executive Committee, and thus there was less chance that their recommendations would be debated or reversed. This strategy was used several times in the 1970s as a way of dealing with important and controversial issues. One illustration will be detailed here, that of the Ad Hoc Committee on Foreign Payments created in 1975 to respond to proposals for new legislation or administrative regulations to control the problem of illegal payments to foreign governments by United States corporations.[37]

The issue of improper foreign payments had arisen in the aftermath of Watergate, when evidence was uncovered of corporate slush funds used both to make illegal campaign contributions and to pay off foreign officials in order to get contracts.[38] As these payments amounted to large sums of money, and were not disclosed to stockholders, the SEC began its own investigations on the grounds that corporations had violated disclosure requirements. The SEC action opened a can of

---

37. There were others, however, including an ad hoc committee established in the mid-1970s to examine the role of lawyers in securities transactions in the light of increased pressure from the SEC for lawyers to adopt the role of auditors of their clients' statements and representations. See "Report of the Special Committee on Lawyers' Role in Securities Transactions," *The Record of the Association of the Bar* 32 (1977): 345–364.

38. For background to this issue, see *Congress and the Nation: A Review of Government and Politics* (Washington, D.C.: Congressional Quarterly, Inc., 1976), p. 884.

worms, with more than four hundred corporations voluntarily admitting having made illegal payments to foreign officials. Among these payments were bribes paid to highly placed officials in governments friendly to the United States, causing political scandals in those countries and embarrassing both the foreign governments and the United States. Congress launched its own investigation, which increased the likelihood of a legislative solution to the problem, much to the consternation of the corporations involved.

The Ad Hoc Committee on Foreign Payments was appointed to address the issue of what sorts of controls should be placed upon corporations to ensure that this illegal behavior did not recur. There were two clear alternatives. The first, anathema to the corporations, was to treat illegal foreign payments as criminal actions and as such subject to criminal investigation and sanction. The second alternative would regulate foreign payments through disclosure requirements whereby corporations making such payments would have to report that fact to their stockholders and the SEC. Though clearly preferable to criminalization, more rigorous reporting requirements were not particularly popular with the corporations because they would increase the regulatory authority of the SEC at a time when, under an activist enforcement chief, it was feeling its oats.[39]

By the time the ABCNY ad hoc committee produced its report, there were bills in both the House of Representatives and the Senate that combined increased disclosure requirements with criminal sanctions. These bills threatened the worst of both worlds as far as the corporations were concerned. In its report, the ad hoc committee argued that criminalization was of doubtful legality and would be difficult to enforce as it would extend the reach of the criminal law to extraterritorial conduct. Moreover, the committee argued that combining disclosure requirements with criminal sanctions was fundamentally inconsistent because the two methods of social control were based on quite different assumptions. Instead, the committee unanimously endorsed a "generic disclosure system" without criminalization, which it held was "the most effective and practical approach to an American solution to the problem."[40]

---

39. The mid-1970s was a period of particularly active enforcement efforts by the SEC under the leadership of Stanley Sporkin, who was chief of its enforcement division. See Seligman, *The SEC and the Future of Finance*.

40. Report on Questionable Foreign Payments by Corporations: The Problem and Approaches to a Solution, Ad Hoc Committee on Foreign Payments, The Association of the Bar of the City of New York, 1977.

The ABCNY report constituted "a strong statement favoring a reporting requirement," but it failed to budge Congress from its determination to combine disclosure and criminalization. In 1977 the Foreign Corrupt Practices Act was signed into law by President Carter with substantial criminal sanctions for officials found guilty of violations.[41] In supporting increased disclosure and opposing criminalization, the ad hoc committee recommended the solution favored by the corporations themselves. At the very time when other sections of the ABCNY were pushing for increased sanctions for antitrust violators and for pro-conservation and consumer legislation, the ad hoc committee adopted a clearly conservative stance. As with the securities committee, the perspective of the reformist younger members, so evident on other matters, did not penetrate this committee. Their absence was not surprising as the driving force behind the ad hoc committee was its vice-chairman, who happened to be the general counsel of General Electric, a large corporation with substantial foreign-trade interests and one naturally very concerned about developments in this area.

The creation of ad hoc, special-purpose committees provided a means by which the president of the ABCNY, should he so desire, could avoid the internal conflict and unpredictable outcomes that might ensue from leaving a controversial public issue such as illegal corporate payments in the hands of a standing committee. Not only did the president enjoy complete discretion to create such committees should he see the need, but he also was unfettered in the appointment of the committee members. By establishing a special committee to review such an issue, the president effectively took it off the agenda of standing committees that might otherwise have addressed it.

CO-OPTATION, DISSENSUS, AND DECISION-MAKING ABILITY

A high proportion of the newcomers to the ABCNY were graduates of elite national law schools and practiced in the large firms as we saw in Chapter 2, but many brought with them new ideological positions and substantive concerns. This was particularly true of young lawyers influenced by the social movements of the 1960s and 1970s who were co-opted into the ABCNY in the early 1970s. New committees were formed to give expression to their interests, and young members were

---

41. Foreign Corrupt Practices Act, 1979. The criminal sanctions included a $10,000 fine or five years' imprisonment for corporate officials found guilty of violations.

appointed to existing committees. This policy of co-optation was certainly successful in averting any continued hostility from young associates. However, as Philip Selznick demonstrated in his classic study of the Tennessee Valley Authority, co-optation has its costs.[42] Inviting new elements into the organization and allowing them to participate in decision making frequently results in goal changes and the adoption of new policies. In the case of the ABCNY, the co-optation of the young, reformist element of the New York bar resulted in both increased internal conflict and the adoption of new policies, some of which differed starkly from previous policy positions. It was not just that new personnel were added to the committees, or came to participate in organizational decision making, but that the new members represented a diversity of practice settings, clienteles, and interests. Law professors, government lawyers, and lawyers from legal clinics were appointed to committees and given a voice in the Association. Although large-firm lawyers remained dominant, divergent viewpoints were increasingly expressed.

The ability of these newcomers to affect ABCNY policy was greatly enhanced by the election of a series of reformist presidents, beginning with Plimpton, who used their considerable discretionary authority to establish new committees and appoint new committee leadership. The effect was long-term. Changes initiated by Plimpton, for instance, continued to affect the development of ABCNY policy into the 1980s. The first chairs of both the new Committees on Environmental Law and Consumer Affairs established by Plimpton proceeded to serve on the Executive Committee in the mid-1970s and to bring their perspectives to that body's deliberations; the academics originally appointed to the Committee on Trade Regulation eventually became chairs themselves and, in their turn, continued the more inclusive policies of their predecessors. The Committee on Consumer Affairs became a strong advocate of reform in a number of areas, including professional regulation. The appointment power of the president's office, then, was a powerful means for bringing about changes in policy outcomes in a relatively short period of time.

The introduction of new committees in new areas of law and the incorporation of divergent viewpoints on existing committees resulted in increased dissensus within the ABCNY. This occurred to the point where in some cases conflicting reports were presented to external publics by different committees, thereby undermining the ABCNY's ability to influence policy. In other cases, intracommittee disagreement

---

42. Philip Selznick, *TVA and the Grassroots* (Berkeley: University of California, 1949).

prevented committees from taking any position at all on controversial legal issues. In general, then, the increased diversity of viewpoints represented in the ABCNY in the 1970s made its exercise of influence with respect to legal change more problematic.

Heinz et al. suggest that this is the fate of mass-based, comprehensive professional associations, such as the CBA.[43] They contend that conflicting interests within internally heterogeneous organizations act as internal veto groups, effectively limiting the organization's policy-making initiatives to relatively minor or technical issues on which some consensus can be found. In Karl Mannheim's view, the same process occurs when a single unified elite disintegrates into multiple, competing elites.[44] Competition and conflict among these plural elites similarly undermine the ability of any one elite to provide clear leadership.

Had the ABCNY become so riven with internal conflict in the 1970s that its ability to act was undermined? Although increased diversity of social background and the co-optation of the young reformers resulted in increased internal dissensus and greater difficulty in reaching agreement on controversial issues, the ABCNY was by no means paralyzed by conflicting interests.

The young lawyers newly admitted to the ABCNY during the 1970s were not too dissimilar in terms of law school and practice type to their older fellow members. Their views on substantive legal and professional issues frequently differed from those of their elders, but more in degree than in direction. By the 1970s, the ABCNY had already established a reputation as being liberal and reformist on social and professional issues. Although the younger members certainly wanted to go farther than their elders, they were heading in essentially the same direction—improved access to justice, removal of racial and sexual discrimination, and the protection of the environment. A new coalition emerged between the older, liberal members of the large-firm elite and the younger, often Democratic, Jewish, and female newcomers to that elite, enabling the ABCNY to take clear positions on many social and professional issues during this time.

Furthermore, there are strategies and devices whereby the leadership of internally divided organizations is able to maintain control and ensure continued effective functioning. Indeed, Terence Halliday demonstrates that even the heterogeneous and representative CBA was

---

43. Heinz et al., "Diversity, Representation, and Leadership in an Urban Bar," *American Bar Foundation Research Journal* (1976): 771–775. For a conflicting viewpoint with respect to the same organization, see Terence C. Halliday, *Beyond Monopoly*.

44. Karl Mannheim, *Man and Society in an Age of Reconstruction* (New York: Harcourt, Brace, 1940).

able to "transcend" its inclusiveness and overcome potential internal stalemate on consequential issues by utilizing various organizational stratagems. He contends that by maintaining some control over recruitment to the leadership, by ensuring that authority is centralized, and by developing a degree of autonomy from constituent units, the leadership can gain the flexibility and discretion to contain disintegrative consequences and deadlocking tendencies that might have followed inclusiveness.[45]

As long as the core areas of concern to the corporate legal elite—securities regulation, corporate governance, banking and financial regulation—were protected from takeover by radically different viewpoints, the older leadership of the ABCNY could live with the newcomers and their reformist predilections. The use of avoidance strategies by enclave committees operating in prestigious but highly technical and specialized fields of law enabled these core areas to escape disruption brought about by conflicting interests and values. In addition, the use of special ad hoc committees to address immediate and controversial issues made it possible for the ABCNY to continue to speak with one voice on matters of particular importance. By combining avoidance with accommodative strategies, then, the ABCNY was able to limit the uncertainties brought about by a more diverse membership.

Of course, as we have observed, the extent of the ABCNY's new heterogeneity was in fact limited. Those segments of the bar that might have brought into the ABCNY radical disagreement about issues of substantive law and professionalism remained for the most part outside its walls. The ABCNY may have become more diverse, but not all subgroups of the bar were represented, let alone incorporated. The perspectives and interests of the plaintiffs' personal injury and derivative class-action bars remained unrepresented, and other local segments of the bar were merely included, with the results that the ABCNY was still able to take strong positions on critical matters of professional policy during these postwar decades.

---

45. Terence C. Halliday, *Beyond Monopoly*, p. 334. For Halliday's detailed argument, see chapter 11.

PART THREE

Regulating the Profession and Reforming the Legal System

Chapter Five

The Moral Authority of the Professional Elite

Commenting on the condition of the legal profession in the middle of the nineteenth century, Roscoe Pound observed that it was "not so much a Bar, but so many hundred or so many thousand lawyers, each a law unto himself."[1] With admission to the bar open to "all men of good character," and the absence of any accepted standards of professional conduct, the "professional idea" was at its nadir at this time. Crucial to the revival of professionalism, according to Pound, was the emergence of organizations of lawyers to set standards for entry into the bar and to regulate the conduct of those admitted. These new associations would form grievance, or discipline, committees to investigate complaints against members' conduct, formulate codes of ethics to guide lawyers' behavior, and maintain standards for admission to the bar. The creation of bar associations and the subsequent emergence of social-control mechanisms within those associations was central to the whole process of professionalization that the bar embarked upon in the twentieth century.

Recent revisionist treatments of this process of professionalization, such as that of Jerold Auerbach, present a much less benign view.[2] According to this view, bar associations were established by a WASP upper-class elite to control the rest of the bar and shape its development. Certainly the early bar associations were exclusive organizations intended for the "best men" of the bar. By the early years of the twentieth century leadership of the major metropolitan bar associations had

---

1. Roscoe Pound, *The Lawyer from Antiquity to Modern Times* (St. Paul: West Publishing Company, 1953), p. 248.

2. Jerold S. Auerbach, *Unequal Justice: Lawyers and Social Change in Modern America* (New York: Oxford, 1976); Magali Sarfatti Larson, *The Rise of Professionalism: A Sociological Analysis* (Berkeley: University of California, 1977).

passed into the hands of the new legal elite, the corporate lawyers who worked in large firms and served the powerful business corporations. Equally WASPish and upper-class in social origin as their advocate forebears, this class-based elite, by reason of its dominance of the major professional associations, enjoyed "an unsurpassed opportunity to articulate their wishes as professional values."[3] In other words, according to Auerbach, a minority of upper-class lawyers, whether leading advocates or corporate lawyers, was able to shape the development of professional regulation through their control over the newly established bar associations. From this perspective the regulatory mechanisms and ethical codes of the bar associations should not be viewed as neutral instruments, or as reflecting the combined interests of all members of the bar, but rather as the expression of the class interests of the legal establishment. Not only were the proscriptions included in the Canon of Ethics adopted by the ABA in 1908 directed at the nonelite, more marginal members of the bar, but also the enforcement activities of the grievance committees focused on these same peripheral members of the profession. As the more marginal lawyers in the large cities of the twentieth century were increasingly Jewish or Catholic practitioners, professional self-regulation meant not only elite control over the nonelite majority but also WASP upper-class control over an ethnic professional underclass.[4]

If any single bar association fitted this class theory of the professionalization process it was the ABCNY. Established, as we have seen, by the upper-class members of the New York bar, this first of the modern bar associations attempted to regulate the bench and bar of the city. Much of its effort was directed at those segments of the bar composed largely of more marginal, ethnic practitioners.[5] It was active in prosecuting so-called ambulance chasers, personal injury lawyers who solicited clients among accident victims. Twice during the interwar period the ABCNY initiated crusades against ambulance chasers, many of whom were Jewish or Catholic solo practitioners. In addition, the ABCNY attempted unsuccessfully to have the state legislature amend the judiciary law so as to give the state supreme court the power to modify contingent-fee arrangements made with clients.[6]

3. Auerbach, *Unequal Justice*, p. 64.

4. For an elaboration of this position, see Auerbach, *Unequal Justice*, chapter 2.

5. Carlin's data on the lawyers investigated and disciplined by the ABCNY in the 1960s indicate that they predominantly came from the ranks of solo and small-firm practitioners who were significantly underrepresented in the ABCNY's membership. See Jerome E. Carlin, *Lawyers' Ethics: A Survey of the New York Bar* (New York: Russell Sage Foundation, 1966), chapter 9.

6. George Martin, *Causes and Conflicts: The Centennial History of the Association of the Bar of the City of New York* (Boston: Houghton Mifflin, 1970), pp. 374–377.

Contrary to what might be expected from elite theories of professional control, however, the legal establishment did not act alone on ambulance-chasing but rather in concert with local bar groups, which were also concerned about its incidence. Established local practitioners were hurt by the cutthroat competition for personal injury work encouraged by unethical solicitation. Thus the NYCLA and the Bronx County Bar Association cooperated with the ABCNY in these investigations in the interwar period and shared in their costs. Nor was the WASP minority very successful in achieving their regulatory goals: Like the poor, ambulance chasers were always there, and the grievance committee disciplined a minuscule proportion of unethical attorneys.[7] Yet the initiative clearly lay with the upper-class elite of the bar as represented by the ABCNY. It was the ABCNY that took the lead in raising standards for admission to the bar, in formulating codes of ethics, and in enforcing professional norms through disciplinary committees.

In the 1970s the moral leadership of the large-firm elite of the ABCNY was subjected to greater external challenge and internal uncertainty than in the past. As a consequence, by 1980, the ABCNY no longer occupied such a clear position of authority within the New York bar. External challenge to the ABCNY's moral authority came from local bar groups unhappy with the ABCNY's hegemony, and internal uncertainty from changes in its membership and the consequent introduction of new values that affected its ability to agree on new directions for professional regulation. Nevertheless, the ABCNY still struggled to maintain control over lawyer discipline and attempted to exercise leadership throughout the 1970s with respect to professional self-regulation.

Although in the interwar years the local bar groups had by no means been merely passive observers of the regulatory initiatives of the corporate bar, the leadership of the ABCNY was not seriously threatened. In the 1960s and 1970s, however, local bar elites were better able to assert their interests. In Chicago, for instance, the leaders of the local trial bar were successful in fully penetrating the leadership of the CBA in the 1960s and 1970s, to the extent that some lawyers referred to a trial lawyers' coup, and thus were able to influence the direction of changes affecting their constituents.[8] On the national level, the increased importance of local bar elites was manifested in the emergence of the American Trial Lawyers Association during the 1970s as an active national organization with local chapters intent on defending the

7. See Carlin, *Lawyers' Ethics*, chapter 9.
8. Charles L. Cappell and Terence C. Halliday, "Professional Projects of Elite Chicago Lawyers, 1950–1974," *American Bar Foundation Research Journal* (1983): 291–340.

interests of the local trial bars.[9] Though the local practitioners were never to be fully incorporated into the ABCNY as they were in the CBA in Chicago, they eventually were able to undermine the formal authority the ABCNY had long held over lawyers' conduct in New York City.

LOCAL BAR ELITES AND LAWYER DISCIPLINE

In Chapter 1, I outlined the formation and early development of the ABCNY's Committee on Grievances. To recapitulate briefly, in 1884 the committee asserted jurisdiction over all lawyers practicing in New York City whether members of the ABCNY or not. From the mid-1880s, then, a voluntary organization of lawyers, with a small minority of the bar as members, claimed the right to investigate complaints about the conduct of all lawyers in the city. This assertion of citywide authority by the ABCNY was given de facto recognition by the Appellate Division of the New York Supreme Court, [10] which had ultimate authority over the conduct of lawyers in the state but which had neither the desire nor the resources at this time to develop lawyer disciplinary mechanisms of its own. By the beginning of the twentieth century the ABCNY grievance committee was well established as responsible for lawyer discipline in Manhattan and the Bronx. Even the formation and rapid growth of a rival organization of lawyers in the city, the NYCLA, failed to disturb its dominant position. The advantages of priority that the ABCNY enjoyed by being first into the field, its substantial financial resources, and the cooperation of the Appellate Division enabled the ABCNY to develop a monopoly over lawyer discipline in the city. Jerome Carlin found in 1960 that 98 percent of all complaints about lawyers' conduct in New York City were referred to the ABCNY committee for investigation.[11]

In 1937 the official legal status of the ABCNY committee was confirmed when the Appellate Division granted it the subpoena powers it had eagerly sought to strengthen its investigatory efforts. Providing access to the coercive power of the state, subpoena power enabled the

---

9. The American Trial Lawyers' Association conducted a vigorous campaign in opposition to proposals for a new code of ethics put forward by the ABA in 1980, and local branches strongly opposed the adoption of no-fault liability statutes in many states in the 1970s.

10. The Appellate Division of the New York Supreme Court is an intermediate appellate court in the statewide system. Above it is the Court of Appeals and below it are the various trial courts. Responsible for the admission and discipline of lawyers, the Appellate Division is divided into four departments, each of which covers a part of the state. The First Department has jurisdiction over Manhattan and the Bronx.

11. Carlin, *Lawyers' Ethics*, p. 150.

grievance committee to compel witnesses to attend hearings and to testify. The ABCNY consolidated the public status of its grievance committee by convincing the New York City government in the 1960s that it was performing a public service in regulating lawyers and therefore should be reimbursed for a substantial part of its expenditures on lawyer discipline.[12]

The institutionalization of the Committee on Grievances certainly provided a mechanism through which the elite ABCNY could exercise control over the nonelite majority of the bar. The effectiveness of this mechanism, however, was by no means clear. The sanctioning powers of the grievance committee were limited: It could investigate complaints against attorneys and, if probable cause of unethical conduct were found, initiate action before the Appellate Division, but it had no authority to suspend or disbar from practice. Only the court had the authority to disbar attorneys, although as time progressed the ABCNY committee, in common with grievance committees elsewhere, took it upon itself to issue admonishments and censures to lawyers who were first-time offenders or against whom the committee lacked sufficient evidence to press charges. Also, of course, the decision to investigate, and then perhaps to prosecute, involved the exercise of considerable discretionary authority that could greatly inconvenience the attorney who was the subject of the complaint, even though the process was completely hidden from the public.

Furthermore, as was noted earlier, only a small number of attorneys were ever investigated, let alone disciplined. In his study of the ethics of New York lawyers, Carlin found that the formal disciplinary machinery of the ABCNY uncovered and punished only a tiny proportion of the total amount of unethical conduct in any one year. Whereas the Committee on Grievances received an average of 1,450 complaints per annum from 1952 to 1961, only 60 per year were brought to a formal hearing before the committee. Of these 60 cases, only an average of 19 per annum, little more than one percent of the original complaints, were sent on to the Appellate Division for adjudication, of which an average of 10 cases resulted in the disbarment of the responding attorney.[13] By the late 1970s the number of complaints received had increased substantially—to 2,362 in 1978, for instance—and the number of referrals to the Appellate Division had also risen significantly—to 79 in 1978, representing more than 3 percent of the total number of com-

---

12. In the mid-1960s, New York City reimbursed the ABCNY for about one-third of its total expenditures on lawyer discipline. Martin, *Causes and Conflicts*, p. 378.

13. Carlin, *Lawyers' Ethics*, p. 151.

plaints. Yet the number and proportion of final disciplinary actions taken by the Appellate Division remained relatively low. In 1978, thirty-one lawyers were disciplined in some way by the Appellate Division, including a total of 17 disbarments, which was not many more proportionately than were disbarred in the 1950s.[14] Such a small number of lawyers were disciplined in any one year that it is clear lawyer discipline could scarcely serve as a significant deterrent to unethical conduct or as an efficient means of oppressing the underclass of the bar. More important, perhaps, than the actual power that control over discipline bestowed on the ABCNY was the symbolic authority it carried. Control over discipline could be seen as a form of status competition in Joseph Gusfield's terms, symbolically suggesting the superior moral standing of those responsible for maintaining the ethical standards of the bar.[15] Certainly, the ABCNY's performance of this social-control function contributed to the Association's prominence in the city and the bar.

The ABCNY's monopoly over the operation of lawyer discipline in New York City was not to be challenged until the late 1960s. Following considerable public criticism of the organized bar's performance in lawyer discipline, attention was directed toward the operation, or inoperation, of professional disciplinary committees. An ABA commission reported in 1970 that a "scandalous situation" existed in lawyer discipline nationwide and expressed the concern that if bar associations did not improve their performance public authorities might intervene in professional regulation.[16]

In response to these concerns, Cyrus R. Vance, president of the ABCNY, established in 1974 an internal committee of association members to review the procedures of the ABCNY grievance committee and to make recommendations for improvements. Known as the Silverman Committee, it recommended several far-reaching changes while affirming that lawyer discipline should remain a matter of self-regulation and that the ABCNY was the appropriate body to perform that necessary function in New York City. Recognizing that the unrepresentativeness of the ABCNY was a problem, the Silverman Committee recommended including nonmembers of the Association on the grievance committee to make it more representative of the New York bar at large. It also

14. "Analysis of the Grievance System of the Association of the Bar of the City of New York," Final Report by the Economic Development Council of New York City, Inc., Task Force, *Record of the Association of the Bar of the City of New York* 34 (1979): 5–6.

15. Joseph R. Gusfield, *Symbolic Crusade* (Urbana: University of Illinois Press, 1963).

16. Report of the Special Committee on Evaluation of Disciplinary Enforcement, American Bar Association, June 1970, pp. 1–9.

recommended lay participation as a response to the criticism that the bar could not be trusted to discipline its own.[17]

Within the Appellate Division of the New York Supreme Court the issue was also being discussed at this time. A committee of justices, chaired by Justice Francis T. Murphy, Jr., reviewed the Silverman Committee report and responded with recommendations of its own, to many of which the ABCNY acceded.[18] Shortly thereafter, Justice Murphy became presiding justice of the First Department of the Appellate Division, which had jurisdiction over Manhattan and the Bronx. Justice Murphy, an Irish Catholic from the Bronx, had been a judge since early in his legal career, and his father had been a judge before him. A graduate of a local law school, he had little in common with the corporate legal elite who led the ABCNY. With his personal interest in professional discipline, Presiding Justice Murphy pressed the Appellate Division's authority at the expense of the ABCNY.

When New York City had to retrench its expenditures in 1976, it ceased paying for the costs of the grievance committee, leaving the burden to fall on the already financially strapped court system. In 1979, the ABCNY was finally successful, with the help of the Appellate Division, in getting through the state legislature a requirement for the registration of all lawyers, with an annual registration fee to be paid into the court's coffers to meet the costs of lawyer discipline. The court thus acquired financial responsibility for the disciplinary system and the wherewithal to fund it. It was only to be expected, then, that the Appellate Division would take a closer interest in the operation of the grievance system by the ABCNY, particularly with Justice Murphy at the helm and the backdrop of national criticism of bar association performance in this area.

In 1977, the ABCNY announced the first appointment of lawyer nonmembers and of laypersons to its grievance committee, following the recommendations of the Silverman Committee and the Appellate Division. These steps were the first in the attenuation of the control of the large-firm elite over lawyer discipline in New York City. The court, pressing further, wanted it clearly and formally understood that the ABCNY grievance committee was also the Disciplinary Committee of the First Department of the Appellate Division of the New York Supreme Court. This was true in a new and vital sense now that the Appellate Division was responsible for funding the operation of the

---

17. The Association of the Bar of the City of New York, Ad Hoc Committee on Grievance Procedures (Chairman, Leon Silverman), 1976.

18. Appellate Division Committee Report on Grievance System, May 1976.

ABCNY committee. In line with an understanding of the grievance committee's dual identity, the Appellate Division first insisted that appointments to the committee should be made only after consultation between the two bodies, and then began nominating its own candidates for vacancies on the committee. Some of these were members of the ABCNY and others were not. The ABCNY refused to appoint some of the court's nominees, claiming that several lacked the requisite experience and qualifications.[19] In what amounted to a power struggle over whose committee it was, the Appellate Division insisted on having its way and the ABCNY was forced to back down and accept the appointment of persons it did not approve. The ABCNY was now in the unhappy position of having a committee the appointments to which it did not control.

The final parting of the ways was to come over the issue of who actually employed the staff of the committee. Though the Appellate Division bore the costs of the grievance committee, it reimbursed the ABCNY in one lump sum for expenses incurred. Thus the staff of the committee continued to be employees of the ABCNY, hired and paid by it, and receiving its benefits. Wanting greater control over its expenditures, the court proposed that it pay the salaries of the committee's staff directly, whereby they would effectively become employees of the court. The court also suggested that if members of the staff were court employees, it would tend to mute the criticism that the disciplinary process, under the control the ABCNY, was inevitably biased in favor of the large law firms. Having already lost final control over appointments to the committee, the ABCNY found the court's proposal unacceptable because it would have further reduced the ABCNY's authority over the committee and its operations to the point where it would be purely nominal. Stating that it was unable to lend its name to a process over which it no longer had any real control, the ABCNY surrendered responsibility for discipline to the Appellate Division in March 1980.[20] The Committee on Grievances of the ABCNY thus became the Disciplinary Committee of the court, ending the ABCNY's role in this area after 110 years.

The ABCNY's loss of control over disciplinary activities in Manhattan and the Bronx was part of a nationwide trend whereby the discipline of lawyers moved outside the bar associations to independent

---

19. This outline of the struggle between the ABCNY and the Appellate Division over control of lawyer discipline has been constructed from personal interviews with leaders of the ABCNY.

20. News Release, Appellate Division of the New York Supreme Court, First Department, and The Association of the Bar of the City of New York, March 1980.

commissions directly responsible to the state supreme courts.[21] But, unlike the situations in many states where bar associations' disciplinary systems were sadly lacking, the ABCNY had established a professional operation. The issue in New York was not so much the quality of discipline under the ABCNY, although certainly the question of its bias toward those not represented in the ABCNY was raised. An independent analysis of the grievance system conducted in 1979 by the Economic Development Council of New York City at the request of Presiding Justice Murphy found that, although the ABCNY grievance committee had a substantial backlog of cases and its attorneys carried a heavy caseload in comparison to the situations in other states, its procedures were less complicated and time-consuming. Funding and adequate staffing seemed the major problems. Furthermore, the Economic Development Council's report recommended that control over discipline remain vested in the hands of the ABCNY, given its proven track record and the "lack of a superior organization model."[22]

Rather, events in New York reflected historic tensions between the large-firm, corporate elite of the ABCNY and local bar elites, whose interests were represented in the local bar associations and the local courts. The Appellate Division of the Supreme Court was essentially a local court although it ranked below only the New York Court of Appeals in the state court system. Most judges on the Appellate Division bench were originally local lawyers, generally with political connections that gained them positions on the electoral slate in the first place. Closely connected to local bar elites, and to the local political clubs, the members of the Appellate Division bench were natural allies of the local bar associations, not of the Wall Street leadership of the ABCNY.

Historically, the large-firm elite of the New York bar had felt that only they were suitably qualified to run the disciplinary machinery of the bar. There was the implicit assumption that as most of the infringements to be investigated occurred among more marginal practitioners, an assumption reinforced by the actual pattern of complaints received by the Committee on Grievances, control over the disciplinary machinery needed to be in the hands of lawyers removed from those areas of practice where the pressure to act unethically, as defined by the Canon of Ethics, was greatest. In his strident opposition to the integrated bar concept in 1926, and his open defense of elitism, William D. Guthrie asserted that the entry of the mass of lawyers into the or-

21. See Michael J. Powell, "Professional Divestiture: The Cession of Responsibility for Lawyer Discipline," *American Bar Foundation Research Journal* (1986 Winter): 31–54.

22. "Analysis of the Grievance System," Final Report by the Economic Development Council, pp. 3–7.

ganized bar would dilute its ethical standards. He referred to "thousands of lawyers in New York . . . who are restive under the standards of professional conduct which the Grievance Committee of the Association of the Bar . . . has now maintained for a quarter of a century."[23]

While never explicitly stated, this same assumption underlay the strong resistance within the ABCNY to surrendering control of discipline to the Appellate Division. The courts were perceived as being too closely associated with local politics and too embedded in the local bar to maintain a strong front on disciplining lawyers. There was an implicit concern within the leadership of the ABCNY that local politics and court patronage would lessen the quality of the discipline committee and weaken its resolve to enforce the code of ethics. For its part, the Appellate Division responded by charging that the ABCNY grievance committee had always been soft on corporate lawyers in large firms. The struggle between the Appellate Division and the ABCNY for control over lawyer discipline in New York City reflected the tension in New York City between the large-firm elite and local bar groups. As the regulation of lawyers' conduct was, ultimately, a local issue, under the control of the state courts, the local bar groups finally won out. Given the ABCNY's long-standing monopoly in this area, its loss of control over lawyer discipline in New York City represented a major blow to the moral authority of the large-firm elite.

MORAL CHARACTER AND ADMISSION TO THE BAR

Another area of professional self-regulation subject to reexamination during the 1970s was that of character requirements for admission to the bar. In the interwar years when the large-firm elite, together with its allies in the local bar, successfully pressed for more stringent requirements for admission to practice, it demanded not only higher education standards but also investigation into the moral character of applicants to the bar. Applicants for admission to the bar were required to pass a bar examination administered by boards of law examiners in each state and undergo an investigation as to moral character conducted by "Character Committees" established for this purpose by either local bar associations or state supreme courts. Both academic and character admissions requirements were intended to present barriers to those deemed unfit to practice law by dint of lack of either knowledge or moral fitness.

---

23. William D. Guthrie, "Discussion of Report of the Committee on Organization of Entire Bar of State," *Proceedings*, New York State Bar Association (1926): 279.

In addition to passing the bar examination, then, applicants for admission in New York had the burden of satisfying the justices of the Appellate Division, through its character committees, that they possessed "the character and general fitness requisite for an attorney and counsellor-at-law."[24] To achieve this latter end, the applicant was required to file three substantial affidavits as to moral character, complete under oath a lengthy questionnaire that delved into many aspects of the applicant's past private life, and undergo a personal interview with members of the character committee.

Despite the fact that few applicants were rejected on character grounds,[25] these rather elaborate requirements were burdensome for applicants and not at all subject to the constraints of established, written procedures. There were no published guidelines indicating what the character committee would consider indicative of unfit character. Consequently, the room for the exercise of discretionary authority and arbitrary judgment was considerable. Furthermore, the questionnaires to be completed by the applicants included questions about membership in organizations opposed to the American form of government, political activities, and draft registration, leaving open the possibility of the character examination's being used as a means of excluding politically undesirable applicants. Indeed, it was used in this way during the 1950s, with the most celebrated example being the Illinois Supreme Court's unwillingness to admit George Anastaplo to the bar because of his refusal to answer questions as to membership in the Communist party.[26]

During the 1970s, both the political and moral inquiries of the character committees were challenged in court by young lawyers throughout the United States. Questions related to membership in radical organizations and to draft registration, to which answers were to be provided under oath, were threatening to many applicants who had been engaged in resistance to the Vietnam War; others simply felt that such inquiries had little relevance to whether they possessed the character requisite to practice law.[27] At the same time, there was increased

---

24. "Review of Existing Procedures to Determine Character and Fitness for Admission to the New York Bar, and Recommended Changes," Report of The Committee to Regularize Bar Admission Procedures, Appellate Division of the Supreme Court of New York, 1980, p. 4.

25. Carlin reports that of 1,712 applicants investigated by the Committee on Character and Fitness of the First Department from 1944 to 1948, only 55, or less than .03%, were rejected on grounds of unfit character. Carlin, *Lawyers' Ethics*, n. 1, p. 162.

26. For a lengthy discussion of the Anastaplo case, see Auerbach, *Unequal Justice*, pp. 251–253.

27. See *Law Students Civil Rights Research Council, Inc.* v. *Wadmond*, 401 U.S. 154 (1971).

dissatisfaction on the part of younger lawyers with the moral standards deemed appropriate by the character committees. Service on a "Character and Fitness Committee" was certainly not very exciting and did not attract active younger lawyers. Rather, it tended to attract older members of the local bar, often members of the "ethnic" bars of the city, who had little sympathy for the upper-middle-class draft evaders and protesters of the 1960s and early 1970s. They were appointed by the Appellate Division and served for long, indefinite periods of time as there was no fixed term of service. Applicants complained that these elderly committee members were out of touch with the changing norms and mores of American life and persisted in applying outmoded standards of behavior. Societal norms changed much more quickly than did the character and fitness examinations.

In a time when living in "mixed" apartments with roommates of the opposite sex became commonplace, recent graduates found questions requiring the listing of roommates archaic and invasive of privacy. The assumption that living with someone other than one's spouse was evidence of moral turpitude and should disqualify an applicant from admission to the bar was challenged in court, eventually resulting in a 1979 United States Supreme Court decision overturning a decision not to admit an applicant to the bar on such grounds.[28] In addition, the presumption that minor misdemeanors should of themselves preclude a candidate from admission to the bar was attacked. The 1960s and 1970s were decades of great uncertainty in moral standards in American society; character examinations based on a prior certainty seemed inflexible and irrelevant.

With this debate in the background, the ABCNY appointed a Special Committee on Professional Education and Admissions to examine the work of the New York character and fitness committees. The ABCNY special committee joined forces with the Committee on Legal Education and Admissions to the Bar of the New York State Bar Association to produce a joint report in 1978 advocating sweeping changes in the whole process.[29] The initiative lay with the ABCNY but, as the rules governing admission to the bar were established by the state supreme court, the Association needed the support of the state bar if it was to carry the day. With the intention of rationalizing the process, the two bar associations sought the establishment and promulgation of written guidelines indicating the circumstances that would justify denial of admission, the adoption of procedural rules limiting the discretion of the

---

28. *New York Times*, April 21, 1979.

29. "The Character and Fitness Committees in New York State," *The Record of the Association of the Bar of the City of New York* 33 (1978): 20–90.

character committees and protecting the rights of the applicants, and the delineation of the rights of appeal available to rejected applicants. Moreover, the two bar committees advocated the removal from the questionnaire of some of the more personal questions that inquired into the private lives of applicants. The committee also recommended the elimination of the required personal interview and character affidavits, which they considered to be of little value.

These were radical proposals, and in response the Judicial Conference of the State of New York appointed its own committee, the Committee to Regularize Bar Admission Procedures, to examine the bar association proposals and, in turn, make recommendations to the conference. Chaired by a solo practitioner with considerable experience in bar admissions work, the Committee to Regularize rejected almost all the bar associations' most sweeping proposals.[30] It recommended keeping the personal interview and the character affidavits and opposed the idea of promulgating guidelines as to the types of problems that might lead to the denial of admission. The Committee to Regularize did recommend, however, the adoption of the less radical changes proposed by the bar associations, including the codification of procedural rules, the explicit delineation of rights of appeal, and the institution of an advance ruling procedure whereby students could establish the likelihood of meeting any character and fitness problems prior to entering law school. Additionally, the Committee to Regularize recommended the removal from the questionnaire of some of the more dated and irrelevant items, although not the questions about membership in radical political organizations.

The Appellate Division adopted in its entirety the report of the Committee to Regularize, and in 1980 moved to have the changes recommended by that committee incorporated into the admissions process. In so doing, the Appellate Division rejected the bar associations' proposals for more radical surgery. The character and fitness process was rationalized and codified, the questionnaire was refined and reduced in size from eleven to nine pages, and an advance warning system instituted; but the process essentially remained unchanged.[31]

In deciding a 1971 case brought by law students challenging the constitutionality of the political inquiries of character and fitness examinations in New York State, the United States Supreme Court raised, but did not answer, the question of whether "wise policy" would suggest

---

30. "Review of Existing Procedures to Determine Character and Fitness," Report of Committee to Regularize, 1980.
31. "New Rules Adopted for Panels on Character and Fitness," *New York Law Journal,* June 19, 1980.

a system of "extremely minimum checking for serious, concrete character deficiencies" rather than the elaborate system currently in place.[32] The two bar committees advocated such minimal checking prior to admission whereas the Appellate Division remained on a more conservative course, retaining the elaborate screening system with only minor modifications.

It is somewhat ironic that the two bar associations, led by the special committee of the ABCNY, should have pressed for fundamental changes in the admissions process, since it was the ABCNY that originally pushed for extensive character examinations of prospective members of the bar in the 1920s and 1930s. By the late 1970s, however, the ABCNY was advocating the substantial dismantling of the elaborate review system constructed by the courts. The reasons for this change in position lie both in the incorporation into the ABCNY of young, liberal lawyers who graduated in the 1960s and were opposed to intrusive political and moral investigations, and in the markedly different normative environment of the 1970s. Not only had popular values changed, but the United States Supreme Court had shown itself unwilling to uphold an unnecessarily intrusive character and fitness investigation. The local practitioners who served on the character committees, however, opposed the emasculation of the process they operated and adopted a much more conservative position than did the ABCNY/NYSBA committee. Given the state court system's close links with the local bar, it is not surprising that the Appellate Division should spurn the more radical proposals of the two bar associations for the conservative path advocated by their local committee.

The debate over the character and fitness examination for prospective members of the New York bar once again pitted the large-firm elite of the ABCNY, together with its allies in the State Bar Association, against the state judiciary and the local bar groups. Somewhat ironically, the large-firm elite advocated the relaxation of character investigations, and the committee representing the local bar defended the maintenance of restrictive entry procedures. As very few applicants were ever turned down on character grounds, the insistence of the local bar and the court on retaining much of the substance and form of the character examination provides an example of symbolic politics by which members of the bar demonstrated their moral superiority over other occupations. It is not only the large-firm elite of the bar that engages in status competition; indeed, symbols of status that distinguish lawyers as professionals are likely to be more important to lower-echelon lawyers as establishing their special standing in their local

---

32. *Law Students Civil Rights Research Council, Inc.* v. *Wadmond.*

communities than to corporate lawyers who share in the high social standing of their corporate clients. For members of the local bar, the maintenance of character requirements for admission to practice apparently was of considerable symbolic significance. Consequently, reforms originating from the ABCNY and its new coalition of young reformers and older liberals achieved limited success in the face of opposition from the local bar and judiciary.

NEW DIRECTIONS IN LEGAL ETHICS

A major concern of many young lawyers who graduated from the elite national law schools in the late 1960s was access to justice and the provision of legal services to the poor. This was the period of the legal-services movement and of the emergence of the "new public-interest lawyer."[33] Neighborhood legal clinics, providing legal services free or at very reduced costs, were created at this time, giving rise to considerable controversy within the organized bar. Many local bar associations opposed the establishment of these clinics and the formulation of prepaid legal plans, ostensibly because they contravened ethical norms relating to solicitation and lawyer-client relations.[34] In addition, however, members of local bars were worried about the loss of business that might follow the institutionalization of these new modes for the provision of legal services. Local, general-practice lawyers feared that low-income clients would seek free or reduced-rate legal services from federally funded clinics or through prepaid plans, thereby reducing the demand for their own services. It was in response to the vigorous opposition in Illinois of the organized bar to the expansion of group legal services, for example, that in 1971 the Chicago Council of Lawyers first became involved in questions of legal ethics.[35] Concern over the provision of legal services led the Council to conclude that many traditional professional norms were based on outmoded considerations and thus hindered access to justice. Indeed, some ethical constraints appeared designed more to protect the professional monopoly and economic well-being of lawyers than to protect the public or encourage ethical conduct. For reasons such as these, the Council successfully blocked the adoption of the new ABA Code of Professional Responsi-

---

33. See F. Raymond Marks (with Kirk Leswing and Barbara A. Fortinsky), *The Lawyer, the Public, and Professional Responsibility* (Chicago: American Bar Foundation, 1972).

34. Earl Johnson, *Justice and Reform: The Formative Years of the OEO Legal Services Program* (New York: Russell Sage Foundation, 1974).

35. Chicago Council of Lawyers, "Report on Code of Professional Responsibility" (February 1972).

bility in Illinois sponsored by the CBA and the Illinois State Bar Association because it unduly restricted the development of group legal services.[36]

The influx of young lawyers into the bar in the 1970s, a significant proportion of whom were ideologically committed to increasing the availability of legal services, made it difficult for the older leadership of the organized bar to defend traditional professional values that seemed to obstruct access to legal counsel. It should be noted that it was only a particular segment of younger lawyers who advocated such changes; the leaders of the Chicago Council of Lawyers overwhelmingly were graduates of elite national schools, and either worked in legal-aid settings or as associates with large law firms.[37] Similarly motivated young lawyers in the New York Council of Law Associates pressed for a greater commitment of the New York bar to public-interest law. It was these young lawyers, co-opted into the ABCNY and increasingly active in its leadership, who pushed the ABCNY toward reconsidering those ethical proscriptions, which they regarded as hindering access to legal services. There was also a movement within the ABCNY directed at requiring more stringent obligations incumbent upon all lawyers to serve the public as well as their private interests. The following two issues, lawyer advertising and the obligation of members of the bar to provide legal services to the poor, were subjects of considerable internal debate within the ABCNY during the 1970s.

Lawyer Advertising

Both the old Canon of Ethics and the new Code of Professional Responsibility adopted by the ABA in 1969 imposed blanket prohibitions on lawyer advertising. Viewed as manifesting a spirit of commercialism foreign to the quiet dignity of the profession, advertising was treated as a form of unprofessional conduct. It suggested "touting" and the solicitation of business, and promised to encourage the needless "stirring up" of litigation. The ban on lawyer advertising did not become a major ethical issue until the 1970s, when the growing consumer and legal-services movements argued that it artificially raised the costs of routine legal services by reducing intraprofessional competition and obstructed the flow of information about available legal services. According to legal-aid lawyers, advertising was required to inform potential clients as to what services were available at what price. For the

---

36. Michael J. Powell, "Anatomy of a Counter-Bar Association: The Chicago Council of Lawyers," *American Bar Foundation Research Journal* (1979): 535.

37. Ibid.

promoters of low-cost legal clinics advertising was essential to their economic viability. Thus the attack on the professional restriction on advertising was led by consumer advocates together with legal-clinic entrepreneurs.[38] Between 1975 and 1977, more than ten lawsuits were brought against bar groups on the issue around the country, largely by consumer advocates.[39]

Further, the Antitrust Division of the Justice Department was investigating the restraint of trade tendencies of professional ethics and the activities of professional associations. Following the 1975 United States Supreme Court decision in *Goldfarb* v. *Virginia State Bar Association*, which held that the minimum fee schedules enforced by the bar association violated the Sherman Act, the Justice Department sued the ABA in 1976. It alleged a combination and restraint of trade through the operation of the Code of Professional Responsibility, especially as it related to lawyer advertising.[40] Consequently, the ABA began to rethink its traditional blanket prohibition on advertising, eventually proposing amendments to the Code of Professional Responsibility that would permit a minimal amount of lawyer advertising in directories, law lists, and the Yellow Pages.[41] Faced with expressions of dissatisfaction from the consumer advocates newly in its midst, the ABCNY was also under pressure to modify its position.

In 1976 the ABCNY Executive Committee appointed a small subcommittee to consider the issue and recommend what position it should take on the ABA proposed amendments. Recommending that the ABCNY delegates to the State Bar Association should support the adoption of the minimal changes proposed by the ABA as "a cautious first step," the subcommittee suggested that the Executive Committee should avoid taking a more definitive position on the whole advertising issue because it was too controversial, and, instead, should allow different committees to express and publish their conflicting views.[42] But one member of the subcommittee, a former chairman of the Special Committee on Consumer Affairs, submitted a minority report in which he differed with both the substantive recommendations of the subcom-

38. Michael J. Powell, "Developments in the Regulation of Lawyers: Competing Segments and Market, Client, and Government Controls," *Social Forces* 64 (1985): 284–287.

39. Lori B. Andrews, "Lawyer Advertising and the First Amendment," *American Bar Foundation Research Journal* (1981 Fall): 967–1022.

40. Powell, "Developments in the Regulation of Lawyers," p. 294.

41. For the text of the ABA proposals, see Lori B. Andrews, *Birth of a Salesman: Lawyer Advertising and Solicitation* (Chicago: American Bar Association, 1980), pp. 91–134.

42. Report to Executive Committee, Ad Hoc Committee on Advertising, ABCNY, 1976.

mittee and its suggestions as to procedure within the ABCNY. Advocating a much more liberal position on advertising, the dissenter criticized the majority report of the subcommittee for recommending that the Executive Committee take no action in the immediate future. This signified to him abdication of leadership on the part of the Executive Committee and the ABCNY that is not "consistent with the preeminent position which the Association seeks—and asserts—in matters of professional discipline."[43]

The Executive Committee, however, approved the majority report of its ad hoc subcommittee, and thus the delegates of the ABCNY voted in favor of the State Bar Association's adoption of the minimal relaxation of the restrictions on advertising proposed by the ABA. Three committees of the ABCNY subsequently published reports in the March 1977 *Record* of the Association on the question. Two of the reports urged that the ban on advertising should be completely lifted and only false and misleading advertising barred.[44] One of these reports was that of the Special Committee on Consumer Affairs, which defined lawyer advertising almost entirely as a consumer issue; ethical questions were involved only to the extent that advertising raised issues of truth and honesty. Arguing that advertising was "a necessary precondition to the effective delivery of legal services to those of moderate or limited means," the Special Committee on Consumer Affairs placed access to services over more abstract professional values and contended that only false and misleading advertising should be prohibited.[45]

The Association as a whole still had not taken a position when the United States Supreme Court shot down the advertising ban in June of 1977 with its decision in *Bates and O'Steen v. Arizona State Bar.*[46] This case was an appeal brought by two young legal clinic operators against the Arizona Supreme Court's decisions upholding the imposition of sanctions on them by the Arizona State Bar Association for advertising. The United States Supreme Court decided for the advertisers, opining that advertising was a form of free speech and thus protected by the First Amendment. Furthermore, the Supreme Court held that advertising was a useful method of getting information about the type and cost

---

43. Ibid., Minority Report.

44. Reports of Committee on Professional Responsibility and Special Committee on Consumer Affairs in *Record of the Association of the Bar of the City of New York* 32 (March 1977): 114–118.

45. Statement of Position Regarding Advertising by Lawyers, Special Committee on Consumer Affairs, January 1976.

46. *Bates and O'Steen* v. *Arizona State Bar*, 433 U.S. 350 (1977).

of legal services to those with legal needs. In the opinion of the Court, the needs of consumers for information weighed more heavily than did any postulated damage to professionalism inherent in advertising.[47]

Even though the *Bates* decision leaned toward relatively permissive standards on advertising, it left the development of specific regulations to the organized bar. Two groups within the bar opposed any drastic relaxation of advertising restrictions: the old traditionalists horrified by the entrance of crass commercialism into the profession, and the solo practitioners and small-firm lawyers engaged in personal-plight areas of law who stood to lose business to high-volume legal clinics with large advertising budgets. It was a coalition of these two conservative elements that led the ABA to adopt a proposal for the minimal relaxation of the profession's ban on advertising consonant with the *Bates* decision. The new ABA position retained restrictions on both the type and the content of lawyer advertisements, limited the information that could be provided with respect to fees, and prohibited television advertising completely.[48]

Meantime, the ABCNY formed a new, larger Ad Hoc Committee on Lawyer Advertising to reconsider its position. In sharp contrast to the ABA, this committee adopted the "false and misleading" standard advocated by the Special Committee on Consumer Affairs some two years earlier, recommending the removal of all restrictions on lawyer advertising other than requirements of truth and accuracy. In October 1977 the Executive Committee adopted this report of the ad hoc committee even though it represented a substantial change in its position.[49]

The significant role played by the Special Committee on Consumer Affairs in this reversal of the ABCNY's official position is evident from the Executive Committee's statement on lawyer advertising. Accepting the consumer definition of the issue almost completely with only a passing reference to questions of professional ethics, the Executive Committee observed that "the rights of free speech and of access to legal services are values too important to sacrifice to elusive and perhaps illusory gains in dignity."[50] There was considerable debate within the ABCNY on this issue, but in the final analysis the large law firms stood neither to gain nor lose from lawyer advertising. The Sullivan & Cromwells of Wall Street had no need to advertise in order to gain

---

47. Ibid. For a brief discussion of the Court's opinion, see Andrews, *Birth of a Salesman*, pp. 3–6.

48. See Andrews, *Birth of a Salesman*.

49. "Advertising by Lawyers," Report by the Executive Committee in Support of Its Resolution Regarding Lawyer Advertising, October 1977.

50. Ibid., p. 18.

legal business. Indeed, in the world of the large law firm advertising would be quite counterproductive even for newer firms seeking to establish themselves. Corporate clients are too sophisticated about their legal needs to be moved by media advertising; what mattered was reputation and success, aided and abetted by good personal connections. Large firms did engage in self-promotion through their public activities, their bar association work, and the club memberships of their members, but it was of a very different kind from that covered by the prohibition of advertising. Thus the issue was of relatively low priority to the large-firm lawyer, especially because, following the *Bates* decision, there was a degree of inevitability about the relaxation of restrictions. The older members of the ABCNY, however, did not lose their distaste for the whole concept of lawyer advertising and were not enthusiastic supporters of the proposed changes. Indeed, it was the hesitation of the older members that led to the indecision demonstrated by the Executive Committee's early refusal to commit the ABCNY to a firm position.

In advocating minimal restrictions on lawyer advertising the ABCNY went out on a limb. The New York State Bar Association had quickly followed the ABA, adopting its conservative and restrictive proposed amendments to the Code of Professional Responsibility. Other local and county bar associations could be expected to support this position, because this was an issue that directly affected the material interests of local solo and small-firm lawyers. Widespread advertising threatened to increase competition for lower-income clients and reduce fees for the bread-and-butter legal work of the general practitioner. In February 1978 the Appellate Division of the New York Supreme Court adopted as a court rule the restrictive proposal of the State Bar Association, allowing minimal lawyer advertising rather than the open, "false and misleading" standard advocated by the ABCNY.[51] In the final analysis, then, the ABCNY failed to determine the standards instituted to regulate lawyer advertising in New York City.

Although the older members of the large-firm elite, the traditional leaders of the ABCNY, may not have favored the introduction of lawyer advertising, it was an innovation that did not threaten their interests. After the *Bates* decision they were willing to sit back and allow the consumer and legal-services advocates to carry the day within the ABCNY. Thus the ABCNY emerged with a radical position at odds with the rest of the New York bar, a position rejected by the Appellate Division. Again, as with the reform of the character and fitness exam-

---

51. "Rules for Lawyers' Ads Uniform for State," *New York Law Journal* (March 15, 1978).

ination, the local bar groups were in the position of advocating minimal change while the new leadership of the ABCNY pushed for radical surgery. And, again, the ABCNY was unsuccessful in having its position adopted.

Pro Bono Publico Obligations of the Bar

Similar differences of opinion within both the ABCNY and the wider New York City legal community were evoked by the issue of the pro bono publico (for the good of the public) service obligations of the bar. Idealistic notions of the professions emphasized their "collectivity orientation," their alleged willingness to place the public interest before their own material interests.[52] The "sliding scale" fees of physicians in days gone by were a manifestation of the medical profession's commitment to the provision of health services to all, independent of their ability to pay. All the professions enshrined the rhetoric of public service in their ethical codes, but it was in the legal profession that there emerged the idea of a specific public-service obligation incumbent upon all members of the profession. According to this notion, all lawyers had an obligation to donate time pro bono publico. In actuality, the obligation to provide public legal services free or at a substantially lowered cost remained completely voluntary, and for most lawyers an aspirational ideal rather than a practical reality.[53]

In the late 1960s and early 1970s, along with the legal-services movement and the emergence of "public-interest law," there was born a new emphasis on the pro bono obligations of lawyers. Under pressure from graduating law students, many large law firms began to give official recognition to their responsibility to assist in meeting the needs of the poor for legal services. Such recognition moved beyond the mere invocation of the higher ideals of the profession to making structural changes to facilitate permitting members of the firms to fulfill their public-service obligations. Some firms nominated a partner to be responsible for coordinating the public-service work of members of the firm; others adopted the practice of sending a young associate to work for six months in a neighborhood legal-aid office; and most firms recognized pro bono work as a legitimate charge on their accounts indirectly subsidized by regular billings to their corporate clients.[54]

---

52. For example, Talcott Parsons, "The Professions and Social Structure," in *Essays in Sociological Theory* (New York: Free Press, rev. ed., 1954).

53. Barlow F. Christenson, "The Lawyer's Pro Bono Publico Responsibility," *American Bar Foundation Research Journal* (1981 Winter): 1–20.

54. Marks, *The Lawyer, the Public, and Professional Responsibility.*

The New York Council of Law Associates was established for the explicit purpose of facilitating arrangements for young associates to fulfill their public-service interests. It also served as an organizational base from which young lawyers could press the ABCNY to develop and encourage "public-interest" law opportunities as a means of meeting the huge, unfilled need for legal services assumed to exist among the New York poor. One such proposal originating from younger members associated with the Council of Law Associates was that the ABCNY sponsor a public-interest law firm to be staffed with salaried attorneys and funded by levies drawn on the large firms. In this concrete manner the ABCNY and the large firms would become involved in the provision of legal services to the poor. Although nothing came of this proposal in the long run, it was seriously considered by the Executive Committee. The implications of a voluntary association such as the ABCNY getting directly involved in public-interest law with all the potential of highly controversial litigation, class-action suits, and so forth, were considered too serious for the public-interest law-firm project to proceed. Instead, the ABCNY sponsored in 1977 a more neutral organization called the New York Lawyers for the Public Interest, which merely sought to channel public-interest law opportunities to the large law firms. It was funded by donations from the large firms, in the same way that the public-interest law firm was to be, but it would not get involved directly in legal representation itself and thus would not embroil the ABCNY in controversy and possible litigation.

Responding to continued interest in public-interest law, and to a concern that lawyers and law firms were still not meeting their pro bono obligations, the president of the ABCNY appointed in 1977 a special committee to study the issue and make policy recommendations. Composed of members from a variety of practice settings, including two solo practitioners, the Special Committee on Lawyers' Pro Bono Obligations presented the ABCNY in 1979 with a lengthy report adopting the position that public service ought to be a mandatory obligation of every lawyer enforced by the disciplinary machinery of the bar and the courts. Pro bono publico was not to be treated merely as an aspiration inscribed in ethical codes and then largely forgotten; rather, it was a requirement incumbent on all lawyers. Furthermore, the special committee insisted that there be some quantification of this obligation, suggesting thirty to sixty hours per annum, with lawyers required to report annually to some central authority the amount of time spent on public-service work. Failure to fulfill the public-service requirement would result in sanctions being imposed.[55] Though the committee's

55. "Toward a Mandatory Contribution of Public Service Practice by Every Lawyer," Report of the Special Committee on Lawyers' Pro Bono Obligations, 1979.

proposal was radical in its implications, it could not be dismissed lightly, especially since the ABCNY still controlled the disciplinary machinery of the New York City bar. In addition, the idea of mandatory pro bono obligations was taken up by the Special Commission on Evaluation of Professional Standards of the ABA, which was charged with drafting a new code of ethics for the profession.[56] In this way, the New York proposal became the subject of national debate and controversy, interwoven with discussion as to the general ethical responsibilities of the bar.

In New York, considerable debate followed the publication of the special committee's report. The opposition to mandatory pro bono requirements was led by a solo practitioner who, in addition to his membership in the ABCNY, was on the board of directors of the NYCLA and chairman of its Committee on Legal Services.[57] The two solo practitioners on the ABCNY's special committee also had filed dissenting minority reports opposing mandatory pro bono requirements. Thus the two sides in the debate appeared neatly polarized, with the special committee of the ABCNY, led by its large-firm members, on one side, and the solo practitioners in opposition.[58]

There was some logic to the apparent polarization. The imposition of mandatory pro bono on the bar at large would be, in fact, a tax on all practitioners. At first the special committee insisted on a levy of time, as that was a commodity available to all lawyers whether wealthy or poor, in large firms or small. All lawyers would have the same obligation to provide a certain number of hours' service, and wealthy large-firm lawyers would not be permitted to buy off that time by making monetary contributions to public-interest law efforts. Later, however, the special committee withdrew its insistence on a labor levy and accepted that the obligations could be met by a monetary donation of an equivalent amount. This compromise made sense as corporate, "office" lawyers from the large firms could scarcely provide adequate "personal-plight" legal services to the poor. Clearly, many large firms and corporate lawyers would buy off their obligation with tax-deductible donations, leaving the onus for actual public service to fall largely upon the small-firm and solo practitioners who could not afford to make monetary contributions. It all appeared too much like elite reform proposed by large-firm lawyers in cahoots with idealistic

56. Discussion Draft, Proposed Model Rules of Professional Conduct, Commission on Evaluation of Professional Standards, American Bar Association, 1980.

57. See "Compulsory Pro Bono Work Opposed by County Bar Panel," *New York Law Journal* (April 10, 1980).

58. Dissenting comments are attached to the majority report of the Special Committee on the Lawyer's Pro Bono Obligations, 1979.

"public-interest" lawyers and academics, who could afford either the time or the money. And, indeed, that is what the proposal was. The ABCNY special committee was representative of a variety of practice situations, but it was a coalition of large-firm and "public-interest" lawyers, together with a solitary academic, which gave the policy the majority it needed within the committee.[59]

The large-firm elite, however, was by no means unanimous in its support of this radical proposal. Some large-firm lawyers opposed the whole notion as impractical and coercive. Mandatory pro bono would necessitate a huge bureaucracy to enforce it and undermine the voluntarism they saw as central to the spirit of public service, moving professional ethics from their voluntary and aspirational origin toward contractual obligation. With considerable dissension within the ranks, the leadership of the ABCNY found it difficult to force the issue and come to any authoritative decision. In the end, the special committee's recommendation of mandatory pro bono obligations was voted down at a members' meeting.

A little later the Executive Committee published a statement as to its position on pro bono legal services in the form of a comment addressing a proposed new ethical code under consideration by the ABA. Stating strongly the lawyer's obligation to participate in providing public-interest legal services, the Executive Committee nevertheless did not support the use of disciplinary sanctions to enforce performance. The Executive Committee argued that a lawyer "cannot choose to ignore this duty and remain in compliance with the rules of professional conduct."[60] But it was clear that without any enforcement mechanism the performance of pro bono legal services remained dependent on the goodwill of members of the bar. The Executive Committee's position was a weaker version of that of the special committee, without any compulsion or reporting requirements. Whatever the ABCNY decided, however, a proposal for a mandatory obligation enforced by discipline would almost certainly have been rejected by the Appellate Division of the New York Supreme Court.

Although the mandatory pro bono proposal eventually failed even within the ABCNY, the special committee's advocacy of it engendered considerable debate over the obligation of lawyers to provide free legal services to those who cannot afford to pay. In so doing, it had substantial symbolical significance in that it drew attention to the bar's stated

---

59. Ibid.
60. "Pro Bono Legal Service: An Executive Committee Position," *The Record of the Association of the Bar of the City of New York* 36 (1981): 10.

commitment to provide representation to all, irrespective of their ability to pay. In reality, the bar's periodic concern with its pro bono responsibilities can be viewed as more an exercise in symbolic politics than a real concern to meet the needs for legal representation of the poor. After all, in the 1960s most of the organized bar had strenuously resisted efforts to expand legal services to the poor through neighborhood clinics. Moreover, pro bono work always had amounted to a minute proportion of the total amount of legal work done by the private bar, and, as a voluntary commitment, could never be more than a drop in the bucket of legal needs. A survey of law firms in the early 1970s showed that pro bono work amounted to a very small proportion of all their work, less than 0.5 percent and less than four hours per lawyer annually, even in those firms that made a substantial commitment to it.[61] This would change, of course, if the pro bono obligation was made mandatory to the extent suggested by the ABCNY special committee (thirty to fifty hours annually for each lawyer). The provision of the equivalent of one week of free legal services by the 40,000 lawyers in New York City would amount to a substantial amount of legal representation. It was not to be, however, as a majority of ABCNY members preferred to keep pro bono work a symbolic aspiration rather than transform it into a material obligation. However, the movement for mandatory pro bono within the ABCNY was elite reform in its clearest form, advocated by elite members of the bar who could most afford the material commitment it would have entailed.

LIMITS TO ELITE CONTROL

In the preface to the second edition of his classic work on the causes and consequences of the division of labor in modern society, Emile Durkheim suggested that specialized occupational "corporations" or groups would serve as new centers for social integration and moral order.[62] According to Durkheim, individuals within modern industrialized societies needed new foci for cohesion and identification as the authority of religious institutions was increasingly attenuated and domestic control became ever less salient with labor force mobility and the clear separation of work and home. Durkheim thought that occupational groups would become moral communities in societies characterized by an extensive division of labor, establishing their own moral orders to which individual members of the occupations would be sub-

---

61. Auerbach, *Unequal Justice,* p. 282.
62. Emile Durkheim, *The Division of Labor in Society* (New York: Free Press, 1933), pp. 1–31.

ject. Developing sets of moral rules and rituals that would serve both to solidify the occupational community and to distinguish it from other collectivities, occupational "corporations" would emerge as new sources of moral authority and, indeed, as essential organs of public life and government in modern society.

Although his vision of a syndicalist form of government was not to be fulfilled, and his prognostications about the integrative significance of occupational groups were overstated, modern professions have come closest to approximating Durkheim's model of occupational moral communities to which individual members are bound through socialization, common rituals, and shared symbols. Not only have the modern professions developed strong, self-governing organizations, but they claim moral authority over all those inducted into their membership. Induction rituals and professional ideology encourage the belief that professions are special moral communities, quite separate from other occupational collectivities, and that membership in these communities entails responsibilities and standards of behavior beyond those of society generally. Thus professions like law instituted character and fitness examinations to ensure that admittees were of good character, formulated codes of ethics specifying the moral obligations of practitioners, and constructed self-regulatory systems to enforce, albeit minimally, the sets of rules thereby established.

Durkheim never paid much attention to how the moral order of these occupational communities would emerge, nor did he attempt to predict who would define the content of the obligations included therein. The implication was that occupational identification would naturally flow from repeated workplace interactions, and the moral authority of the occupation would emerge along with the development of group activities focused around shared occupational pursuits and interests. Like all groups, occupational collectivities would develop their own sets of moral rules to govern performance within the group and would thus eventually become sources of moral authority.

To more recent commentators, however, it is clear that occupational or professional elites have been responsible for the development and institutionalization of the moral order of the occupational collectivities. Structural functionalists such as Suzanne Keller point to the necessary role of elites in establishing and maintaining the moral order of both the larger society and the collectivities within it. As Keller sees it, "Moral obligation to ultimate ends . . . is the duty of strategic elites."[63] These elites are responsible, in Durkheim's terms, "to create

63. Suzanne Keller, *Beyond the Ruling Class: Strategic Elites in Modern Society* (New York: Random House, 1963), p. 138.

respect for the beliefs, traditions, and collective practices: that is, to defend the collective conscience from enemies within and without."[64] In so doing, the strategic elites of the professions are ensuring collective solidarity and serving the interests of all members of the professional communities.

Critics of elite dominance likewise point to the central role played by professional elites in the definition of the moral order of the professions and in the construction of professional ideologies.[65] The fact that elites play this role, however, is not functionally necessary in any way but reflects their superior power resources and their alliance with key political elites. From this revisionist perspective, the moral order of the profession, defined and enforced by the elite, does not reflect the interests of all segments of the profession; rather, it serves to enhance the dominant position and interests of the elite itself. Through their control of the major professional associations, elite groups have been able to impose their definition of the profession on the occupational collectivity as a whole.

Whatever the empirical validity of these conflicting explanations of the motivation and interests of professional elites, this chapter has demonstrated the considerable effort and substantial organizational resources expended by the elite ABCNY on developing and upholding the moral order of the legal profession. The extent to which it was successful in establishing a moral community, or in imposing its definitions upon the rest of the bar, is questionable; yet it continued to attempt to exercise leadership in this area throughout the 1970s. Although undoubtedly defining the professional responsibilities of lawyers in their own terms, the leaders of the ABCNY certainly appeared to feel an ongoing responsibility for the moral order of the New York bar and of the profession as a whole.

Distrustful of local judicial control and concerned about the penetration of local bar politics and patronage, the ABCNY struggled to maintain its control over lawyer discipline in the face of insistent pressure from the Appellate Division.[66] In 1980, the ABCNY finally and reluctantly surrendered authority over the system it had built. In addition, encouraged by its younger members who were not so bound to traditional notions of professional regulation, the ABCNY advocated radical changes in the character and fitness examination and in the restrictions

---

64. Durkheim, *The Division of Labor*, p. 84.
65. See, for example, Auerbach, *Unequal Justice*, and Philip Schuchman, "Ethics and Legal Ethics: The Propriety of the Canons as a Group Moral Code," *George Washington Law Review* 37 (1968–1969): 244–269.
66. Powell, "Professional Divestiture."

on lawyer advertising. These new directions in professional regulation were pursued notwithstanding considerable debate within the bar, especially over the relaxation of the bar's long-standing prohibition of lawyer advertising.

Furthermore, the ABCNY was a very active participant in the national discussions within the legal community over the formulation of a new code of ethics. Believing that the existing Code of Professional Responsibility no longer addressed adequately the ethical dilemmas facing American lawyers, the ABA in 1977 established the Commission on Evaluation of Professional Standards to draft a new code of ethics. The commission produced a discussion draft in 1980 and called for comments from members of the bar and professional organizations.[67] No fewer than four committees of the ABCNY responded to this call with detailed comments on the discussion draft that were submitted to hearings held in New York City in 1980.[68] Subsequently, the Executive Committee produced two lengthy statements on the final draft of the "Model Rules of Professional Conduct," one dealing with its format and the other with the substance of the proposed rules.[69] In preparing these comments and statements the ABCNY played a much more active role than most other bar associations, which generally restricted themselves to statements of approval or disapproval. The ABCNY's continued high level of activity in the whole area of professional ethics reflects its elite character with the corollary that it had a special responsibility to provide leadership in the redefinition of the moral order of the profession that was occurring in the 1970s.

The large-firm elite of the ABCNY, however, was by no means able to impose its views on the New York bar at large. Notwithstanding Auerbach's account of the development of professional regulation that emphasized the dominance of the WASP upper class,[70] the examples recounted in this chapter indicate that the nonelite majority was able to protect its own interests. As a result of the ABCNY's loss of control

---

67. Discussion Draft, Proposed Model Rules of Professional Conduct, American Bar Association (1980).

68. See Committee Reports Commenting on the January 30, 1980, Discussion Draft of Model Rules of Professional Conduct, Association of the Bar of the City of New York, July 1980.

69. "Proposed Model Rules of Professional Conduct: An Executive Committee Statement," *The Record of the Association of the Bar of the City of New York* 37 (1982): 14–18; "The Substance of the Proposed Model Rules of Professional Conduct: An Executive Committee Statement," *The Record of the Association of the Bar of the City of New York* 37 (1982): 417–435.

70. Auerbach, *Unequal Justice*.

over lawyer discipline, large-firm lawyers no longer enjoyed monopoly control over the disciplinary machinery but rather became only one of many segments of the bar represented on the court's disciplinary committee. Whereas for much of this century the chair of the grievance committee had been a lawyer from an eminent large firm specializing in corporate law, the first chairman of the Disciplinary Committee of the First Department of the Appellate Division was a prominent criminal defense attorney who practiced alone. Such a change symbolized the demise of the historic control by the large-firm elite over lawyer discipline in New York.

In addition, the ABCNYs efforts to shape the direction of professional regulation during the 1970s met limited success. The sweeping reforms of the character and fitness requirements and of the rules concerning lawyer advertising proposed by the ABCNY failed to sway the state courts, which adopted the much more conservative proposals of local bar and court groups. Decisions about these matters were made in the local or state courts, which were much more closely allied to local bar interests and ethnic politics than to the Wall Street elite. At this local level, as we shall see in the next chapter, the large-firm elite was handicapped by its lack of natural allies and connections. Contrary to what elite theorists would suggest, then, the ABCNY demonstrated limited ability to determine the rules governing admission to the bar and the conduct of legal practice.

It was not just a matter of the inability of the elite of the legal profession to impose its definition of the appropriate moral order on the bar as a whole, but also the rejection by the nonelite of that elite definition and the nonelite's defense of traditional conceptions of professionalism. Although Suzanne Keller emphasizes the role of elites as "guardians of the collective life,"[71] the symbols of distinctive collective identity and status may well be more important to those at the margins of particular collectivities than to the elites at the center. The status position of marginal members of collectivities may depend more heavily than that of elite members on their identification with distinctive collective symbols. Thus, local lawyers wanted to retain the character and fitness examination for prospective members of the bar as a symbol of the strict requirements for entry, thereby contributing to special standing of lawyers in the occupational status structure. Clearly, rank and file members, not just elites, place considerable importance on the defense of the traditions and symbols associated with the distinctive identities of their collectivities.

---

71. Keller, *Beyond the Ruling Class*, p. 139.

THE SYMBOLIC POLITICS
OF PROFESSIONAL REGULATION

The ABCNY's ability to promote radical reforms in professional regulation was facilitated by its relatively homogeneous membership, and by the fact that most of the new directions it proposed did not threaten the status or material well-being of its elite large-firm membership in the way they did the interests of solo and small-firm practitioners. Lawyer advertising did not pose a threat to large-firm lawyers with corporate clients, and the prospect of committing a week each year to pro bono activity was much less burdensome to the high-income corporate practitioners of the ABCNY than to marginal practitioners in the personal-plight realm of practice. On these issues the large-firm elite could afford to be more public-spirited than the local and ethnic bars.

Significantly, the ABCNY was much less liberally inclined when it came to proposals for the reform of regulations governing areas of practice in which large-firm, corporate lawyers were frequently involved. In the 1970s, for instance, the Securities and Exchange Commission (SEC) became increasingly aggressive in disciplining lawyers and accountants who practiced before it. Not only did it bring charges against several prominent New York securities lawyers who were partners in established firms, but also pressed for a larger role for lawyers in securities law enforcement. Contending that the investing public as well as the client depend upon a lawyer's representations in the securities field, the SEC called upon the securities bar to recognize its public responsibilities and adopt more of the role of an auditor in presenting a client's legal status. Furthermore, the SEC went so far as to suggest that securities lawyers had an affirmative obligation to report to the SEC a client's violations of the securities laws.[72]

In response to pressure for an expanded conception of the securities lawyer's responsibilities, the ABCNY appointed a special committee to consider the appropriate role of lawyers in securities transactions and their responsibilities to the investing public and the SEC. In its report of April 1977 this committee presented guidelines for lawyers in two central areas of securities practice—the rendering of written legal opinions, and the preparation of registration statements for initial public offerings of stock. Although constituting the "first effort by the Bar to provide guidelines for the lawyer's representation of an issuer in a registered sale of securities," the report fell far short of endorsing the

---

72. See Powell, "Developments in the Regulation of Lawyers," pp. 295–296; "Report of the Special Committee on Lawyers' Role in Securities Transactions," *Record of the Association of the Bar of the City of New York* 32 (1977): 345.

SEC's expanded view of a securities lawyer's responsibilities.[73] Indeed, it explicitly rejected the suggestion that the securities lawyer has an affirmative obligation to report violations of the law or fraudulent activity to a third party, adopting rather the traditional position that a lawyer *may* reveal evidence concerning the possible commission of future crimes by a client should others be endangered.[74] Of course, lawyers may not knowingly assist clients in fraudulent actions, but the special committee did not place any particular onus upon the lawyer to verify the factual material upon which a legal opinion may depend. In other words, the report of the special committee did not advocate any radical changes in securities lawyers' ethical obligations.

Similarly, the main weight of the ABCNY Executive Committee's summary statement on the final draft of the Model Rules of Professional Conduct proposed by the ABA's Commission on Evaluation of Professional Standards was to restrict the more expansive views of lawyers' responsibilities and obligations contained therein. The statement called for many provisions of the model rules to be "limited," "further limited," or "eliminated." For instance, whereas the draft of the model rules would prohibit assisting a client in fraudulent or criminal conduct if the lawyer "knows or reasonably should know that the conduct is fraudulent or criminal," the ABCNY wanted the prohibition restricted to when the lawyer actually knows and therefore called for the removal of the words "reasonably should know." Moreover, the ABCNY wanted further limited the already restricted provisions permitting the disclosure of client confidences to prevent serious bodily or monetary harm to others.[75] In an earlier set of submissions on the Discussion Draft of the Proposed Model Rules, the ABCNY's Committee on Corporate Legal Departments strongly opposed a controversial provision whereby there would be an affirmative obligation on lawyers within corporations to take steps to disclose wrongdoing if members of the corporation persist in violating the law in such a way as to cause it or others harm.[76] The ABCNY was not enthusiastic about proposed revisions of the ethical code that would have impinged directly upon the practices and liabilities of corporate lawyers.

---

73. Ibid., p. 347.

74. Ibid., pp. 361–362.

75. "The Substance of the Proposed Model Rules of Professional Conduct: An Executive Committee Statement," *The Record of the Association of the Bar of the City of New York* 37 (1982): 417–435.

76. Report by the Committee on Corporate Law Departments, in Committee Reports Commenting on the January 30, 1980, Discussion Draft of Model Rules of Professional Conduct, Association of the Bar of the City of New York, pp. 67–73.

One can only conclude from the ABCNY's lack of enthusiasm for more stringent controls over the practices of its large-firm members that there was a significant symbolic component to its substantial engagement in professional regulation. This is not to suggest that the ABCNY's efforts were not sincere or consequential but rather to point to the symbolic functions served by its activity in this area. In general, the politics of professional regulation and social control can be seen as an exercise in symbolic politics and status competition both within and without the profession.[77] In other words, the symbolic value of professional regulation may be much more important to the bar, and to the ABCNY, than its instrumental implementation and actual outcomes.

Professional regulation can serve three distinct but interrelated symbolic functions, two of which are directed toward external publics and one largely intraprofessional in its focus, quite apart from whatever instrumental purposes it serves. The first, and arguably the most important, is to legitimate the autonomy and special privileges of the legal profession in the political economy. As students of the organized bar's disciplinary machinery have frequently observed, the appearance of discipline has been more important than the reality.[78] Certainly, Carlin found the ABCNY's disciplinary actions in the 1950s, despite the cost to the Association and the hard work of voluntary members of its grievance committee, to be too few and far between to have had any significant deterrent effect on lawyers' conduct.[79] Furthermore, the behaviors for which lawyers are typically disciplined tend to be common criminal offenses, such as the embezzlement of clients' funds, not special requirements incumbent on professionals.[80] Yet the discipline system, despite its limited reach, serves to demonstrate to outsiders that the profession engages in self-regulation, even from time to time ex-

---

77. For a seminal discussion of symbolic issues in politics and of status politics, see Joseph R. Gusfield, *Symbolic Crusade: Status Politics and the American Temperance Movement* (Urbana, Illinois: University of Illinois Press, 1970).

78. For example, Marks and Cathcart observed that "when we consider the disciplinary process as a whole we are looking at the ways that the legal profession gives appearance of self-regulation without in fact engaging in the act of self-regulation." F. Raymond Marks and Darlene Cathcart, "Discipline Within the Legal Profession: Is It Self-Regulation?" *University of Illinois Law Forum* (1974): 193. For a similar evaluation, see Richard Abel, "Why Does the ABA Promulgate Ethical Rules?" *Texas Law Review* 59 (1981): 639–688.

79. Carlin, *Lawyers' Ethics*, pp. 160–162.

80. See S. Arthurs, "Discipline in the Legal Profession in Ontario," *Osgoode Hall Law Journal* 7 (1970): 235–270; Eric H. Steele and Raymond T. Nimmer, "Lawyers, Clients, and Professional Regulation," *American Bar Foundation Research Journal* (1976): 917–1019.

pelling one of its own, thereby discouraging interest in implementing external controls. The profession is left to regulate itself. To use Murray Edelman's term, the bar's self-regulatory edifice provides "symbolic reassurance" to its supposed beneficiaries even though its actual performance falls far short of providing the protections to the public that it claims.[81]

The second symbolic function of professional regulation relates to the status of the legal profession in the wider occupational structure and involves competition among occupations for "an honored place in society."[82] We can view the occupational prestige structure as reflecting the outcomes of incessant competition among occupational groups for deference and recognition. From this viewpoint, professions are those occupations that have been successful in this competition and have achieved a certain exalted standing. Codes of ethics and high entry requirements are important symbols of this high status and are accorded considerable significance in movements of occupational upward mobility or professionalization processes.[83] Debates within the profession over ethical codes, character requirements for admission, and the pro bono obligations of lawyers have symbolic significance in demonstrating the profession's concern about moral standards even though the reality may be otherwise. Thus, although few candidates for admission to the bar are denied entry on moral or character grounds, the character and fitness committees serve an important symbolic function in distinguishing the practice of law from other more mundane occupations.

Status competition within the highly differentiated legal profession itself is the third symbolic function served by engagement in the politics of professional regulation. In general, social stratification systems are based not only on the differential allocations of material rewards to individuals and groups but also on the varying amounts of deference or prestige accorded them. Just as sociologists can demonstrate relatively stable prestige rankings of occupations, so have researchers documented the existence of clear intraprofessional prestige orders.[84] Some areas and types of practice are held in higher esteem by their

---

81. Murray Edelman, *The Symbolic Uses of Politics* (Urbana, Illinois: University of Illinois Press, 1964), p. 22.

82. Gusfield, *Symbolic Crusade*, p. 185.

83. Harold L. Wilensky, "The Professionalization of Everyone?" *American Journal of Sociology* 70 (1964):137–158.

84. See Edward O. Laumann and John P. Heinz, "Specialization and Prestige in the Legal Profession: The Structure of Deference," *American Bar Foundation Research Journal* (1977): 155–216.

colleagues than are others. Prestige conferral, however, is not a disembodied process of according respect but always contains moral valuations of the individuals or groups in question and of their roles and activities. In a suggestive essay on the bases of intraprofessional prestige, Andrew Abbott points to the relative purity or impurity of the tasks undertaken by various professional specialties as a central dimension in determining the amount of deference accorded them.[85] As Everett Hughes perceptively observed: "The division of labor among lawyers is as much one of respectability (hence of self-concept and role) as of specialized knowledge and skills. One might even call it a moral division of labor."[86] Subgroups within the bar compete for respect and status.

The moral order of the profession, as is manifested in its rules and codes, does not simply emerge consensually but reflects the interests and values of dominant segments of the profession. There are frequent competition and debate over the content of these rules as in the longstanding struggle between the plaintiff and defense segments of the bar over the propriety of contingency fees in tort actions.[87] Whereas plaintiffs' attorneys characterize the contingency fee system as enabling indigent plaintiffs to seek legal recourse, thereby giving them access to the justice system, the defense bar has historically opposed it as encouraging lawyers to stir up litigation. It is not just a matter of which position will be institutionalized in the moral code of the profession; the association of the contingency fee system with the solicitation of clients and other unethical practices results in the symbolic degradation of the segment of the bar that utilizes it. Consequently, although the contingency fee system has survived despite persistent attacks from the elite defense bar, the personal injury plaintiffs' attorneys, for whom it is the dominant method of payment, occupy a lowly place in the intraprofessional prestige order. Their work has been identified with practices frowned upon by the dominant segments of the profession and therefore derogated.

Control over lawyer discipline in New York was more important for the symbolic status it bestowed upon the ABCNY than for the actual powers it conferred over the bar. Not only did it make the ABCNY an

---

85. Andrew Abbott, "Status and Status Strain in the Professions," *American Journal of Sociology* 86 (1981): 819–835.

86. Everett C. Hughes, *Men and Their Work* (New York: Free Press, 1958), p.71.

87. See Auerbach, *Unequal Justice*, pp. 46–50. The ABCNY attempted from time to time to have the Appellate Division of the New York Supreme Court impose an arbitrary limit on the proportion of damage awards that plaintiffs' attorneys could claim as contingent fees.

organization to be reckoned with, but it also carried the distinct connotation that the ABCNY was the defender of the moral order of the profession. For the most part, the exercise of the ABCNY's disciplinary powers resulted in members investigating and disciplining nonmembers, with the clear implication that virtue rested in the ABCNY and vice beyond its walls. The status competition involved in control over lawyer discipline can be seen in the desire of the First Department of the Appellate Division of the New York Supreme Court to wrest effective control away from the ABCNY. It was not only a matter of representativeness or power but a symbolic issue of where professional virtue would be seen to lie.

The commitment by the ABCNY of considerable organizational resources to professional regulation both historically and in the contemporary period underlines the importance of the whole area to the elite of the bar. Yet the large-firm elite was not alone in according such significance to the rules and rituals of the profession; as we have seen, nonelite segments of the bar also placed importance upon them and successfully defended their own definitions of the moral order of the professional community. In the next chapter we shall further see how nonelite local bar groups responded to ABCNY reform initiatives in legal and public policy arenas.

Chapter Six

Legal Change and Professional Influence: Assets and Liabilities of Elite Organization

Whereas the ABCNY remained an elite and unrepresentative legal association at the end of the 1950s, other metropolitan bar associations, such as the CBA, had adopted an inclusive mass-membership model of organization in the interwar years because of the putative advantages of size and representativeness. Leaders of the integrated bar movement argued vigorously that there were advantages to inclusivity, including greater financial resources and increased legitimacy as representative associations.[1] Furthermore, inclusive associations should be better able to influence external authorities such as legislatures on matters of particular concern to the bar. From this perspective, remaining a minority exclusive organization had costs in terms of resources, legitimacy, and influence capabilities.

Yet, in contrast to this widespread embracement of inclusion and representativeness, the critics of the all-inclusive associations of the organized bar frequently attacked them for their inability to provide decisive and public-spirited leadership. In particular, the supporters of civil rights and legal aid in the late 1960s and early 1970s pointed to the foot-dragging and apparent self-interest of these mass-based associations. Not infrequently, the ABCNY was presented by these critics as a paragon of a progressive, public-spirited, and effective bar association. Indeed, as I noted earlier, the ABCNY served as a model for the young reformers in the Chicago bar who despaired of achieving needed reforms through the CBA and formed the Chicago Council of Lawyers as a reformist alternative.[2] To these reformers, the necessity

---

1. For an outline of the arguments behind the integrated bar movement, see Theodore J. Schneyer, "The Incoherence of the Unified Bar Concept: Generalizing from the Wisconsin Case, "*American Bar Foundation Research Journal* (Winter 1983).

2. Michael J. Powell, "Anatomy of a Counter-Bar Association: The Chicago Council of Lawyers, "*American Bar Foundation Research Journal* (Summer 1979): 501–539.

of satisfying multiple interests and internal constituencies prevented inclusive associations from taking bold initiatives and strong stands on important and controversial policy issues. The CBA, for instance, dragged its feet on civil rights legislation in the early 1960s because of internal discord, giving only minimal support to the 1964 civil rights bill. Whereas the CBA "performed the minimum possible role to maintain a semblance of public credibility," the ABCNY was a strong supporter of civil rights legislation from the outset, and played a critical role in defending the constitutionality of the 1964 Civil Rights Act.[3]

We are presented, then, with two models of a successful bar association: one that advocates inclusiveness and representativeness as the means to collective professional influence, and the other that holds to an elite model of organizing as providing the necessary basis for professional power. It may well be that the influence resources available to each type of association will be differentially effective according to the nature of the issue, the characteristics of the decision makers, and the peculiarities of the decision-making forum. The prestige and connections of an elite association may have more utility on some issues, and in some arenas, whereas the representativeness of an inclusive body may be more advantageous in others. In this chapter, I look at some major attempts by the ABCNY to shape the legal system and the direction of legal change in the post–World War II decades in order to determine the conditions under which the elite, nonrepresentative association is able to convert its resources into influence. What are the advantages and disadvantages, the assets and liabilities of elite status and homogeneous membership as demonstrated by the ABCNY's interventions in public policy-making? Has this elite association enjoyed the success that elite theorists and reformers might lead one to expect?

One would not expect bar associations, or professional associations in general, to exercise equal influence in all policy domains or in all areas of social change. Rather, we would expect organizations of professionals to have greater influence on issues in those areas in which their members have specialized and recognized expertise, areas that comprise what Halliday has termed their primary sphere of influence.[4] In broader matters of public policy, however, their secondary sphere of influence, professional associations lack a monopoly of expertise and have to compete with other interests having equal or greater claims to authority. Thus medical associations would be ex-

---

3. Terence C. Halliday, "The Idiom of Legalism in Bar Politics: Lawyers, McCarthyism, and the Civil Rights Era, "*American Bar Foundation Research Journal* (Fall 1982): 964–973.

4. Terence C. Halliday, *Beyond Monopoly: Lawyers, State Crises, and Professional Empowerment* (Chicago: University of Chicago Press, 1987), pp. 41–51.

pected to be more influential on narrow matters of medical policy than on general public policy matters such as environmental issues and nuclear war, and bar associations to be accorded greater authority on policies relating directly to the legal system than on all matters coming before a legislature. Even matters clearly within the primary spheres of influence of professional associations, however, generally involve political ideologies and interests as well as questions of the allocation of scarce resources. Thus the collective expertise of the professional association may not carry the day even on issues demonstrably within its realm. In this chapter, the relative effectiveness of the involvement of the ABCNY in policy matters in both its primary and secondary spheres of influence is examined.

First, we shall look at effective policy interventions or initiatives of the ABCNY, all of which occurred in its secondary sphere of influence and at the national level, before considering interventions and initiatives at the state level, which were markedly less successful. Finally, we shall address two additional policy initiatives at the state level in which the ABCNY was eventually successful and examine the conditions facilitating its successful intervention.

THE ASSETS OF ELITE STATUS AND THE SUCCESSFUL EXERCISE OF INFLUENCE

There were certain organizational advantages associated with maintaining an elite identity. The ABCNY's accumulated prestige meant that it remained attractive to potential members. Although the Committee on Membership created to replace the old Committee on Admissions was mandated to encourage new membership applications, it did not engage in the vigorous campaigns to increase membership frequently pursued by other associations. It did not need to offer special incentives, such as reduced dues, to attract new members. The membership of the ABCNY continued to rise throughout the 1970s without any promotional gimmicks, eventually outstripping the inclusive NYCLA. In addition to the selective benefits available to the membership, such as access to the excellent library of the ABCNY and professional liability group insurance, new members shared in the high status of the organization to which they now belonged. Organizational prestige could continue to serve as an inducement to membership so long as the ABCNY was perceived as an elite organization even if it no longer took the form of an exclusive upper-class club within the bar.

Furthermore, the maintenance of an elite organizational structure with small, select committees also retained the participation of leading members of the bar. As membership on the committees remained selective rather than open, prominent lawyers were willing to serve because their expertise was recognized and rewarded. Demand for committee positions remained high, far exceeding their availability, and appointment to a committee continued to confer status. While the inability to gain a committee appointment was undoubtedly frustrating for some members, scarcity in the supply of positions kept their value high.

Ease of decision making is an advantage conferred by relative membership homogeneity. Large, representative associations that include all the diverse interests of the profession may well experience considerable difficulty in reaching agreement on controversial issues. Even then, the positions adopted are likely to reflect the conflicting interests within the association and represent the lowest common denominator.[5] In the period prior to the 1960s, the ABCNY enjoyed considerable homogeneity and internal consensus and was thus able to make decisions quickly without having to adopt compromise positions. Despite the increased dissensus introduced into the ABCNY in the 1970s by the new elements in its membership, particularly the younger members, the ABCNY was still able to take strong reformist stances on several matters affecting professional regulation and the delivery of legal services, even if only after considerable internal debate. Bar associations fully representative of the legal profession, such as the CBA, could not adopt such policy positions because the interests of local segments of the bar heavily represented in their membership were directly and negatively affected.

Crucial to the exercise of influence over policy issues are the resources an organization can mobilize and utilize in its influence attempts. Not all organizations have the same or equal resources at their disposal and, consequently, will not be capable of exercising the same amount of influence over the making of policy. What are the resources an elite association such as the ABCNY can mobilize in an attempt to influence the direction of legal change? There are at least four generalized resources available to most professional associations in varying amounts. As an association of the large-firm elite, the ABCNY is particularly well-endowed with these resources, although, as we shall see, they may have variable utility with respect to particular issues or particular decision makers.

The first of the four resources available to bar associations is that of legal expertise, both technical and substantive. It is the resource of

---

5. See John P. Heinz et al., "Diversity, Representation, and Leadership in an Urban Bar," *American Bar Foundation Research Journal* (1976): 771–775, for a development of this argument with respect to the CBA.

technical legal expertise that frequently permits the bar association to intervene in the policy-making process in the first place. Changes in public policy often mean legislative change, or changes in rules and procedures, and lawyers, as experts in the drafting of rules and laws, are involved from the outset. Indeed, on occasion legislative leaders will recognize that bar associations are repositories of expertise in drafting laws and will invite them to draw up new laws for presentation to the legislatures for enactment. The Illinois legislature, for example, delegated to the Illinois bar associations the responsibility for drafting a new criminal law code for the state. The product of the bar associations was enacted almost in its entirety.[6] Bar associations vary in the areas in which they have expert resources, with the ABCNY having ready access to expertise in business and financial law. Comprehensive, inclusive associations had members with expertise in all areas of the law, providing them with authority in areas unrepresented in the ABCNY.

Of course, it is difficult to draw the line between technical and substantive advice. Frequently, what appear to be technical concerns have important substantive implications. The wording of a statute or rule, even the positioning of punctuation, can determine what behaviors are or are not covered. Recognizing that their technical expertise provides an avenue for legitimate entry into the policy-making process, lawyers may in fact emphasize their technical contributions when in fact they are also interested in the substance of the issues involved.[7] This was certainly the case when the CBA drew up a new criminal code for Illinois. Bar associations, of course, also have resources of substantive expertise in many areas because lawyers accumulate considerable experience in different fields of practice. Tax lawyers, for instance, know a great deal not only about the technical aspects of the tax laws but also their substantive implications for their clients. So, too, are divorce lawyers likely to hold views about the efficacy of particular divorce laws and proposed reforms. Lawyers and legal associations, then, frequently become involved in debating the merits of changes in the substantive law. In its advocacy of more liberal divorce laws in the 1950s, the ABCNY certainly did not restrict itself to the technical quality of particular laws but proposed a substantial broadening of the acceptable grounds for divorce. When substantive changes are involved, the bar association will be simply one of many groups vying for influence. We may expect, then, that bar associations in general will be more successful in their exercise of influence, the more technical the legal change.

---

6. Halliday, *Beyond Monopoly*, pp. 245–253.

7. See Halliday's argument about bar associations' use of technical expertise to influence substantive law in Terence C. Halliday, "The Idiom of Legalism," *American Bar Foundation Research Journal* (1982).

The second resource available to professional associations is money. Membership dues provide resources that can be used to fund committee activities and to support special projects. The ABCNY charged relatively high dues, and with the growth of its membership in the postwar period its income increased substantially. The total income of the ABCNY exceeded $3.5 million in 1980.[8] In addition to its regular income from membership dues, the ABCNY was able to count on the voluntary contributions of its members and their law firms for special expenses. Given the character of its membership, and the revenues of the large firms to which many members belonged, the ABCNY had access to greater financial resources than most professional associations of similar size.

In the postwar period, the ABCNY has also been able to tap a new source of financial support in the form of grants from private foundations headquartered in New York City. The connections of the leaders of the ABCNY—many of whom serve on foundation boards—facilitate its access to foundation grants with which it has underwritten several major research and policy studies.[9] With money from these grants the ABCNY instituted a new model for developing policy proposals. Instead of relying upon busy volunteers from among its membership, the ABCNY provided special committees with paid professional staffs under the supervision of experts, usually law professors, to research and write reports on important policy issues. In this way the quality, and potential influence, of the report was greatly enhanced. Several of the ABCNY's major attempts at achieving legal change utilized the highly professional work of such special committees funded by foundations grants.

With their membership of highly educated and successful members of the surrounding society, professional associations generally enjoy relatively high social standing. Arthur Stinchcombe, in his classic essay on the history of organizational forms, suggests that organizations vary along a prestige order in much the same way as individuals.[10] Talcott Parsons, in his treatment of influence as a medium of exchange, further suggests that an organization's position in a prestige hierarchy will

---

8. Annual Report of the Treasurer, *Yearbook,* 1981–1982, The Association of the Bar of the City of New York.

9. For a list of all the major projects the ABCNY has mounted with the assistance of foundation grants in the postwar period, see George Martin, *Causes and Conflicts: The Centennial History of the Association of the Bar of the City of New York* (Boston: Houghton Mifflin, 1970), Table 2, pp. 393–394.

10. Arthur L. Stinchcombe, "Social Structure and Organizations," in *Handbook of Organizations,* ed. James G. March (Chicago: Rand McNally, 1965).

largely determine its influence capability. Similarly, William J. Goode views prestige as "a means to the goals of individuals, groups and corporate agencies.[11] It follows that the more prestige an organization has, the more successful it will be in exercising influence. It may well be, however, that high prestige is more influential with some decision makers and in certain decision arenas than in others.

Organizations may come by their prestige standing in different ways, but voluntary associations derive it largely from the social standing of their members. An elite association, then, like the ABCNY, the leadership of which has included from time to time five secretaries of state and several United States cabinet members, will have considerable prestige resources, whereas mass-based associations may have less because of their all-encompassing membership. In addition, the history and reputation of the ABCNY as an exclusive patrician association contributed to its ongoing high status.

Goode notes that organizations or individuals with considerable prestige are more likely to gain admission to desirable circles and thereby establish the contacts that enable them to have access to important decision makers.[12] Gaining access is the necessary first step in any attempt to exercise influence, and an organization having members with connections in important places will have an advantage over those that do not. The generalized prestige of the ABCNY was such, for instance, that it could at least gain a hearing with the majority leaders of the state legislature even though those leaders might refuse to defer to the ABCNY or to its constituency. Prestige, then, was an important resource for the ABCNY, which contributed to its influence capacity.

Connectedness is another influence resource that organizations have in varying degrees. As we have seen, connectedness may mean the opportunity to present a viewpoint to key decision makers, but it may also mean access to insider or timely information that may be very useful in the attempt to exercise influence. Law-school ties have been an important integrative mechanism within the legal profession, especially for graduates from Ivy League schools. These ties enable lawyers to keep in touch with classmates as they move vertically and laterally within the profession, government, and private industry. At the very least they provide avenues for access. Given the rapidity with which lawyers move in and out of government, law-school and law-firm ties

---

11. Talcott Parsons," On the Concept of Influence, "in *Sociological Theory and Modern Society* (New York: Free Press, 1967); William J. Goode, *The Celebration of Heroes: Prestige as a Social Control System* (Berkeley: University of California Press, 1980), p. 6.

12. Goode, *The Celebration of Heroes*, p. 6.

help bridge the chasm between the public and private domains. The fact that the legal counsel to the governor of New York has nearly always come from a large firm in New York, for instance, has given the ABCNY ready access to the governor's office. And the fact that commissioners of the Securities and Exchange Commission have frequently been recruited from the New York securities bar, and have frequently served on one of its corporate committees, has greatly enhanced the ability of the ABCNY Committee on Securities Regulation to work effectively with that agency. These connections facilitate the passage of information back and forth between the private bar and government agencies and provide access to valued indications as to future directions of government policy. Furthermore, the leaders of the ABCNY, as partners in prominent Wall Street firms, are well connected to financial and business elites through their legal roles as advocates of large corporations and financial entities.

The ABCNY, then, possesses considerable resources of expertise, money, prestige, and connectedness that can be mobilized in its attempts to exercise influence over policy-making processes. In the remainder of this section, I shall examine three successful attempts by the ABCNY to initiate legal changes, or to influence the outcome of ongoing policy debates, and thereby demonstrate the utility of these resources. It was not always successful, however. Later in this chapter, I shall examine influence attempts that largely failed, or at least failed to achieve the end desired by the ABCNY. The resources of the ABCNY were of variable utility according to the subject matter of the issue (the extent to which it was esoteric and technical), the number and strength of interests mobilized on the issue, and the "site" or arena in which the decision was made.

The Bricker Amendment

In the 1950s the ABCNY mobilized the Northeastern establishment in opposition to the attempt of Senator John W. Bricker of Ohio to restrict the treaty-making authority of the executive branch and to limit the effect of any treaty or international agreement on domestic law.[13] The actual constitutional amendment introduced by Senator Bricker would have made all treaties and executive agreements entered into by the president subject to the regulation of Congress, made of no effect

---

13. For extensive discussions of the politics surrounding the Bricker amendment, see Stephen A. Garrett, "Foreign Policy and the American Constitution," *International Studies Quarterly* 16 (1972): 187–220; Loch K. Johnson, *The Making of International Agreements: Congress Confronts the Executive* (New York: New York University Press, 1984).

within the United States any treaty provisions that conflicted with the Constitution, and limited the ability of Congress or the executive branch to use treaty provisions as internal law. The Bricker amendment was only one of several proposals that varied in details but all of which sought similar ends which were introduced in the Senate in the early 1950s. These legislative proposals enjoyed considerable support among Republicans and conservative Democrats and together constituted a serious threat to the president's discretion in foreign policy-making. The debate over the Bricker amendment represented a major struggle over the control of foreign policy-making between the executive and legislative branches of government.

Behind the Bricker amendment lay widespread fears that the provisions of various international treaties and agreements entered into by the president might usurp domestic law because of Article VI of the Constitution—the so-called supremacy clause—which recognized treaties as "the supreme Law of the Land," binding judges in every state of the nation.[14] Southerners were particularly concerned that the Human Rights Declaration of the United Nations might be used by the federal government or the courts to subvert traditional states' rights in this area and overturn segregation. There was also, however, opposition to the executive branch's committing the United States to policies through executive agreements that were not submitted to Congress for approval. President Roosevelt's controversial agreement with Stalin at Yalta was the classic example that incensed the right wings of both parties.[15] In general, supporters of the Bricker amendment were isolationist in sentiment, and opposed too strong an executive, and, in particular, viewed the United Nations and such experiments in "world government" as anathema.

Powerful groups supporting the Bricker amendment and its corollaries included the American Medical Association, the Daughters of the American Revolution, the American Legion, the Veterans of Foreign Wars, the Chamber of Commerce, and the American Bar Association's Committee on Peace and Law.[16] The support of the ABA committee was particularly important because the debate over the Bricker amendment developed into a lawyer's squabble as it involved complicated questions of the division of powers and the relationship among treaty provisions and federal and state law. Led by a former ABA president, Frank E. Holman of Oregon, who was passionately committed to the

---

14. See Garrett, "Foreign Policy and the American Constitution," p. 191.
15. Johnson, *The Making of International Agreements*, p. 109.
16. Ibid.

proposal,[17] the ABA committee's endorsement provided the amendment with an aura of legal legitimacy, suggesting it did not pose any constitutional or legal problems.

Two committees of the ABCNY studied and opposed the Bricker amendment as posing an unwarranted limitation on the president's ability to conduct foreign policy.[18] Their joint report was approved by the members in May 1952 and was widely distributed. The chairmen testified several times against the amendment in Washington, and the president of the Association explained its opposition in a speech before the American Newspaper Publishers Association. The legal arguments developed and presented by the ABCNY were used by major figures in the Eisenhower administration in their opposition, so much so that Holman of the ABA accused the administration of taking its cues from the internationalists at the ABCNY. Holman asserted:

> The president not being a lawyer, his views merely reflected the views of the Secretary of State and the Attorney General, which, in turn, were based on the out-of-date Report of the City Bar of New York supported by eastern seaboard internationalists like Professor Corwin of Princeton.[19]

There was some truth in Holman's accusation. Both the secretary of state, John Foster Dulles, and the attorney general, Herbert Brownell, who led the fight for the administration, were prominent New York lawyers and members of the ABCNY. Indeed, Brownell was to become president of the ABCNY a decade or so later.

The ABCNY's opposition to this proposed constitutional amendment flowed naturally from the internationalist sentiment of the corporate lawyers in the large New York firms. After all, the first substantive committee formed by the ABCNY was the Committee on International Law, established in 1920. Many New York lawyers engaged in the practice of international law and, indeed, some had participated in the drafting of the international agreements under attack by Bricker and his allies. John Foster Dulles, Eisenhower's secretary of state and a strong opponent of the Bricker amendment, was a senior partner in the Wall Street firm Sullivan & Cromwell and had personally drafted the Japanese Peace Treaty.[20] Furthermore, the sympathy of the

17. Holman later wrote a book on the dispute in which he bitterly attacked the opposition of the "internationalist" ABCNY; Frank E. Holman, *Story of the Bricker Amendment* (New York: Committee for Constitutional Government, 1954).

18. These were the Committees on Federal Legislation and International Law. For a brief outline of their report, see Martin, *Causes and Conflicts*, p. 288.

19. Holman, *Story of the Bricker Amendment*, p. 23.

20. On Dulles, see Stephen E. Ambrose, *Eisenhower: The President* (New York: Simon and Schuster, 1984), pp. 20–22.

ABCNY leadership lay much more naturally with the executive branch than with the legislative, as it was in the executive branch that many ABCNY leaders had served.

In addition to publishing its own report, which strongly opposed the amendment, the ABCNY used its connections to form a committee of important legal and nonlegal figures to oppose it. Named the "Committee for Defense of the Constitution," it was headed by Professor Edward Corwin of Princeton, an expert on the Constitution, General Lucius Clay, a close friend of President Eisenhower, and John W. Davis, perhaps the best-known practicing lawyer at that time. This committee undertook to raise funds and bolster opposition to the amendment.[21] Formation of the committee widened the base of opposition to Bricker's proposal and permitted the outright lobbying that would have threatened the ABCNY's tax-exempt status.

Although Bricker had first introduced the amendment in 1952 with the cosponsorship of fifty-eight other senators, it did not finally come to a vote until February of 1954, when it was handily defeated. By that time support had ebbed away from Bricker's radical proposal to a more restrained amendment in the same direction sponsored by the patriarch of the Senate, Walter George. Senator George, with his considerable power in the Senate, had substantially more support, and his amendment failed by only one vote to get the two-thirds majority needed to pass a constitutional amendment. It was a close call for the administration, and that encouraged supporters of the amendment to reintroduce it, but they were never able to muster enough support to bring it to a vote again.[22]

Although President Eisenhower had hesitated to come out strongly against the Bricker amendment for fear of splitting the Republican party, his eventual recognition of the threat it posed to presidential authority in foreign policy-making led him to marshal his forces against it. One could scarcely argue that the ABCNY's role was determinative of the outcome, yet its opposition was significant. As we have seen, its arguments were widely used by the administration, and its successful mobilization of the Northeastern establishment provided the opponents of the amendment with much-needed support. Furthermore, its expert testimony as to the constitutional and legal implications of the proposed amendment was critical to counter the legitimacy endowed upon the amendment by the ABA's support. As the ABCNY president

---

21. For a brief discussion of this committee's activities, see Martin, *Causes and Conflicts,* p. 290.

22. The struggle in Congress over the amendment is related in Garrett, "Foreign Policy and the American Constitution," pp. 196–199.

in 1953–1954 observed, the Association provided the "intellectual sinews" of the campaign.[23]

The ABCNY's opposition to the Bricker amendment illustrates its ability to convert its resources of expertise, prestige, and connections into influence over the development of public policy on the national level. It had access to experts in constitutional law and was able to capitalize on its connections among the business and cultural elites of the Northeast. This was an issue ideally suited to the ABCNY. It was of a sufficiently esoteric legal nature to provide lawyers with a legitimate entree and, indeed, to give them an authoritative voice. Furthermore, it was a national issue, and it was at the national level that the ABCNY and the large-firm elite had their greatest influence.

The Carswell Nomination

A similar example of the ABCNY's ability to convert its resources of prestige and national connections into influence in the United States Congress occurred twenty years later. Following the Senate's rejection of his first nominee, Clement F. Haynesworth, Jr., for a vacant seat on the United States Supreme Court in 1969, President Nixon nominated G. Harrold Carswell, a judge on the United States Court of Appeals in Florida, for the position. Despite testimony to the effect that Judge Carswell had been an incorporator and member of a private club in Tallahassee that excluded blacks, and notwithstanding his distinctly mediocre record as a federal judge, the Committee on the Federal Judiciary of the ABA found him "qualified" for this high position. Subsequently, the Judiciary Committee of the Senate overwhelmingly approved his nomination, and there appeared to be little opposition on the floor of the Senate. Carswell's confirmation appeared likely to be assured until several leaders of the New York bar began a campaign in February of 1970 to oppose the nomination. Leading the opposition was Francis T. P. Plimpton, the activist president of the ABCNY at the time. These opponents of the Carswell nomination circulated a statement of opposition to leading lawyers and legal scholars nationwide, gaining over five hundred signatures in the process, and then sent copies to each member of the Senate.[24] This display of concern over the Carswell nomination by so many prominent lawyers caused some serious questions to be raised in the Senate and, suddenly, the administration found its candidate in trouble.

---

23. Martin, *Causes and Conflicts,* p. 291.

24. For an outline of the events surrounding the Carswell nomination, and Plimpton and the ABCNY's involvement, see Geoffrey Hellman, "Periodpiece Fellow," *New Yorker,* December 4, 1971.

Traditionally the ABCNY had not evaluated or commented on nominations for the U.S. Supreme Court, leaving that to the Federal Judiciary Committee of the ABA. It had not, then, involved itself in the dispute over the Haynesworth nomination, but now found itself entangled in the growing furor over Judge Carswell as a result of the leadership role played by its president in the opposition to this second Nixon nominee. Plimpton participated, along with former president Samuel Rosenman, in a news conference in Washington attacking Carswell's credentials and then, when the nomination came up on the floor of the Senate for debate, sent telegrams to all the senators calling on them to vote against confirmation. While the Senate debate continued, the Executive Committee of the ABCNY broke new ground by finally agreeing to take a position on Carswell's credentials and joined the growing chorus of opposition to his confirmation.

Early in April 1970, the Senate voted against confirmation of Judge Carswell, an outcome that had not been expected two months previously, and which was attributable in large part to the opposition movement orchestrated by the leaders of the ABCNY. Even though the ABCNY formally did not enter the fray until late in the piece, its presence was highly visible from the beginning. That the leadership of such a distinguished and established bar group should oppose so strongly the confirmation of Judge Carswell countered the earlier finding of "qualified" by the ABA and raised serious doubts as to his qualifications for a seat on the highest court of the land. Once again the ABCNY leadership demonstrated its ability to mobilize the Northeastern legal elite on matters of national significance and was able to utilize successfully its assets of prestige and connectedness.

Conflict-of-Interest Statutes

Like the Bricker amendment, the interest of the ABCNY in the laws governing the conflicts of interest encountered by government employees while in government or once they move out rose naturally from the professional careers of the large-firm members of the ABCNY. As we have noted, lawyers from the large New York firms frequently moved in and out of government positions in Washington and so had a natural personal interest in the laws that governed the potential conflicts of interest that followed that movement. Many served in Washington out of a sense of public duty and responsibility, accepting much lower incomes for significant periods of time. For others, government service was an important credential, adding to their professional standing and facilitating their representation of clients with the federal government through contacts made and knowledge accumulated. Many lawyers, however, found the existing laws governing potential conflicts of interest of government officials too restrictive, making movement in and out of government difficult and costly. Laws that were too restrictive discouraged successful people in the private sector from contributing their abilities to the public good. Holding that restrictive conflict-of-interest statutes were contrary to the public interest, leaders of the ABCNY sought their revision.

Unlike the Bricker amendment, when the ABCNY had reacted to a legislative initiative taken by someone else, the ABCNY itself initiated the review of the conflict-of-interest statutes. In 1956 the ABCNY established a special committee to undertake research in the area and to make recommendations. Funded generously by a private foundation, the Special Committee on Federal Conflicts of Interest had its own staff and a Yale Law School professor as director. After four years' work, the Special Committee reported, recommending the consolidation of all the scattered statutes relating to conflicts of interest into one statute and presenting a model act for introduction into Congress. Published by the Harvard University Press as *Conflict of Interest and Federal Service* (1960), the Special Committee's report was widely covered in the press and met with general approval.[25]

The chairman of the Special Committee noted in retrospect that the basic premise of the report was "to facilitate people going in from outside."[26] The underlying concern was to maximize the federal government's ability to recruit talent and at the same time maintain public trust in government officials. Outright graft while in the government was not a major concern of the Special Committee, which clearly repudiated such abuse of fiduciary responsibility on the part of government officials and recommended strict provisions dealing with it. The committee saw several major problems, other than outright corruption, for people entering the government for limited periods of time with the expectancy of reentering private life, and it was to overcome these problems that the committee particularly wanted new legislation.

The first problem under the existing statutes, according to the committee, was the lack of a clear-cut distinction between long-term and short-term government employees.[27] These two categories of employees were subject to conflict requirements of the same severity, making it difficult for lawyers and others to enter the government for short

---

25. See Roswell B. Perkins, Jr., "The New Federal Conflict-of-Interest Law," *Harvard Law Review* 76 (1963): 1113–1169.

26. Roswell B. Perkins, Jr., personal interview with author, July 3, 1979.

27. The following discussion follows closely Perkins, "The New Federal Conflict-of-Interest Law."

periods of time. The ABCNY report called for a clear distinction between the two types of employees and for less strict requirements upon short-term employees.

The second problem was how to safeguard the financial security of individuals from the private sector who accepted decreased income to enter government service. Clearly, the continuation of partial salary support from the former, private sector employer could not be countenanced, but the Special Committee recommended that the continuation of all the supplementary payments received while in private employment—pension plans, insurance benefits, stock options, and the like—should be permitted. Uncertainty about the legality of continued contributions to such plans by private employers had been a serious stumbling block for corporate executives and lawyers invited to join the government in some time-bounded capacity.

The third problem area involved post-employment restrictions. These posed a major problem for lawyers and other professionals likely to be involved in the representation of clients before the government at some future point. The ABCNY sought to reduce the stringency of the statutes governing the representation of clients before the agencies in which lawyers had served, arguing that any broad prohibition of representation of clients on issues that had been pending while the individual was in office would seriously impede recruitment into the government. This was an area obviously of immediate relevance to lawyers who planned to enter, or return to, private practice once out of the government and represent clients before governmental agencies.

Related to this problem was the treatment accorded partners of a current or former government employee. The question was whether restrictions placed on an employee should also cover his law firm. The Special Committee wanted this area dealt with also, not wanting exclusions affecting individual employees to be automatically transferable to partners. Clearly, if restrictions on a former government employee limiting his practice with the government agency or department he had just left were generalized to the partnership as a whole, law firms would suffer considerably.

Enjoying support from a wide variety of sources, the ABCNY report proved to be very influential. When President Kennedy appointed a three-man advisory panel in 1961 to review the conflict laws and recommend possible revisions, its members included the director of the ABCNY study, and its eventual report was based largely on that of the ABCNY Special Committee The advisory panel's report, in turn, formed the basis of a special presidential message to Congress in April 1961 calling for the enactment of new conflict-of-interest legislation.

Eventually, in 1963, a new conflict-of-interest act governing employees of the federal government that conformed closely to the recommendations embodied in the ABCNY report was enacted by Congress and signed by the president.[28] The new act codified in one set of statutes the previously scattered conflict-of-interest requirements and dealt favorably with the problem areas that had been of particular concern to the ABCNY Special Committee.

Like the Bricker amendment, the conflict-of-interest issue was tailor-made for the ABCNY. It arose naturally out of the professional interests of the ABCNY leadership, some of whom had extensive experience in government service and knew firsthand the difficulties of moving back and forth between the public and private sectors. Members of the Special Committee were able to bring to bear their own experience in government service and the connections they had established in Washington. Its chairman, Roswell Perkins, Jr., had worked on Capitol Hill as a congressional aide and so had contacts among congressional staffs, and the ABCNY enjoyed good access to the Kennedy administration, which had appointed many northeasterners to important executive positions. Thus the Special Committee was able to gain the administration's endorsement of reform in this area and the adoption of virtually all its recommendations. *Business Week*, in reviewing the report of the Special Committee when it was first published, observed that "the thoroughness of the study and the prestige and political influence of the bar group assures that the recommendations will get careful consideration in Congress."[29] On a federal-level issue like this, the ABCNY was able to parlay successfully its resources of foundation support, expertise, prestige, and connections into influence.

In addition, there was no significant organized opposition to the proposed reform. Business and professional groups, whose members moved in and out of government regularly, supported the recommendations because they promised to liberalize, and make more predictable by codifying, the conflict-of-interest requirements. Consumer and public-interest groups, such as Common Cause and Ralph Nader's organization, which might have opposed the recommendations as relaxing the conflict statutes too much, were not yet formed, so there was no significant consumerist opposition. Several individual senators and congressmen feared the law was too liberal, but they lacked any substantial support within Congress because the reform did not threaten any particular organized interest.

28. For details as to the content of the new act, see Perkins, "The New Federal Conflict-of-Interest Law," pp. 1122–1162.

29. *Business Week*, 27 February 1960, p. 32.

In contrast, when the ABCNY, encouraged by the successful outcome of this reform effort, undertook a similar study of conflicts of interest within Congress itself and produced a report suggesting new statutory law to deal with this aspect of congressional ethics, it met with a marked lack of interest on the part of members of Congress.[30] Certainly, the self-interest of large-firm lawyers did not motivate the ABCNY in establishing this committee; instead, it saw itself as providing a public service by applying its resources to this important question. In preparing and presenting this report, the ABCNY was able to mobilize the same resources as with the earlier conflict-of-interest study, with the exception of experience. Like the earlier study of conflict of interest in the executive branch, the project on congressional ethics was funded by a private foundation and a special committee established to oversee the work of a paid professional staff, including again a professor of law. The prestige of the ABCNY and the connections of its leaders were assets that were used again in promoting the report of the Special Committee on Congressional Ethics, but this time they were not to prove so effective.

The members of Congress had little interest, and members of state legislatures even less, in rationalizing and strengthening the existing laws having to do with their conflicts of interest. Consequently, the ABCNY initiative in this instance came to naught. It would seem that even at the federal level, where the ABCNY's resources of expertise, prestige, and good connections were most likely to be convertible into influence, the ABCNY's success depended upon the nature of the issue and the receptiveness of the key decision makers.

THE LIABILITIES AND LIMITATIONS OF ELITE STATUS

Exclusivity and high social status not only provide resources that can facilitate the exercise of influence but also carry liabilities which can hinder successful intervention in the policy-making process. This is not always recognized by social scientists when pointing to the putative power of societal elites. Instead, the overwhelming emphasis is on the ability of elite groups to determine decision outcomes through the mobilization of their superior resources.[31] Though elite groups certainly have access to "more" resources, nonelites may have access to different resources than elites, allowing them to exercise countervailing influ-

---

30. James C. Kirby, Jr., *Congress and the Public Trust* (New York: Atheneum, 1970).

31. In general, see the work of G. William Domhoff, particularly *The Powers That Be: Processes of Ruling Class Domination in America* (New York: Vintage Books, 1978), and *Who Rules America?* (Englewood Cliffs, N.J.: Prentice-Hall, 1967).

ence. Indeed, on some issues, with some decision makers, and in some arenas, elite assets may in fact be liabilities. The ABCNY's restricted membership and identification with the large-firm elite of the New York bar have had some negative consequences for the success of its policy initiatives, particularly those at the local and state levels of decision making.

In the first place, as the ABCNY has not incorporated all segments of the bar into its membership, its claim to represent the interests of the New York bar as a whole has been frequently challenged. Viewpoints of those lawyers unrepresented are unlikely to be reflected in its policy positions, undermining the ABCNY's legitimacy especially with local and state authorities who, well aware of the elite composition of the ABCNY, may tend to discount ABCNY policy recommendations as those of a minority of the bar. The ABCNY's lack of representativeness may enable it to take decisive reform initiatives, but it may also handicap it in its attempts to implement those initiatives.

In addition, the lack of incorporation of local bar groups within the ABCNY encourages their external opposition to ABCNY proposals. In fully inclusive associations such as the CBA, conflict among various interests in the bar takes place within the organization, thereby on occasion rendering it ineffective; with exclusive organizations, that conflict takes place in public decision-making arenas. In New York, then, with the ABCNY representing one, albeit powerful, segment of the profession, conflict over legal changes affecting the interests of lawyers was more likely to be fought out in public arenas than inside the Association.

The second limitation that follows the ABCNY's identification with the corporate, large-firm elite is a lack of familiarity with local political organizations and leaders. From the beginning the upper-class ABCNY was hostile to the Irish Catholics and the local Democratic machine. Its periodic reform efforts, which clearly involved an element of status politics whereby the upper-class elite demonstrated its superiority, contributed to its distance from local political leaders; and its upper-class culture and restrictive admissions procedures kept out the ethnic lawyers who were well connected with the local political clubs and ethnic organizations. Furthermore, the upper-class leadership of the ABCNY was overwhelmingly Republican, whereas the dominant local party was Democratic. Consequently, the prewar, upper-class ABCNY lacked even minimal contact with local political organizations.

Even though the ABCNY's membership composition became more diverse in the postwar period, its lack of integration with local judicial and political leaders persisted as the predominantly large-firm membership of the ABCNY had national rather than local interests and connections. With corporate clients whose interests transcended state boundaries, large-firm lawyers were increasingly engaged in the practice of law at the national or even international level—before federal courts and agencies, and with respect to national and international markets. Leaders of the ABCNY were much more likely to have held government office in Washington than in Albany, and to have national political and governmental linkages rather than local or state connections. Lacking the contacts at the local level that facilitate the exercise of influence, the ABCNY's accumulated prestige was often insufficient to carry the day on isssues determined at the local or state levels.

In contrast, local bar groups were oriented toward the local and state courts and to local government bodies and the state legislature. Their connections were strongest with these entities and could be mobilized in opposition to initiatives of the large-firm elite of the ABCNY. Active in local political circles, many local lawyers were elected to state legislatures while continuing to practice part-time and retain their membership in local bar associations. Lawyers who practiced regularly in the local and state courts developed close ties with the judges and court personnel. Large-firm lawyers, however, who appeared rarely in the local courts and were unlikely to be active in local political clubs, generally lacked these local connections. Lack of integration into local political and judicial networks served to limit the ABCNY's ability to exercise influence at the local and state levels in both the pre- and postwar periods.

The lack of local political involvement led not only to a lack of "clout," but also to a lack of local political know-how. In addition, elite lawyers were frequently unwilling to become involved at the local level, demonstrating an unwillingness to "get their hands dirty in local politics," as one observer put it.[32] The ABCNY did not spend a great deal of energy in developing contacts at the local level or show a willingness to "work" the local political system. Unlike the CBA, which frequently sponsored dinners for state assemblymen and senators to inform them of their legislative concerns, and even on occasion has hosted dinners for local ward committeemen, the ABCNY has remained relatively aloof. There has been no regularized contact with even the state legislative representatives from Manhattan, let alone from other parts of New York, and certainly no formalized attempts to contact and influence those involved in local political organizations. The ABCNY's attitude in this area is evident in its consistent unwillingness to hire a permanent lobbyist at the state capital to represent the

---

32. Marion Ames, former president of the New York State League of Women Voters, personal interview with author, November 15, 1979.

ABCNY's interests and to develop those linkages that might facilitate the passage of desired legislation. Indeed, a lobbyist for the League of Women Voters who had been engaged in many battles for court and judicial reform indicated that she could not remember working with any representatives of the ABCNY on anything in Albany.[33]

The following section demonstrates the detrimental effect of the lack of representativeness, the lack of local connections, and the lack of local political experience on the ability of the ABCNY to implement its policy initiatives and influence the direction of legal change at the local and state levels during the postwar period. From a different perspective, the examples discussed in this section show the ability of local bar groups to limit the influence of the large-firm elite in order to protect their interests. It should become plain that local bar groups, the non-elite of the New York bar, are not without their own resources with which to influence decision makers.

We shall first examine the efforts of the ABCNY in what was perhaps its major concern during the entire postwar period—court reform. The three major elements of court reform upon which the ABCNY expended considerable resources during this period were court reorganization, civil procedure, and judicial selection. Recognizing that to take on all aspects of the court system at one time would arouse too much opposition, the ABCNY applied itself first to court reorganization and revision of the rules of procedure in the early 1960s, and then to the methods of judicial selection in the latter part of the decade. In undertaking to reform the court system, the ABCNY was seeking to change local and state institutions. The courts and rules of procedure that it sought to reform were not those of the federal system, with which its leaders were most familiar, but those of the local and state systems with which they had much less experience. The limitations of the elite status of the ABCNY were apparent in these reform efforts.

Court Reorganization

By the 1950s the courts of New York were in a chaotic condition. There were multiple courts, local and state, with confusing and conflicting jurisdictions and procedures.[34] In New York City alone eight local courts existed in addition to the state courts. The numerous local courts enjoyed considerable autonomy in their operation as there was no cen-

---

33. Ibid.
34. For an excellent discussion of the unreformed condition of the New York courts, see Barbara Botein, "Court Reorganization in New York: The Role of Bernard Botein, 1958–73," *The Justice System Journal* 3 (1978): 126–142.

tralized authority or administration. As Martin notes: "No one was in charge of all the courts. In most of them each judge was his own master and answerable to no one."[35] Local financing meant local political control of the courts with serious consequences for their autonomy and coherence. There had been no general or systematic reforms of the court system since the adoption of the Field Code in 1846; instead, multiple incremental accretions resulted in a disorganized patchwork of courts and rules. Reforming and rationalizing this chaos took on the character of a moral crusade in the 1950s and 1960s for the ABCNY and "good government groups."

In response to pressure from reformist groups, and in answer to increasing public criticism, the state legislature in Albany created in 1953 a Temporary Commission on the Courts to investigate the criticisms of the court system and to make recommendations for improvements.[36] Reflecting the role of the ABCNY as a leader in the agitation for court reform, Harrison Tweed, former president of the ABCNY, was appointed chairman of the Temporary Commission, and its membership included several other prominent members of the ABCNY. From the outset, then, the Temporary Commission as well as the larger court reform movement was identified with the large-firm elite and the ABCNY.

Once again utilizing its access to financial resources, the ABCNY established two special committees funded by foundation grants, with professional staffs, to conduct research into the conditions of the New York courts and make recommendations for their reorganization. Each of these committees presented lengthy reports that were published as books documenting the chaotic conditions prevailing in the various courts and calling for systemwide reforms. The first report, published as *Children and Families in the Courts of New York City* (1954), recommended the creation of a single, statewide family court to have jurisdiction over all family-related legal matters in place of the confusing jumble of courts dealing with children and families.[37] Similarly, the second report, *Bad Housekeeping: The Administration of the New York Courts* (1955), recommended a simplified, unified court system with a central administrative office as a necessary rationalization of the numerous courts with overlapping jurisdictions and without any centralized authority.[38] In producing these reports, which provided ample

---

35. Martin, *Causes and Conflicts*, p. 300.

36. Botein, "Court Reorganization in New York."

37. Walter Gellhorn, *Children and Families in the Courts of New York City* (New York: Dodd, Mead, 1954).

38. Association of the Bar of the City of New York, *Bad Housekeeping: The Administration of the New York Courts* (New York: The Association of the Bar, 1955).

evidence of the deleterious state of the courts, the ABCNY made full use of its resources of money and expertise. The reports were solid documents, well researched and presented, and were widely used by the advocates of court reform for the next decade.

Recognizing the weaknesses implicit in its limited constituency, the ABCNY also sought to broaden the basis for court reform during this period by forming the Committee for Modern Courts in 1955 to bring together civic and business leaders in support of court reform. By demonstrating that it was not only the large-firm lawyers who desired court reform but also responsible elements of the community, the ABCNY hoped to blunt the criticism that court reform was merely the creature of the large-law-firm elite. Financed by contributions from individuals, law firms, and business corporations, the Committee for Modern Courts was to undertake research on the courts, to monitor court performance, and to support legislation intended to improve the operation of the courts.[39].

Even with a broader basis of support, the ABCNY's attempts to achieve the reorganization of the courts in the 1950s died of legislative inaction. Legislation prepared by the Temporary Commission to pave the way for court reform never made it out of committee, and in 1958 the legislature refused to appropriate any more money for the commission's staff. The only positive achievement of the commission was the creation of a statewide Judicial Conference composed of the chief judge of the Court of Appeals and the presiding justices of the four Appellate Divisions.[40] Although having only minor administrative responsibilities, the Judicial Conference was a halting first step toward a centralized administration of the courts in the state and became the locus of further reorganization efforts.

Despite the almost complete failure of the Temporary Commission, civic groups, led by the newly created Committee for Modern Courts and by the League of Women Voters, continued to bring pressure to bear on the legislature to undertake court reform. In 1958 the Judicial Conference was authorized to study the existing court structure and to make recommendations. Although different in some respects from that of the Temporary Commission, the Judicial Conference's plan shared the same underlying theme: the need for a unified court structure with a centralized administration. Responding again to public pressure, the legislature submitted the issue of court reorganization to the public in the form of a referendum in 1961. After the voters of New York overwhelmingly endorsed the proposal, a Joint Committee on Court Reor-

---

39. See Martin, *Causes and Conflicts*, p. 303.
40. Ibid., pp. 304–305.

ganization was established by the legislature and set to work drafting and sponsoring the legislative bills necessary to implement change. There was a great deal of lobbying and political activity on the content of these bills, but toward the end of 1962 the Court Reorganization Act, instituting the reform of the court structure, was passed by the legislature and signed into law by Governor Rockefeller.[41] Court reform had finally arrived.

Martin suggests that the 1962 act creating a new court structure "brought the tangle of individual and independent courts to an end and substituted a unified system."[42] His prognosis is overly optimistic, however, in that the legislative reforms did not lead to the fully unified, integrated statewide court system that the reformers had advocated; instead, several specialized courts remained and others retained considerable administrative and financial autonomy.

There were three major reforms enacted in 1962.[43] The first was the creation of a centralized, statewide court administration. The legislature created an Administrative Board of the Judicial Conference, which would oversee personnel practices, financial affairs, and calendar scheduling. In addition, each of the four departments of the Appellate Division of the Supreme Court was empowered to provide for an administrative justice to regulate all the courts within the department. Thus the courts were given a centralized administrative structure for the first time, but the local financing of the courts continued. The ABCNY and other reformers sought the end of local control, but that was not to be achieved until state financing for the whole system was finally introduced a decade later.

The second major change was the creation of a statewide Family Court to replace the overlapping Children's Court and Domestic Relations Court. All family matters were to come under the jurisdiction of the one court, as the ABCNY special committee had recommended back in 1954. The new Family Court was an example of the type of statewide unified court the ABCNY and other reformers had advocated, with the exception that it was still a separate, independent court. The reformers had wanted a unified, generalist trial court of first instance rather than several separate specialized courts. The Family Court was a major improvement over the preceding situation, where jurisdiction over family matters was scattered over several courts, but its separate existence was evidence of the continued absence of a fully unified court system.

---

41. See the outline of events in Botein, "Court Reorganization in New York."
42. Martin, *Causes and Conflicts*, p. 306.
43. The discussion here follows Botein, "Court Reorganization in New York."

The abolition of some courts and the consolidation of others marked the third major change instituted in 1962. Many local and county courts were eliminated, with their cases, personnel, and facilities transferred to the New York Supreme Court. In New York City a new civil court was created to replace various city and municipal courts. But the civil and criminal courts remained quite separate, as did the two courts with immense patronage power, the Court of Claims and the Surrogates' Court. The situation was worse upstate, where local interests had successfully pressed for the retention of miscellaneous village and county courts. A truly unified statewide court system threatened both local control over the courts, from which members of the local bar and judges benefited, and the independent authority and status of local court judges who would be merged into a larger court system and probably subject to rotation from court to court. The Court Reorganization Act of 1962 resulted in the consolidation of some disparate courts with overlapping jurisdictions, but a unified court of first instance foundered on local particularism and the vested interests of the specialized courts.

The road to court reorganization proved rocky for the ABCNY and its fellow reform organizations. Unsuccessful in the 1950s, the ABCNY had to accept a reorganization in the 1960s that was considerably less than what it had wanted. A fully integrated, unified court structure was not achieved. But if the ABCNY had to settle for half a loaf in its efforts to reorganize the courts into a unified system, it achieved even less in its attempt to revise the rules of civil procedure and to transfer rule-making authority from the legislature to the courts.

The Rules of Civil Procedure

An integral part of court reform was procedural reform. The New York Civil Practice Act of 1921 and the accompanying Rules of Civil Procedure governed the representation of clients in the civil courts of the state. Like the courts, the Practice Act stood in dire need of rationalization and revision having undergone unplanned growth since 1921, with bits and pieces tacked on by amendments and supplements without any regard for the whole.[44] The result was a patchwork of often inconsistent and disorganized rules and procedures, containing many obsolete and unnecessary provisions. Furthermore, authority to promulgate new rules under the 1921 act did not rest with the courts but was vested in the legislature, allowing for political control over rule-

---

44. Jack B. Weinstein, "Proposed Revision of New York Civil Practice," *Columbia Law Review* 60 (1960): 50–103.

making. This latter feature of the existing structure was of considerable concern to the ABCNY elite, which consistently sought to separate the political and judicial spheres.

The Temporary Commission on the Courts established in 1954 an Advisory Committee to study civil procedure and to draft an entirely new civil practice act for the state. Given that civil procedure involves a great deal of arcane and specialized knowledge and experience, the Advisory Committee was composed entirely of lawyers. Not willing to leave matters in the hands of the Advisory Committee, and agreeing on the urgent need for revision, the three major bar associations of the state, the State Bar Association, the NYCLA, and the ABCNY, formed a Joint Committee on the Civil Practice Act to work with the Advisory Committee. This Joint Committee of the bar assocations developed an excellent working relationship with the Advisory Committee, which was happy to have the assistance of the bar associations in its task. Consequently, the Joint Committee had access to all the internal memoranda and working reports of the Advisory Committee and was able "to furnish the Advisory Committee with its opinions on the revisions prior to their incorporation into drafts of legislative bills."[45] As a consequence, the Joint Committee exercised considerable influence over the final shape of the proposed new practice act. Indeed, in its report the Joint Committee noted that "the Advisory Committee has reconsidered its position in the light of this Committee's comments and has accepted a large number of changes suggested by this Committee."[46]

The Advisory Committee presented its proposed revision of the 1921 Civil Practice Act and associated rules of procedure to the legislature in 1961. Endorsed by the bar associations' Joint Committee, the proposed revision would have replaced the old act and rules completely, and in the process consolidated about 2,000 different sections and provisions into about 850. The proposed revision, however, was not merely a codification of existing rules and procedures, but included many new provisions, some of which had important substantive implications. Perhaps the most controversial feature of the Advisory Committee's proposal was the provision that the rules would not be embodied in statutes, and thus not require statutory revision as they did under the 1921 act, but rather be left in the hands of the judiciary as court rules.[47] The intention not only was to separate legislative and judicial authority clearly, but also to increase the rules' flexibility and amenability to change.

---

45. Report of Joint Committee on the Civil Practice Act, 1960, p. 27.
46. Ibid.
47. Weinstein, "Proposed Revision of New York Civil Practice."

The revised practice act also included major changes in pretrial procedures including the increased use of pretrial conferences to encourage settlements, broader discovery requirements along the model of
the federal rules, and more detailed pleadings on the part of those
bringing actions so that both the court and the defendant knew well in
advance what the evidence was for the allegations. Despite the confidence of the Joint Committee that "these proposals should not engen-
der political controversy,"[48] they met with the vigorous opposition of
the plaintiffs' bar, which felt they were intended to weight the scales
of justice against them and their clients. The fears of the plaintiffs' bar
had some basis as the requirement for more detailed pleadings, for
instance, was directed at the negligence bar and was much more oner-
ous than that under the old practice act.[49] It would also provide more
information for the defense to work with at an early stage in a claim,
thereby strengthening the hand of the defense attorney at the expense
of the plaintiff. Furthermore, proposed restrictions on the number and
types of appeals to be allowed from the lower courts to the Appellate
Division—intended to reduce the caseload of the higher court—were
viewed by the plaintiffs' bar as circumscribing their rights of appeal.
Consequently, the New York State Association of Plaintiffs' Trial Lawyers strongly opposed the proposed new practice act and rules of procedure.

The plaintiffs' bar viewed the whole reform effort as elite reform
emanating from the establishment bar, which it viewed as incurably
pro-defense in its orientation.[50] Not only was the Advisory Committee
composed of "distinguished lawyers," but its staff was drawn from Columbia University Law School under the leadership of an academic expert in civil procedure. Similarly, the Joint Committee, organized by an
ABCNY member and former president of the State Bar Association
who was a senior partner in the Wall Street firm Davis, Polk & Wardwell, was dominated by established practitioners with a strong representation from the large firms. Regarding themselves as practical experts on civil procedure, plaintiffs' attorneys felt excluded from the
revision process. A former president of the Association of Plaintiffs'

---

48. Report of Joint Committee, p. 44.

49. For details on these added requirements, see Report of Joint Committee, p. 32.

50. Jack B. Weinstein, Chief Judge, United States District Court, Second Circuit, personal interview with author, November 24, 1980. Judge Weinstein was the academic
expert who worked with the Advisory Committee and supervised the drafting of the
proposed new civil procedure law.

Trial Lawyers complained that "our opinions are not solicited, nor are they invited."[51]

The lawyer members of the legislature, primarily local practitioners themselves, were receptive to these criticisms and probably would have preferred to make no changes at all. Many feared that a new practice act and revised rules of procedure would require them to re-learn their civil procedure and would make their eventual return to practice more difficult. They also disagreed over the locus of rule-mak-ing authority, not only for reasons of power but also because they feared that the Judicial Conference, which would have this responsibil-ity under the proposed new act, would be unduly conservative and biased toward the defense bar. By keeping control over rule-making, the legislators would be able to shape the development of civil practice. There was little enthusiasm, then, for the substantial revisions wanted by the Advisory Committee and its bar association allies.

Consequently, the new practice act that was eventually adopted by the legislature in 1962 was much modified from that originally intro-duced by the Advisory Committee and endorsed by the ABCNY. Gone were requirements for pretrial conferences, broadened pretrial discov-ery, and more detailed pleadings in negligence complaints, and the restrictions on the rights of appeal were dropped. The legislature's bill did modernize and codify the rules, but all the controversial substan-tive revisions were removed. Although this bill was a distinct improve-ment over the *status quo ante* in terms of the consistency and coherence of the procedures, the ABCNY and the Joint Committee opposed it vigorously. Particularly galling to the bar associations was the adamant refusal of the legislature to surrender authority over rule-making, with the legislature's bill placing the act and the rules back together again within the statutory law. The ABCNY opposed the new bill at hearings and lobbied legislators, but to no avail, as it was "enacted with little difficulty and few improvements."[52] Following its failure to stop the bill in the legislature, the ABCNY took the step it reserves for unusu-ally important issues, sending all nine of its living former presidents to Albany in an effort to persuade the governor to veto the bill. Despite such heavy pressure from the ABCNY and the establishment bar, the governor signed the bill and New York had a new civil practice act

---

51. Proceedings of New York State Association of Plaintiffs' Trial Lawyers, 1958, p. 272.

52. Annual Report of the President, *Record of the Association of the Bar of the City of New York* 17 (1962): 374–410.

with the rule-making authority left squarely in the hands of the legislature.[53]

Why this defeat for the legal establishment? The struggle over a new civil practice act was peculiarly a lawyers' battle, arousing little interest outside the legal community, and yet the ABCNY and its allies in the State Bar Association and the NYCLA were unable to carry the day. When the Advisory Committee's new practice act first failed in the legislature in 1961, the president of the ABCNY pointed to the "selfish interests of some segments of the Bar" as responsible.[54] He was undoubtedly pointing to local bar interests, which had been able to counter effectively the establishment's resources of prestige and expertise. The fact that this issue was determined in the state legislature, with which local bar groups had more contacts than had the Wall Street elite, was critical. Local interests in the legal system won this battle and demonstrated emphatically that they could severely limit the reform effectiveness of the large-firm elite of the bar.

Judicial Selection

Since the 1846 constitution, almost all local and state judges in New York had been elected to the bench rather than appointed. The 1962 Court Reorganization Act left the existing system of judicial election unaltered.[55] While overtly democratic, the electoral process placed great discretion in the hands of the political parties, who slated candidates for judicial vacancies. Often the electorate was left without a choice as the parties divided up the vacancies between them and jointly slated each other's candidates. Consequently, rather than judges being chosen by the electorate at large, they were, to all intents and purposes, selected by the slating committees of the political parties. Even when there was a contested election for a judicial position, the voters had difficulty in determining who was the better candidate. Consequently, voting generally followed party lines. It was very difficult for a Republican candidate to win a contested election in New York City and for a Democrat to win in the suburbs or upstate. The selection of judges by local politicians, the division of judicial vacancies among the parties like the spoils of victory, and the election of judges according to their party identification rather than merit affronted all the

---

53. For a discussion of the new civil practice act, see Samuel M. Hesson, "The New York Civil Practice Law and Rules," *Albany Law Review* 27 (1963): 175–193.

54. Annual Report of the President, *Record of the Association of the Bar of the City of New York* 16 (1961): 350–384.

55. Martin, *Causes and Conflicts*, p. 307.

norms the establishment bar of the ABCNY held about the dignity and quality of the judiciary.

Moreover, local political control meant that neither the upper-class ABCNY of the earlier period nor the elite ABCNY of the 1970s was able to act as gatekeeper to the bench, despite the work of its Committee on Judiciary. The evaluations of judicial candidates by the judiciary committee were frequently ignored by the local political organizations in slating candidates for judicial positions and, therefore, did not serve to keep unqualified persons off the bench. Attempts by leaders of the ABCNY to gain the cooperation of the political parties in not slating unqualified candidates consistently ended in frustration.[56]

The ABCNY made two major efforts in the 1960s to change the method of judicial selection from election to appointment, and both ultimately failed. After court reorganization became a reality in 1962, the Special Committee on Judicial Selection and Tenure proposed and sponsored a plan for the appointment of judges in New York City based on the so-called Missouri Plan, a merit-selection plan first instituted in Missouri.[57] All judges were to be appointed by the relevant elected official, the mayor or the governor, from a panel of names submitted by a nonpartisan judicial selection commission. Although the plan proposed by the Special Committee would have affected only three local New York City courts, it received little support in the legislature, and for two successive years never reached the floor of the Assembly or Senate.[58]

The second effort of the ABCNY came in 1967, the year in which a constitutional convention was called to redraft the state's constitution, raising the possibility of having a whole new judicial article incorporating merit selection. At the Constitutional Convention the ABCNY proposed essentially the same plan for the merit selection of judges as that formulated by the earlier special committee except that its scope was not restricted to New York City but broadened to encompass the whole state. Once again, however, the political leaders were successful in thwarting the ABCNY's efforts, and the reformers could not muster enough votes to have the plan adopted. The elective system remained in force.[59]

The reasons for the failure of the ABCNY to have the merit selection adopted in New York despite two major efforts in the 1960s are similar

---

56. Ibid., pp. 308–309.

57. For an outline of the Missouri Plan and its operation, see Richard A. Watson and Randall G. Downing, *The Politics of the Bench and Bar* (New York: Wiley, 1969).

58. Martin, *Causes and Conflicts*, p. 311.

59. Ibid., pp. 311–312.

to those behind the ABCNY's limited success in court reform and re-vision of the civil procedure. Any attempt to change the method of selecting judges ran up against the opposition of those elements of the bar and polity that benefited from the *status quo*. The elective system served well the interests of the local political parties, as it provided them with a ready source of patronage with which to reward faithful supporters. Merit selection, with its nonpartisan judicial selection com-missions, threatened the control of the local political organizations over the judicial selection process and would entail the loss of considerable patronage opportunities, and all that that implied in terms of control over the courts. Of course, that was exactly what the reformers had in mind: The ABCNY and reform groups saw merit selection as not only a way to get better judges but also a means of attenuating local political control over the courts. There was no disguising the intent and likely outcome of merit selection. In advocating an appointive system, then, the ABCNY was challenging the vested interests of entrenched local political leaders. Despite its ability to mobilize the support of business leaders and civic groups, the ABCNY was unable to overcome the local strength of the political parties.

Individual lawyer-legislators could also be counted upon to oppose any change in the method of selecting judges. Closely connected to the leaders of the local political organizations, the legislators saw their in-terests in a similar way. Just as the political leaders preferred not to have to abide by the recommendations of a selection commission, so did the lawyer-legislators who aspired to be judges. Noting that "nearly every member of the legislature who is a member of the bar has such aspirations," former judge and president of the ABCNY, Samuel Rosenman, commented that "this kind of self-interest makes it a most difficult job to obtain the passage of our proposal."[60] The intro-duction of an appointive system with a greater emphasis on legal abil-ities and experience would certainly work to the disadvantage of those legislators who had been primarily politicians rather than lawyers.

Support for merit selection has been largely confined to the defense bar and large-firm lawyers throughout the United States. Watson and Downing found that support for the appointive system in Missouri came almost completely from the defense bar.[61] Members of the plain-tiffs' bar and less established lawyers feared that defense-oriented, large-firm lawyers would inevitably dominate the nonpartisan judicial selection panels, thereby limiting their opportunities for judicial posi-

---

60. Ibid., p. 311.
61. Watson and Downing, *The Politics of the Bench and Bar*.

tions. Remember that local and state judicial positions were highly valued by nonelite local lawyers as they offered a secure income and guaranteed benefits and prestige in the local community. The small ethnic and minority bar associations of New York City also believed that under an appointive, or merit, system their members would have fewer chances of getting on the bench. The words of a humorous ditty sung, ironically, at one of the ABCNY's evenings of light entertainment in the early 1960s, illustrates the fears of local ethnic lawyers:

If you're not from Fair Old Harvard
They will toss you in the can . . .
Oh, the Old Missouri Plan
Oh, the Old Missouri Plan
It won't be served with sauerkraut nor sauce Italian
There'll be no corned beef and cabbage
And spaghetti they will ban
There'll be no such dish
As gefilte fish
On the Old Missouri Plan[62]

Though it was unclear what exactly the outcome would be under a merit system controlled by the elite of the profession, there were concerns that minorities would be disadvantaged. At least the political parties could be counted on to nominate candidates from local ethnic communities, if only to reward them for their electoral support. By this means many Jewish and Italian lawyers, and some blacks, had gained judicial positions. Thus the local and ethnic bar groups could be expected to oppose the ABCNY's plan for merit selection.[63]

Merit selection of judges was opposed more strenuously than court reorganization because of its immediate impact upon access to highly valued positions in the legal system. Merit selection was clearly identified with the large-firm legal establishment as represented in the ABCNY, with the result that local interests could oppose it as yet another example of elite reform. The ABCNY did not make any headway at all in its campaign for merit selection until a decade later, when the shock of an unpleasant contested election for the position of chief jus-

---

62. Ibid., pp. 4–5.
63. Ibid., pp. 343–348. In fact, Watson and Downing found, after an extensive study of the Missouri Plan in operation, that there was no significant difference in the social and educational backgrounds of judges selected by either the appointive or the elective system. Graduates of elite national law schools were equally as absent from the ranks of the appointed judges as from the elected.

tice of the Court of Appeals provided yet another opportunity to press for reform.

No-Fault Automobile Insurance

Another long-standing reform interest of the ABCNY was tort reform. In the early 1970s the ABCNY actively supported a movement to implement a system of no-fault automobile insurance in New York. The essential idea of no-fault automobile insurance was to remove the necessity of demonstrating fault from the process of accident compensation.[64] Under the existing system of tort liability, the victims of an automobile accident had to prove the other party to be at fault, and to demonstrate the lack of contributory negligence on their own part, if they were to receive full compensation for medical costs incurred and the pain and suffering endured. Based on the finding of fault, the tort liability system encouraged the adversarial representation of the parties to the accident, and thus was a great source of work for lawyers. A no-fault system would make the question of responsibility for the accident irrelevant. All parties would be compensated for their losses without first having to demonstrate fault and the absence of contributory negligence. Consequently, there would be no need in the vast majority of accidents for either party to have recourse to the courts or to hire lawyers to represent them. Disputed cases would be decided by an administrative process rather than by adjudication in the courts.

No-fault systems were increasingly advocated throughout the United States in the 1970s as a solution to overcrowded courts and the expense of adversarial dispute resolution. They were advocated not just in the area of torts but also in divorce and marital disputes, leading to the adoption in a number of states of no-fault divorce laws.[65] In the realm of tort law, no-fault provisions were particularly supported by business corporations subject to multiple liability claims and by insurance companies, which ended up paying out most of the awards under the traditional adversary system of adjudication. The attractiveness of no-fault systems to these interests lay in the increased predictability it provided insurers and business by avoiding the uncertainties introduced by trials and juries. Awards would be standardized and estab-

---

64. For a general discussion of the principles involved in no-fault automobile insurance, see Report of Special Committee on Automobile Insurance Plans, *Record of the Association of the Bar of the City of New York* 27 (1972): 245–274; see also Charles F. Krause, "No-Fault Alternatives—The Case for Comparative Negligence and Compulsory Arbitration in New York, Part I," *New York State Bar Association Journal* 44 (1972): 535–544.

65. See Lenore J. Weitzman, *The Divorce Revolution: The Unexpected Social and Economic Consequences for Women and Children in America* (New York: Free Press, 1985).

lished by experts instead of by impressionable juries, would be more likely to be "reasonable," and would certainly be predictable. Furthermore, the incentive of the contingency fee, which encourages the plaintiff's attorney to seek out clients and aggressively pursue claims, would be removed as the claiming process is taken out of the adversarial system and no longer requires demonstration of fault. Even though not all insurance companies supported no-fault systems, some preferring to slug it out in the adversarial system where the advantage still lay with the defendant, no-fault was generally perceived to be in the interest of the insurance industry.

Opposing the introduction of no-fault provisions in the tort area were the considerable number of personal injury lawyers who pressed the claims of accident victims. This was a sizable segment of the New York bar, many of whom depended on automobile cases for their livelihood and whose immediate financial interests would be hurt by the replacement of the tort liability system with a no-fault accident compensation plan. Viewing no-fault schemes as denying the accident victim his or her day in court, and fearing economic loss, members of the local trial bar, particularly the plaintiffs' bar, were violently opposed to any no-fault legislation and strenuously resisted its passage in the New York legislature.

In 1970, following an extensive study of automobile accident compensation, the New York Department of Insurance had a no-fault bill introduced into the legislature which, in due course, was easily defeated by the allies of the trial lawyers.[66] That same year the ABCNY appointed a Special Committee on Automobile Insurance Plans to investigate the report on alternative methods of compensating accident victims. This "blue-ribbon" committee of the Association, which included some leading large-firm lawyers, reported to the Executive Committee in 1972 recommending that "the present right of action based on negligence against the owners and operators of automobiles should be abolished."[67] The Special Committee advocated a total no-fault plan in which the right of action, and the notion of fault, would be completely removed from the system of compensation. It disapproved of partial no-fault plans, which would retain compensation based on proof of fault for some proportion of accident claims, as internally inconsistent and only serving to perpetuate the shortcomings and expense of the tort liability system.

---

66. State of New York Department of Insurance, "Automobile Insurance . . . For Whose Benefit?" 1970; see also Ralph D. Semarad, "The New York State Insurance Department's Auto Insurance Plan," *New York State Bar Association* 43 (1971): 164–174.

67. Report of Special Committee on Automobile Insurance Plans, p. 249.

The ABCNY was the only bar association in the state to propose the implementation of a total no-fault plan. To its president, this was evidence that the ABCNY was above self-interest and was prepared to put the larger view first in that a no-fault system would clearly reduce the amount of available legal work.[68] But, in fact, the ABCNY's position reflected its composition as much as its high ideals. Few members of the ABCNY, and none of its leaders, were negligence lawyers. The introduction of no-fault was certainly not going to affect the practices or pocketbooks of many of the members of the ABCNY. Its Special Committee on Automobile Insurance Plans included only two negligence lawyers out of fifteen members, and they both dissented from the majority report of the committee.[69] David Peck, the chairman of the Special Committee, was a senior partner at Sullivan & Cromwell, a prominent Wall Street firm that could not have been farther removed from the practice of negligence law. Indeed, the ABCNY did not even have a standing committee on negligence law. Certainly, there was no group within the ABCNY to advocate the position of the plaintiffs' bar, which saw no-fault plans such as that proposed by the ABCNY as threatening their very livelihood. The ABCNY, in its advocacy of no-fault insurance, was entering the territory of another segment of the bar completely, and proposing to alter fundamentally the conditions of practice for that segment.

The Special Committee did not draft its own legislation, but soon after its report appeared another no-fault bill was introduced into the legislature in 1972. Known as the Gordon bill, it proposed a partial no-fault plan with a minimum threshold above which the old tort liability system would come into play.[70] Although this bill was contrary to the recommendations of the Special Committee in that it advocated only partial no-fault, it promised at least to introduce the principle of no-fault into the statutes and remove some of the minor disputes from the courts, and so the ABCNY endorsed it.[71]

Organized opposition to the no-fault bill came from the local county bar associations, such as those in Brooklyn and Queens, and from the newly emergent trial lawyers' organizations such as the New York State Trial Lawyers Association and the Plaintiffs' Trial Lawyers Asso-

---

68. Annual Report of the President, *Record of the Association of the Bar of the City of New York* 27 (1972): 455–517.

69. See Report of Special Committee on Automobile Insurance Plans, Dissents.

70. See Charles F. Krause, "No-Fault Alternatives—The Case for Comparative Negligence and Compulsory Arbitration in New York, Part II," *New York State Bar Association Journal* 45 (1973): 30–35.

71. Minutes of the Executive Committee, Association of the Bar of the City of New York, March 8, 1972.

ciation. Using the rhetoric of rights and justice, the trial lawyers elevated opposition to no-fault from a lowly concern about dollar awards
and employment for lawyers to fundamental questions of justice and
individual rights.[72] Opponents of no-fault insurance plans had considerable support in the legislature and were able to defeat the Gordon
bill. A considerably weakened version of it was to be enacted later, but
it did not pose any threat to the plaintiffs' bar.[73]

Though the local bar groups, then, were unsuccessful in stopping
no-fault completely, they were able to limit its applicability to those
accident victims who suffered very minor injuries. The threshold figure
was low enough to exclude a large proportion of accident victims, significantly mitigating the impact on the trial bar. Working on a contingency-fee basis, plaintiffs' attorneys did not have time, anyway, to lav-
ish on minor cases that were productive of small awards. As the editor
of the *Brooklyn Barrister* concluded: "All things considered, the total effect on the Bar of this law will be slight."[74] The local trial bar again
managed to withstand the reform efforts of the large-firm elite and to
defend successfully the principle of fault.

ELITE REFORM AND LOCAL CONNECTIONS

The ABCNY's failure to achieve a completely unified court system, its
inability to push through a substantially revised civil practice act, its
failure to change the method by which judges were selected, and the
passage of a minimal no-fault bill all demonstrate the limitations of the
influence resources of an elite association. Because the views of local
bar groups, which had a direct interest in any changes in the local and
state courts in which they practiced, were not incorporated in the
decision-making processes of the ABCNY, reform proposals emanating
therefrom were identified from the beginning with the large-firm elite
of the bar. These proposals, then, were open to attack as elitist and
contrary to the interests of substantial segments of the bar.

Even the formation of the Committee on Modern Courts as a quite
separate entity in order to broaden the base of support for court reform
did not overcome the identification of court reform with the elite of the
bar and the ABCNY. The staff of the Committee on Modern Courts,
realizing that the sponsorship of the ABCNY not only carried little
weight with upstate legislators and local political leaders but was likely
to arouse their antipathy, sought to distance themselves from the

---

72. For an outline of the arguments of those opposed to no-fault automobile insurance, see Rosemary R. Gunning, "No Fault Insurance," *Queens Bar Bulletin* 35 (1972).
73. See Krause, "No-Fault Alternatives."
74. John Corbett, "The Bar and No-Fault," *Brooklyn Barrister* 24 (1973): 165–166.

ABCNY and the large-firm elite.[75] They had difficulty doing so, how-ever, as the large firms and their senior partners were the committee's most consistent financial supporters, and many of the leaders of the ABCNY served on its board of governors. In addition, the committee was housed in the Bar Building, an office building next door to and owned by the ABCNY. Furthermore, although the Committee on Modern Courts was successful in recruiting business and civic leaders to the cause of court reform, these persons themselves were from the upper segments of New York society and may have only served to reinforce the notion that court reform was the hobby of the business and professional elite.

The large-firm elite lacked the representativeness, the local connections, and the local political experience to implement its reform agenda. Note that all the failures or limited successes outlined briefly in this chapter occurred at the local or state levels of decision making. It is at these levels that the elite resources of the ABCNY appear to be least effective and that local interests are best able to capitalize on their resources of local connections and political experience. On the few occasions when the ABCNY has been able to develop and utilize strong local connections, its efforts at exercising influence in local decision-making arenas have met with more success. However, even on these occasions its relative success has come because the issues involved have not aroused the strong opposition of local bar groups.

The Appointment of Judges to the Court of Appeals

The story of court reform in New York did not end with the failures of the ABCNY to achieve its ends in the 1960s. Following an unusual, and particularly colorful, electoral battle in 1973 for the highest judicial position in the state, that of chief judge of the New York Court of Appeals, the ABCNY once again took up the cudgels of merit selection. This time the ABCNY called for the appointment of judges to the Court of Appeals.

Traditionally the position of chief judge went to the most senior member of the Court of Appeals without reference to political affiliation. The political parties had generally respected this tradition, and there was rarely any electoral contest; the most senior member of the court was duly slated and elected unopposed. In 1973, however, with a Republican, Charles Breitel, due to be elevated to the position of chief judge, the New York City Democrats broke with tradition and signaled

---

75. Fern Schair, executive director of Committee on Modern Courts, personal interview with author, October 25, 1979.

their intention to contest the position.[76] A successful and flamboyant personal injury lawyer, Jacob D. Fuchsberg, won the Democratic primary despite lacking any previous judicial experience, thereby becoming the Democratic candidate who would run against the Republican Breitel.

Although a rank outsider to the establishment bar, Fuchsberg had served as president of the American Trial Lawyers Association and had a substantial following among the large number of trial lawyers in New York City. He also had amassed a considerable personal fortune, which he could use to finance his campaign. Disturbed by the prospect of a millionaire plaintiffs' attorney without any judicial experience becoming the chief judge of the state, the ABCNY and the large-firm elite threw their weight and dollars behind the scholarly Breitel, who was an experienced and respected judge. The ABCNY's Committee on Judiciary found Fuchsberg not qualified for the position while finding Judge Breitel to be "well qualified." The lines were clearly drawn: Fuchsberg's support lay in the local Democratic organizations and within the trial bar, whereas Breitel's support came from the legal and business establishment and the Republican party.

It was a bitter and colorful campaign. Fuchsberg infuriated the ABCNY and Wall Street establishment by engaging in an advertising blitz that lauded his courtroom exploits and portrayed him as the friend of the little man. He promised to reform the courts and he attacked Breitel as the standpat candidate of the large law firms. In return, Breitel repeatedly criticized Fuchsberg's lack of judicial experience. In the end, the experience of Breitel and the superior resources of the large-firm elite and its allies won out and Fuchsberg was defeated. He was, however, to win election to a seat on the Court of Appeals a short time later, thereby ending up on the same bench as his former opponent, Chief Judge Breitel.

Finding such electoral battles demeaning to the courts and the judiciary, and fearful that on another occasion another lawyer with no judicial experience and a personal fortune similarly could take advantage of the elective system to gain a seat on the highest court of the state, the leaders of the ABCNY once again enlisted the support of civic and business groups to prevail on the governor and legislature to change the system of judicial selection from election to appointment.

On this occasion the ABCNY's push for merit selection coincided with the election in 1976 of a new Democratic governor, Hugh Carey,

---

76. For a detailed outline of the contest for the position of chief judge, see Cynthia O. Philip, Paul Nejelski, and Aric Press, *Where Do Judges Come From?* (New York: Institute of Judicial Administration, 1976). The following material is drawn from this account.

an Irish-Catholic lawyer-businessman from Brooklyn who had long been active in local Democratic politics. President of the ABCNY at the time was Cyrus Vance, a prominent Democrat with strong connections with the national leadership of the Democratic party. Governor Carey asked Vance to chair a transition task force on the courts and the legal system. Under Vance's guidance the task force recommended further court reforms, including the merit selection of judges, the creation of a single, statewide trial court, and the complete centralization of court administration. Governor Carey agreed to make the task force's recommendations his policy and he introduced these reform measures into the legislature in 1976.[77] Following considerable debate in the legislature and intensive lobbying by pro-court-reform groups, the New York State Assembly and Senate finally agreed to place three major amendments to the judicial article of the State Constitution before the citizens of New York in a referendum in November 1977. Although these amendments were more modest than the original proposals, dispensing with the establishment of a single trial court and with the merit selection of all judges, they did include the appointment of judges to the Court of Appeals.[78] This time the electorate voted in support of the constitutional amendment. As a result the Constitution of New York State was amended in 1977 to incorporate the appointment of judges to the highest court of the state by the governor from a panel of names submitted by a bipartisan nominating commission. After many failures and disappointments, court reform groups, led by the president of the ABCNY, had finally succeeded in having merit selection enacted, albeit only at the highest level.

It was no coincidence that the ABCNY's success came under the leadership of Cyrus Vance. About to be selected by President Carter as secretary of state, Vance was an important channel to the national leadership of the Democratic party for Governor Carey, who harbored presidential aspirations. Active in local Democratic circles, Vance was less ambivalent about involvement in the local political process than were many of his large-firm colleagues, and traveled to Albany to lobby prominent legislators on the task force's court-reform proposals. He paid courtesy calls on the majority leaders, hosted receptions, and

---

77. For an outline and discussion of Governor Carey's proposals for court reform, see *New York Times*, May 4, 1976, 1:3; May 4, 1976, 36:2.

78. In addition to the appointment of judges to the Court of Appeals, the proposed amendments included the institution of a new system for disciplining judges and the establishment of a unified administration of state courts. See *New York Times*, June 29, 1977, II, 2:2. For a report on the outcome of the referendum, see *New York Times*, November 10, 1977, 1:5.

got on the telephone.[79] With Carey's clout behind it, and the support of the good government groups, Vance was successful, and New York eventually had a limited but important measure of merit selection.

Vance's contribution to the outcome was considerable. But there was general unease with elections to the highest court following the unseemly electoral struggle for the chief judge's position. Of course, although the Court of Appeals was the highest court in the state and the level at which legal acuity and judicial experience were most important, it was also the furthermost removed from the aspirations of members of the local bar. Whereas many looked to the local and lower state courts for secure positions, few could aspire to the Court of Appeals. There was, then, less opposition to merit selection at this level than at lower levels. Local bar groups were willing, if push came to shove, to accept an appointed Court of Appeals provided their access to the more numerous lower court positions was not threatened.

Commitment Procedures for the Mentally Ill

In the early 1960s, the ABCNY formed a Special Committee to Study Commitment Procedures with an eye to the revision of the law relating to the commitment of mentally incapacitated people to institutions. Again using an academic expert as director, and a professional staff of researchers, the Special Committee produced a substantial report which was published by Cornell University Press in 1962, and attracted considerable attention.[80] The Special Committee's recommendations were radical, suggesting the abolition of the existing system of court commitment and its replacement with "medical admission" based on the certification of two physicians and the approval of the admitting hospital. In addition, the Special Committee called for increased safeguards to protect patients' rights, including periodic hearings during the duration of commitment in order to determine whether continued institutionalization was required. To undertake these periodic reviews, and to implement other reforms, the committee recommended the establishment of a new state agency independent of the existing Depart-

---

79. This information comes from personal interviews conducted by the author with the following persons: Judah Gribbetz, former legal counsel to Governor Carey; Marion Ames, former president of the League of Women Voters; Arthur Cooperman, former chairman of the Judiciary Committee, New York State Assembly, New York State Legislature.

80. Bertram F. Willcox, *Mental Illness and Due Process* (Ithaca: Cornell University Press, 1962).

ment of Medical Hygiene, which at that time ran the mental health facilities.[81]

Legislation based on the report was introduced in 1963 in an effort "to effect a major revision of a complex of laws which have not been changed in 30 years."[82] Although not passed in 1963, similar legislation was introduced again the following year and enacted, without a great deal of difficulty. The enacted legislation included some modification of the proposals originally proposed by the Special Committee, but the ABCNY pronounced itself satisfied with the outcome, observing that "the legislation as finally introduced and enacted retained all the essentials of the Committee's initial recommendations."[83] In this instance, then, the work of the Special Committee and the initiative of the Association bore fruit quickly, resulting in a recodification and substantial reformulation of the laws relating to commitment procedures.

The rapid success of the ABCNY in this instance undoubtedly reflected the fact that few interest groups mobilized in opposition to the proposed changes in the law notwithstanding their extensiveness. Even though the proposals of the Special Committee promised to remove commitment procedures from the courts and adversarial proceedings and place them in the hands of medical experts, there was no organized opposition from within the bar. Although some lawyers may have specialized in mental health law, it was not a recognized area of specialization at that time and, certainly, lawyers who practiced in the area were not organized. Most commitment work was probably done by local neighborhood general practitioners, and it was unpleasant work without the prospect of substantial financial reward. Furthermore, the proposal allowed for judicial review of disputes and of decisions to continue commitment , and so did not completely remove the whole area from the legal system. Local practitioners, then, lacked a strong material incentive to mobilize in opposition to the ABCNY initiative, and thus this incursion of the establishment bar into local law reform proceeded unimpeded.

---

81. Ibid.

82. Annual Report of the President, *Record of the Association of the Bar of the City of New York* 18 (1963): 427–459.

83. Annual Report of the President, *Record of the Association of the Bar of the City of New York* 19 (1964): 342–378. For a discussion of the new law, see Joyce Daryl Chaikin, "Commitment by Fiat: New York's New Mental Hygiene Law," *Columbia Journal of Law and Social Problems* 1 (1965): 113–124; Duncan R. Farney, "Comments. Incarceration of the Mentally Ill—New York's New Law," *Syracuse Law Review* 17 (1966): 671–687.

Divorce Law Reform

Revision of the New York divorce laws was another story. The reform initiatives of the ABCNY in the postwar years at first met with no success but were eventually adopted. In May of 1948, the ABCNY established a Special Committee on the Improvement of the Divorce Laws, which was authorized "to carry forward the Association's program for liberalising the divorce laws of the state by adding grounds additional to adultery for absolute divorce."[84] This was clearly not noncontroversial technical law reform in which the ABCNY was engaging but major substantive reform aimed at changing the entire character of the divorce law in New York State.

Unchanged for over a hundred years, the divorce laws of New York were variously described by presidents of the ABCNY as "archaic" and "antiquated and medieval," in that they did not permit divorce for any reason other than adultery. There were no provisions for divorce on grounds of separation, irreconcilable differences, or incompatibility. Prospective divorcées either had to demonstrate adultery on the part of one partner or fly to Mexico or Reno, where the divorce laws were more lenient and residency requirements minimal. Either way, the divorce laws did not encourage respect for the law and were out of tune with the times. The Roman Catholic Diocese, a major institution in New York, was the main obstacle to divorce-law reform.

Although there was an identifiable divorce bar in New York City in the 1950s, it was not well represented within the ABCNY. Divorce lawyers do not enjoy high standing within the bar, and divorce practice was traditionally eschewed by the large law firms.[85] Certainly, the leaders of the ABCNY were not divorce practitioners themselves, but they were undoubtedly well aware of the difficulties caused by the strict divorce laws. Some had almost certainly taken the plane to Mexico or Reno themselves, and others had referred senior executives of corporate clients to local divorce lawyers. Yet the leaders of the ABCNY and their corporate clients could well afford to evade the strictures of the New York divorce law; it was people of low income who were trapped by it. Why, then, should the ABCNY initiate reform efforts in this area? It was not a case of status politics, of engaging in

---

84. Annual Report of the President, *Record of the Association of the Bar of the City of New York* 3 (1948): 226–258.

85. On the relative prestige of divorce lawyers, see John P. Heinz and Edward O. Laumann, "Specialization and Prestige in the Legal Profession: The Structure of Deference," *American Bar Foundation Research Journal* (1977): 155–216.

reform in order to shore up their own status or to demonstrate their ethical superiority; nor did the broadening of the divorce law offer any material advantages to their corporate clientele. And although a new divorce law promised to provide more legal work for divorce lawyers, it would not benefit the predominantly large-firm lawyers who led the ABCNY. One can only conclude that the ABCNY engaged in reform in this area for its own sake, recognizing the damage done to respect for the law by the hypocrisy and evasion encouraged by the existing situation.

The Special Committee established in 1948 was a typical ABCNY special committee at that time, a "blue-ribbon" committee including prominent members of the bar and with a corporate law practitioner as its chairman. Though the Special Committee worked hard and managed to line up the support of the news media and of the Protestant churches, it could not break the influence of the Roman Catholic Church over the legislators and its reform proposals went nowhere.[86] By 1959, the "blue-ribbon" committee had failed to effect any substantive changes in the divorce laws and was dismantled.

Five years later the ABCNY created a second Special Committee on Matrimonial Law, but this time with a Jewish divorce lawyer as chairman and members who "were energetic and all of whom had significant expertise in the field."[87] Rosenman, president of the ABCNY at the time, was a former state legislator and a Democrat, and had a pretty good idea of what sort of leadership was required to push divorce law through the legislature. Howard Spellman, the committee chairman, was an experienced divorce lawyer and well connected to local political elites. Furthermore, he was energetic and terrier-like in his efforts and quite willing to lobby personally in Albany to persuade legislators to adopt reform measures. Spellman's Special Committee experienced almost immediate success. The legislature created a Joint Legislative Committee to consider the substantive and procedural aspects of New York's matrimonial law. Working closely with the Joint Committee, Spellman's Special Committee had considerable input into its deliberations.[88] Outside the legislative process, the Special Committee mobilized support for a bill drafted and introduced by the Joint Committee, undertaking an intensive campaign through radio and television appearances and the newspapers. Spellman and the secretary of

---

86. Paul B. DeWitt, former executive secretary of The Association of the Bar of the City of New York, personal interview with author, June 26, 1979.

87. Annual Report of the President, *Record of the Association of the Bar of the City of New York* 20 (1965): 442–491.

88. Annual Report of Special Committee on Matrimonial Law, 1966.

his committee worked hard in support of the reform bill, staying in Albany on the day the bill was on the floor in order to be of assistance to the legislative leaders in facilitating passage of the statute. Spellman's diligent politicking paid off. On April 24, 1966, a new divorce law was enacted, thereby liberalizing "New York's archaic, cruel and unjust matrimonial law."[89]

Obviously other groups and organizations participated in the reform effort, and "the time was ripe for this salutory reform" in that most other states had already liberalized their laws.[90] But the ABCNY played a significant role in initiating divorce law reform and seeing it through to a successful conclusion. Unlike the blue-ribbon Special Committee established in the 1950s, Spellman's committee was composed of leaders of the local matrimonial bar, experts in divorce law who were well connected locally and understood the local political system. Rosenman, himself an active Democrat of considerable local stature, recognized that to achieve divorce law reform you needed a noted divorce lawyer who could work the legislature. Spellman was just that. In addition, of course, support for the intransigent Catholic position had declined, and the divorce bar, which might otherwise have opposed reforms emanating from the ABCNY, stood to gain more than they would lose from the liberalization of the law. Indeed, with more liberal laws it was likely that there would be much more demand for their services. The ABCNY was successful in its advocacy of divorce law reform at this time because of the local knowledge and connections of its Special Committee, and because the reform did not negatively affect the interests of any well-organized local segment of the bar.

ELITE INFLUENCE IN A PLURALISTIC PROFESSION

Elite status conferred on the ABCNY significant resources that it could mobilize in order to exercise influence. Its membership was wealthy and well-connected, had considerable expertise in certain areas of law, and enjoyed high social status. Connections with business leaders and foundation officials provided access to external funding, and on occasion wealthy members or law firms would support particular projects. Such financial resources in addition to regular membership dues enabled the ABCNY to embark on ambitious projects using academic experts and paid professional staffs to do the necessary research and lay

---

89. Ibid. For a discussion of procedures under the new divorce law, see Rosemary E. Bucci, "Procedure under the New Divorce Law," *New York State Bar Journal* 38 (1966): 498–505.

90. Annual Report of the President, *Record of the Association of the Bar of the City of New York* 21 (1966): 433–471.

the groundwork for reform proposals. If ample financial resources provided the ABCNY with the wherewithal to initiate major reform projects and to prepare quality reports, high social standing ensured that its proposals were at least given a hearing. At the national level, the prestige and reputation of the Association and its leaders contributed significantly to the positive reception given its reports.

As a relatively homogeneous organization the ABCNY enjoyed a high degree of value consensus, especially in the 1950s and 1960s before it experienced rapid growth and greater diversification. As a consequence, the ABCNY was able to adopt strong, uncompromising policy positions. In contrast, more heterogeneous and inclusive organizations such as the CBA suffered from considerable internal dissensus; consequently their policy positions reflected the necessity of compromise and bargaining to satisfy internal constituencies that had diverse and even conflicting interests. The ABCNY, for example, could adopt a "pure" no-fault accident-compensation proposal because its membership included few negligence lawyers who stood to suffer from such a change. This was not possible for more representative bar associations that included significant numbers of negligence lawyers who strongly opposed no-fault policies. Consequently, support for no-fault proposals from such inclusive associations was lukewarm at best.

In proposing reform of the tort law and the development of a new system of compensation for the victims of automobile accidents, the ABCNY was attempting to change an area in which few of its members practiced. This was also true of other reform efforts of the ABCNY, such as reorganization of the local and state courts and expansion of the grounds for divorce, which similarly were largely unrelated to the practice areas of most ABCNY members. It is always easier to reform someone else's bailiwick. Local bar associations whose members practiced in these areas found it more difficult to intervene because their members' interests were directly affected. As the executive director of the Committee on Modern Courts noted: "You simply don't get plans for merit selection of judges or the merger of the local courts coming out of the local bar associations."[91] The ABCNY's distance from the objects of its reform efforts facilitated its taking such initiatives.

Membership homogeneity could also be a disadvantage, however. It meant that certain viewpoints and interests were not represented in the ABCNY decision-making process and therefore not reflected in the positions it adopted. This lack of representativeness limited the ABCNY's effectiveness in promoting its policy proposals, particularly at the local and state levels where legislators and judges were well aware of its identification with the Wall Street elite of the bar. In con-

91. Fern Schair, personal interview with author, October 25, 1979.

trast, the more heterogeneous CBA, which could legitimately claim to represent the bar in Chicago, had greater success with the state legislature in its advocacy of court reform. Although also failing to convince the legislature to adopt the merit selection of judges, the CBA, working with the Illinois State Bar Association, did achieve a completely unified court system with a single trial court. Through a new judicial article enacted by the Illinois legislature in January 1964, "the legions of overlapping county, municipal, city, village and town courts . . . were organized into a single, concise court system with three levels: the Supreme Court, and appellate court, and a single, unified trial court of general jurisdiction."[92] The CBA's greater success was in part due to the fact that internal conflicts within the bar were thrashed out first in the association, prior to taking its reform proposal to the legislature, whereas conflicts within the New York bar were often fought out in public decision-making arenas.

The CBA also had closer links to state legislators and a greater involvement in the political process. It maintained a lobbyist in Springfield, Illinois—usually a former lawyer-legislator—and went to great pains to cultivate good relations with legislators from Chicago. The closer relationship between the CBA and the legislature in Illinois was demonstrated by the Illinois Legislature's virtually complete adoption in 1955 of revisions to the civil practice act drafted by a joint committee of the CBA and the Illinois State Bar Association. As a leader of the CBA noted after the fact: "The Legislature took the whole Act largely based on faith in the Committee and in the recommendations of the two Associations."[93] Mind you, the joint committee in Illinois had backed away from the most controversial revision—that rule-making authority be transferred from the legislature to the courts—whereas the ABCNY continued to insist on it to the very end. The elite ABCNY went further in its demands for revision, to the very heart of the autonomy of the state courts, even though it riled the legislature, whereas the representative CBA more readily compromised its position in order to increase its chances of success.

The ABCNY appears to have been more successful in its policy initiatives at the federal level, where its connections have been strongest and its prestige carried the most weight. But major reforms of the state judicial system and tort law, to which the ABCNY actively committed itself, required state legislation and therefore depended upon the support of the local and state political organizations with which the ABCNY traditionally had weak ties. The gap between the Wall Street elite of the ABCNY, with its largely national professional interests, and

92. Halliday, *Beyond Monopoly*, p. 156.
93. Ibid., p. 161.

local political leaders was considerable. But it was with these leaders, and in local and state decision-making arenas, that local bar groups such as the Brooklyn and Queens County bar associations, and the various organizations of trial lawyers, were most influential. Although smaller in size and with more limited financial resources than the ABCNY, these local bar groups could call on both practical experience and local political connections in opposition to grand schemes of elite reform that they viewed as contrary to their interests. Local nonelite interests within the bar were well embedded in local political and ethnic organizations, greatly enhancing their influence capacity on issues requiring local resolution.

Contrary to the image of an all-powerful upper-class or large-firm elite of the bar promulgated by elite theorists, the limited success of the ABCNY in legal system reforms at the local and state levels attests to the limitations of elite resources and to the countervailing influence capabilities of the nonelite majority of the bar. Its superior financial resources and membership homogeneity enabled the ABCNY to take important reform initiatives, and its accumulated prestige guaranteed it a hearing, but the ABCNY could not push through reforms strongly opposed by local interests within the bar. The sharply differentiated and stratified structure of the New York bar was grafted onto a mosaic of religious, ethnic, and neighborhood interests. This mosaic provided opportunity for the less affluent and the nonelite to exert influence over the making of policy, as politicians had to listen to these varied interests, and contributed to the pluralistic and dispersed nature of power that Wallace Sayre and Herbert Kaufman found in their thorough examination of the government of New York City in the 1950s.[94] If large-firm elite of the ABCNY could garner the support and cooperation of local bar groups, however, as they did in the ABCNY's second attempt to reform the divorce laws, then their chances of success were much greater. As Lowell Field and John Higley argue, societal elites need the cooperation of nonelites in order to achieve their ends.[95]

---

94. Wallace S. Sayre and Herbert Kaufman, *Governing New York City: Politics in the Metropolis* (New York: Russell Sage Foundation, 1960). A fascinating study of New York politics at a much earlier time found the same pattern of pluralistic politics and competing elites, even if power was not yet as dispersed as Sayre and Kaufman found it in the 1950s. See David C. Hammack, *Power and Society: Greater New York at the Turn of the Century* (New York: Russell Sage Foundation, 1982). Studies of community power structures in major metropolitan centers in the 1960s and 1970s also found power to be relatively dispersed. For an overview of these studies, see John Walton, "A Systematic Survey of Community Power Research," in Michael Aiken and Paul E. Mott, eds., *The Structure of Community Power* (New York: Random House, 1970).

95. Lowell G. Field and John Higley, *Elitism* (Boston: Routledge and Kegan Paul, 1980).

PART FOUR

Conclusion

Chapter Seven

Elite Professionalism in Modern Society: Its Persistence and Its Limits

FROM PATRICIAN TO ELITE PROFESSIONALISM

Following his visit to the United States in the early nineteenth century, Alexis de Tocqueville projected that lawyers and judges would come to constitute the aristocracy of the new world.[1] Viewing lawyers and judges as inherently conservative and antidemocratic in their commitment to the rule of law, Tocqueville anticipated that the members of the new aristocracy would defend order against change, thereby limiting the negative consequences of excessive democratization. Clearly Tocqueville was not referring to all lawyers and judges, but rather to an elite segment of the bench and bar represented by figures such as Boston's Daniel Webster, who capped his successful legal career with high political office.[2]

If any group of American lawyers inherited the Tocquevillean mantle, it was the New York legal elite of the late nineteenth and early twentieth centuries. At first composed of renowned courtroom advocates such as William Evarts, Samuel Tilden, David Dudley Field, the Choate brothers, and James Carter, and then of highly successful corporate lawyers such as Elihu Root, William Howard Taft, Charles Evans Hughes, John W. Davis, and William D. Guthrie, this WASP legal aristocracy played the Tocquevillean role in grand style. They were not only eminent New York lawyers but also prominent national figures, many of whom sought and held high national political office.

They led the American bar during the critical period of profession-

---

1. Alexis de Tocqueville, *Democracy in America*, trans. Henry Reeve (3rd ed., London, 1838), vol. 2, pp. 102–112.
2. See Jerold Auerbach, *Unequal Justice: Lawyers and Social Change in Modern America* (New York: Oxford University Press, 1976), p. 14.

alization from the turn of the century until World War II. This Tocque-villean aristocracy created and maintained the ABCNY as a patrician legal association with membership requirements akin to those of the upper-class clubs with which they were so familiar. Holding to patrician notions of professionalism, and generally opposed to democratic tendencies within the bar, they advocated higher entry standards and character and fitness requirements for practice, and led the opposition to the movement to establish statewide, compulsory-membership bar associations. The patrician model dominated the ABCNY until the 1960s, when it was seriously challenged for the first time by significant changes in the surrounding bar and its wider societal context, which required major adaptation on the part of this aristocratic association.

In addition to examining the adaptation of this patrician legal association to a radically different normative and professional environment in the postwar decades, this book has addressed several general questions of fundamental importance to modern democratic societies. These questions relate to the persistence and continued place of elite groups and organizations in mass society with its egalitarian pressures and democratizing tendencies. By what means can elite associations such as the ABCNY maintain their distinctiveness and yet retain their legitimacy in the face of such trends? If they are able to survive as distinctively elite associations, what is the extent of their power and influence? Are these strategic elites, to use Keller's terminology,[3] actually able to shape the main contours of their particular institutional domains, as has been suggested by various elite theorists? Are the resources available to elite associations superior to those of nonelite groups so that the elite associations are able to exercise determinative influence over the outcomes of broader policy-making and statutory change?

We have seen that the ABCNY did persist as an elite association in the midst of an increasingly heterogeneous bar. It did not follow the path taken by the CBA in Chicago decades earlier and become a mass voluntary bar association, fully representative of the surrounding bar. Indeed, despite rapid membership growth in the 1960s and 1970s, the ABCNY still, in 1980, included fewer than one out of every three New York lawyers. Graduates from the elite national law schools and large-firm lawyers continued to be overrepresented in its membership, and the powerful president's office remained firmly in the hands of the

---

3. Suzanne Keller, *Beyond the Ruling Class: Strategic Elites in Modern Society* (New York: Random House, 1963).

corporate legal elite. By 1980 there still had not been a president elected from the personal-plight hemisphere of legal practice.[4]

Although the ABCNY remained an elite association, it was less closely identified with the WASP establishment than previously. Fewer of its leaders belonged to the exclusive clubs of the city than in the interwar years, and the anti-Semitism that had earlier characterized the American upper class, and was clearly viewed as a hurdle for Jewish lawyers seeking to play an active role in the ABCNY during this time, was no longer apparent. If Jewish and Catholic lawyers remain underrepresented in the ABCNY, as they appear to be, it is not because of ABCNY admissions policies or procedures but because they continue to be underrepresented in the prestigious large firms from which the ABCNY still recruits a high proportion of its members. Similarly, once completely excluded from membership in the ABCNY, female lawyers are well represented in the 1980s. There was certainly greater diversity in the social backgrounds and ascriptive characteristics of members in the late 1970s compared to the early 1950s.

If the ABCNY opened up its doors in the 1970s, welcoming instead of scrutinizing membership applications, why did not lawyers from the nonelite segments of the bar flood into the ABCNY, thereby radically changing its character? Relatively high initial fees and annual dues, the operation of differential levels of admission (representation, inclusion, and incorporation), and the retention of an elite organizational structure with small, exclusive committees all contributed to discouraging the massive entry of lawyers from the personal-plight bar and permitted the maintenance of the ABCNY's elite character. For many graduates of local law schools, practicing alone or in small firms, the ABCNY offered little more than the status of membership. Its location was inconvenient (a long way from the courts and City Hall), committee appointments were hard to come by, and it lacked a dining room for business lunches. It did not promise to be a good source for referrals, except, perhaps, for the white-collar criminal defense lawyers who regularly get work from the large corporate firms. These disincentives tended to outweigh the incentives of access to excellent library facilities

---

4. Professors and deans, or former deans, of New York's leading law schools, beginning with Russell Niles in 1966, are the only lawyers other than the large-firm elite to have gained access to the president's office in the postwar period. The burdens of the president's office are such that only those lawyers who can afford to commit considerable time to the position can even consider serving, especially as it is almost always a two-year commitment. This considerably restricts the field of potential presidential candidates, excluding the vast majority of solo practitioners and small-firm lawyers.

and status conferral that the ABCNY offered. Consequently, the leadership of the large-firm elite was not seriously challenged by an influx of nonelite lawyers.

On top of these disincentives, the atmosphere at the ABCNY remained overwhelmingly elitist, dominated as it was by large-firm lawyers. As Heinz and Laumann argue convincingly with respect to the Chicago bar, the personal-plight lawyers in small firms and solo practice and the corporate lawyers of the large firms live and practice in two quite separate worlds—or hemispheres, to use their term. They found that "lawyers who serve major corporations and other large organizations differ systematically from those who work for individuals and small businesses" not only in terms of social backgrounds, education, and careers but also with respect to social and political values and friendship networks. They conclude that "most lawyers reside exclusively in one hemisphere or the other and seldom, if ever, cross the equator."[5] At least in Chicago, lawyers from the two hemispheres met in the CBA. In contrast, in New York the ABCNY was almost exclusively identified with the corporate hemisphere, whereas the NYCLA and the local bar associations provided meeting places for personal-plight practitioners. It was difficult to change these patterns and perceptions. Undoubtedly, many local practitioners continued to feel uncomfortable with the dominant large-firm culture of the ABCNY.

During the postwar decades, then, the ABCNY moved from being a patrician legal association to becoming an elite professional organization in which the ascribed characteristics of age, gender, and ethnicity were less important than professional standing. The ABCNY remained, however, an unrepresentative status community in the New York bar in 1980, led by legal *honoratiores* who occupied positions of considerable prestige within the New York legal community.[6] Through the utilization of different levels of admission and the operation of organizational and cultural disincentives to nonelite membership, the ABCNY remained an elite association within the New York bar, albeit with its upper-class WASP identity considerably attenuated.

---

5. John P. Heinz and Edward O. Laumann, *Chicago Lawyers: The Social Structure of the Bar* (New York: Russell Sage Foundation, 1982), p. 319.

6. The term "honoratiores" is drawn from Max Weber's discussion of the legal profession and its leadership. Honoratiores are those persons who enjoy considerable prestige and deference within their communities and are able to occupy positions of leadership or authority without remuneration because of their economic situation. Weber's description fits very closely the leaders of the ABCNY and of other major professional societies. Max Weber, *Economy and Society*, ed. Guenther Roth and Claus Wittich (Berkeley: University of California Press, 1978), pp. 784–792.

Although the ABCNY did not undergo fundamental democratization, its more diverse membership brought new ideas and values into the association. New committees were founded, and older committees drew from a wider pool of lawyers. The consequence was greater internal dissensus and increased difficulty in reaching agreement on important issues. Karl Mannheim predicted that the open, achievement-based elites of modern democratic societies would be either rent by internal divisions or constrained by the demands of proximate nonelite constituencies rendering them unable to provide decisive leadership.[7]

At first glance, it would seem that these negative prognostications were correct. Greater membership diversity did result in increased dissensus within the ABCNY, especially following the co-optation of young reformist lawyers and consumer advocates into new committees in areas of law defined as much by ideology as by substantive legal content. The higher level of conflict was manifested not only in members' meetings replete with contention but also in disagreements within and between committees. On occasion this internal conflict spilled over into the public arena as committees disseminated their conflicting reports, thereby undermining any unified collective influence the ABCNY might have had over policy-making on the issues at stake. Even without the premature publication of conflicting reports, the difficulties the ABCNY experienced in reaching early agreement on controversial professional issues hindered its ability to intervene expeditiously in ongoing policy debates.

Yet, notwithstanding this higher level of internal conflict, the ABCNY was still able to reach decisions on controversial matters even if only after lengthy debate. Furthermore, these decisions were not all of the "lowest-common-denominator" variety, as tended to be the case in fully representative professional associations, but on occasion were decisions that advocated major changes in long-standing professional or public policy. How was the ABCNY still able to take such positions after it had opened up its membership? As we saw in Chapter 4, and as Halliday showed with respect to the CBA,[8] there are ways in which organizations can manage increased levels of internal dissensus without allowing it to impinge upon core activities or to hamstring decision-making. The ABCNY successfully utilized various organizational strategies to manage conflict, including channeling discontent into peripheral sections or relatively isolated subunits; creating new ad hoc com-

---

7. Karl Mannheim, *Ideology and Utopia* (New York: Harcourt Brace, 1955).

8. Terence C. Halliday, *Beyond Monopoly: Lawyers, State Crises and Professional Empowerment* (Chicago: University of Chicago Press, 1987).

mittees to bypass extant committees regarded as too unpredictable or
conflictual; respecting the relative autonomy of highly technical standing committees; and strengthening hierarchical, centralized authority
over committee actions.

Furthermore, the newcomers to the ABCNY were not all that different from the old guard in terms of their educational and professional
backgrounds and practice interests. Although the old patrician leadership undoubtedly disapproved of some of the proposals for legal reform emanating from some of the new committees, by and large these
proposals did not conflict with their real material interests. Rather, the
real opposition remained outside the ABCNY in the wider New York
bar where the sharpest differences in professional values and interests
were to be found. Thus there was little conflict within the ABCNY over
the recommendation of a true no-fault law in the early 1970s; vigorous
opposition came from segments of the bar not at all included in the
ABCNY. Similarly, relaxation of the norms governing lawyer advertising sought by consumer advocates within the ABCNY met its strongest
opposition in state bar politics and in the state courts where the small-
firm and solo practitioners who stood to be negatively affected by such
a policy had considerable influence. The continued relative homogeneity of interests in the elite ABCNY meant it could still consider and
take strong positions on professional and legal policies.

The persistence of the ABCNY as an elite association, despite the
egalitarian pressures of the 1960s and 1970s, and its ability to manage
higher levels of internal dissensus brought on by greater membership
diversity, suggest that the gloomy prognostications of the demise of
elite groups on the part of the prophets of mass society are unfounded.
The example of the ABCNY demonstrates that elite organizations are
able to maintain their elite status even though they relax their formal
admissions criteria and recruit more broadly. Indeed, as Baltzell suggested, the adoption of a more open admissions policy may well enhance the legitimacy of the elite association.[9] Even though the elite
association may stop short of becoming fully representative of the
wider society, it averts criticism by demonstrating its openness to rising elites without regard for their ascriptive backgrounds. The question
remains as to the extent of the influence of these more open elite
groups upon policy-making in both their immediate institutional domains and in the wider society.

---

9. E. Digby Baltzell, *The Protestant Establishment: Aristocracy and Class in America* (New
York: Vintage Books, 1964).

LIMITS OF ELITE AUTHORITY

Elite theorists, whether of society as a whole or of particular institutions, emphasize the continued power of cohesive, integrated elites to determine important policy outcomes. Jerold Auerbach, for instance, contends that the stratification of the bar historically enabled "relatively few lawyers, concentrated in professional associations, to legislate for the entire profession and to speak for the bar on issues of professional and public consequence."[10] These few lawyers were typified for Auerbach by the WASP corporate elite of the ABCNY.

Certainly, the ABCNY historically had attempted to shape the modern legal profession as it emerged in twentieth-century New York. It developed discipline committees, established a judiciary committee to screen candidates for the bench, engaged in periodic campaigns against ambulance chasers, and led the movement for stiffer qualifications for admission to the bar. Yet in all these areas the ABCNY was less than successful: Its discipline committee merely touched the tip of the iceberg of unethical practice; its campaigns failed to rid the city of ambulance chasers; and its attempt to act as a gatekeeper to the local and state benches was notably unsuccessful. Perhaps of greater importance than the extent of its actual instrumental authority over the bar and the legal system was the symbolic significance of its efforts in these areas. The ABCNY, and through it the corporate elite of the New York bar, became identified with legal reform and professional regulation, thereby imbuing its initiatives with considerable moral force.

There is a further question, however, that arises from the ABCNY's postwar transition from patrician to elite professionalism. Did the admission of lawyers from more diverse social and ethnic backgrounds improve the ABCNY's ability to exercise effective leadership in the profession and the wider society? In *The Protestant Establishment*, Baltzell held that an open upper class or elite, incorporating within its ranks rising elites of achievement, would be able to exercise more effective moral leadership than a closed or caste-like upper class because it would be more representative of the wider society and therefore enjoy greater legitimacy.[11] Following Baltzell's logic, then, we could anticipate that the ABCNY's influence capabilities would have been strengthened by its movement away from a caste-like WASP solidarity.

Examination of the ABCNY's activities in the postwar period, however, shows that it was not any more successful than before in imple-

---

10. Auerbach, *Unequal Justice*, p. 4.
11. Baltzell, *The Protestant Establishment*.

menting the professional and legal-system reforms it initiated. Indeed, as we have seen, it lost its century-long control over lawyer discipline in 1980, and was unable to prevail with its advocacy of radical changes in professional policies governing admission to the bar, lawyer advertising, and no-fault automobile insurance. The newcomers to the ABCNY in the 1960s and 1970s were not, by and large, graduates of local law schools who practiced alone or in small firms, and the reform proposals they espoused did not bring the ABCNY closer to the local nonelite bar groups. Indeed, there was an interesting inversion of roles in the 1970s, with the nonelite local lawyers defending traditional professional restrictions and regulations against attacks brought by elite reformers seeking fundamental changes.

Even when the leadership of the ABCNY made a special effort to ensure representativeness on major projects, it could not readily escape its large-firm identity. When the ABCNY decided to tackle seriously the massive problems of the criminal-justice system in New York City in the the late 1970s, it created a special committee to study the situation and recommend changes to the relevant statutory and judicial bodies. Although a wide variety of lawyers and laypersons representing all the diverse interests in the criminal-justice area were appointed to this committee, it was still viewed as reflecting the interests of the large-firm elite. Thus its recommendations were greeted with great suspicion and scepticism by criminal-justice practitioners and policymakers.[12] Labeled in this way, the ABCNY's special committee, although broadly representative, found it very difficult to make any headway against the intractable opposition of special interests in the criminal-justice system. The continued accurate perception of the ABCNY as an organization of the large-firm legal establishment militated against its effective leadership within the sharply differentiated New York legal system.

In addition, the professional and practice interests of most leaders of the ABCNY were directed overwhelmingly toward Washington, D.C., the federal courts, and national political and economic developments. Consequently, the ABCNY was much more effective on the national and federal levels where the natural interests and connections of its leaders were found, than it was at the local and state levels. Not well integrated into local and state political networks, its leaders gen-

---

12. The final report and recommendations of the Special Committee on Criminal Justice were presented in May 1979 and distributed to all members of the Association and to every city employee involved in law enforcement. For reference to criticisms of earlier drafts of the report, see Tom Goldstein, "Criminal-Justice Report Spurs Debate by Experts," *New York Times*, January 19, 1979.

erally lacked strong local connections and political clout. Large-firm lawyers may enjoy high social standing but they do not get the vote out. Cyrus Vance was an exception, and his strong local political ties proved important to the eventual achievement of a modicum of judicial reform. In comparison, solo and small-firm practitioners frequently appeared in the local courts before the local and state judiciary and were more likely to belong to local political clubs and develop close ties to state legislators, many of whom had once been local lawyers themselves. Moreover, they were embedded in community and ethnic relations that overlapped with political and professional ties and therefore were in a position to mobilize local political opposition to elite reform initiatives that threatened their interests. Many of the important professional and legal-system reforms sought by the ABCNY required the action of state judicial or legislative bodies with which local nonelite bar groups had strong connections and therefore could exercise countervailing influence.

It is clear that even after the ABCNY became more of an open elite organization, there remained limits to its authority and its ability to determine professional policy and reform the New York legal system. Nonelite groups within the bar were generally able to counter effectively initiatives from the elite corporate bar. Elite theories of the legal profession too readily overlook the pluralistic character of the bar, concentrating on the obvious influence resources of the professional elite and ignoring the utility of resources available to nonelite segments. Heinz and Laumann demonstrate unequivocally, as did researchers before them, that the urban bar is sharply differentiated and segmented, so much so that they suggest "one could posit a great many legal professions, perhaps dozens."[13] These various segments, or professions of the bar, have different interests that frequently conflict on matters of professional policy, particularly given the sharp distinction between the corporate and personal hemispheres of legal practice. Furthermore, variations of practice characteristics are overlaid with differences in religious and ethnic background that reinforce systematic patterns of differentiation. The structure of the highly differentiated urban bar is clearly pluralistic, with many competing professional interests and identities.

Although the bar may be composed of sharply differentiated groups with plural interests, it does not follow that all groups within it have equal resources or influence capabilities. Heinz and Laumann also demonstrate convincingly that the legal profession is characterized by

---

13. Heinz and Laumann, *Chicago Lawyers*, p. 5.

the unequal distribution of rewards of prestige and income.[14] At the top of the intraprofessional prestige and income hierarchies are the large-firm corporate lawyers of the ABCNY, and at the bottom are practitioners in the personal-plight hemisphere, who predominantly practice alone or in small groups. As a consequence, the large-firm elite enjoys superior financial and prestige resources compared to those available to other segments of the bar. Not only did the ABCNY have access to these resources but it also had long dominated the regulatory structure of the New York bar and so occupied the high moral ground. The distribution of power in the legal profession, then, approximates what Allen Barton refers to as "biased pluralism," with significant but not overwhelming advantages favoring the large-firm elite.[15]

Unable to prevent elite reform initiatives, local bar interests could effectively neutralize and limit their reach. They could do this within the inclusive and representative metropolitan or state bar association before issues ever reached the public, as in the case of the CBA, or through representations in local and state decision-making arenas where their influence resources have particular utility. Given the pluralistic nature of the legal profession, and the importance of local and state decision-making arenas, the ability of the corporate legal elite, even with all its financial and prestige resources, to determine professional and legal-system policy outcomes was distinctly limited.

Furthermore, metropolitan bars are embedded in highly differentiated urban political systems that make it difficult for any one group, whether a class or functional elite, to control decision-making processes and outcomes. Wallace Sayre and Herbert Kaufman's exhaustive study of the government of New York City in the 1950s demonstrates the pluralistic nature of the urban government process at that time, suggesting that even lower-income groups exercised some influence over critical decisions.[16] Politicians could not afford to ignore neighborhood organizations, ethnic groups, or labor unions, all of which contributed to getting the vote out. David Hammack similarly found that around the turn of the century the power of New York's economic and social elites was limited by the fact that political parties even then were controlled by professional politicians who usually hailed from lower- or middle-income, ethnic backgrounds.[17] He found a substantial and

---

14. Ibid., especially chapter 4.

15. Allen H. Barton, "Fault Lines in American Elite Consensus," *Daedalus* 109 (1980): 1–24.

16. Wallace G. Sayre and Herbert Kaufman, *Governing New York City: Politics in the Metropolis* (New York: Russell Sage Foundation, 1960).

17. David C. Hammack, *Power and Society: Greater New York at the Turn of the Century* (New York: Russell Sage Foundation, 1982).

increasing gap between local political leaders, whose orientation was distinctly local, and economic elites, whose interests were becoming more national. The interweaving of local interests and ethnic identities, and the fact that important decisions required the cooperation of local and state political parties which were locally based, made it difficult for any one elite group to determine the making of public policy. It was no less difficult for the ABCNY to determine the direction of professional policy in the contemporary period.

THE ROLE OF THE ELITE ASSOCIATION

If the elite association is unable to exercise a determinative influence in the making of professional policy notwithstanding its considerable resources, what is its role? Is it no more, perhaps even less, effective than mass-based, representative associations? Does it have a distinctive role within the panoply of modern professional organizations?

The elite association generally has access to the resources necessary to undertake major studies of problem areas upon which it can then base reform proposals. The ABCNY frequently utilized its access to foundations to fund such studies and to academics and experts to staff them. Many of its research projects were published in book form and received wide circulation, contributing significantly to the flow of information and ideas on issues of local and national policy concern. Even if not always resulting in the adoption of their policy recommendations, these reports certainly shaped and channeled the discourse over the direction and content of legal change. No other local, metropolitan, or state association has been able to play such a scholarly role within the American bar, especially at the national and federal levels. The elite ABCNY had the resources, the contacts, and the interest to do so.

Furthermore, because of the relative homogeneity and economic security of its members, the elite association may well be able to consider and support quite radical changes that would be inconceivable for heterogeneous and representative associations. Thus the ABCNY was able to tackle, and provide decisive leadership for, controversial professional issues such as federally funded neighborhood legal clinics, lawyer advertising, and no-fault automobile insurance because those segments of the bar that stood to lose most from changes in these areas were not incorporated into its membership. In contrast, fully representative associations, such as the CBA and the national ABA, had to satisfy multiple and conflicting internal constituencies and therefore found it very difficult to adopt positions welcoming change at all. As a consequence, they generally opted for policies of minimal change in response to external pressures. Of course, it was the elite bar's distance from the impact of changes in these areas that allowed it to take positions limiting the reach of the professional monopoly. At the same time, however, its advocacy of the removal of ethical obstacles to experiments in the provision of legal services to persons of low or middle income improved access to justice for these folk. It could be argued that elite occupational groups, freed from immediate economic insecurities, are in the best position to advocate and initiate reforms in the wider public interest that threaten the interests of elements of the occupation itself.

The distance of the leadership of the ABCNY from local ethnic groups also facilitated its national leadership in the civil rights movement of the 1960s. Not only did it provide a platform for Martin Luther King, Jr., in New York, but it also was an early and strong supporter of federal civil rights legislation. Its substantial, and widely cited, report on the 1964 Civil Rights Act provided detailed argumentation supporting its constitutionality and defending its necessity. In contrast, the CBA, with its more conservative leadership and close connections to local white ethnic communities, was very reluctant to endorse major civil rights legislation and provided only lukewarm support for the Civil Rights Act itself. Of all the nation's major bar associations, the elite ABCNY was probably the most active in support of the extension of rights to minority groups.

Similarly, the elite association's prestige and legitimacy may endow it with greater autonomy from political authorities and therefore enable it to be more outspoken in opposition to repression or violations of rights. Although elite corporate lawyers scarcely rushed to represent unpopular political defendants during the height of McCarthyism in the early 1950s, the ABCNY did intervene in an attempt to protect individual rights in the face of abuses by congressional investigating committees. It first issued in 1948 a widely circulated and influential report on the procedures of congressional investigations that recommended the adoption of due-process protections for those under investigation. Several years later, it was one of the very few bar associations to oppose publicly the ABA's proposal that all lawyers should be subject to loyalty oaths, and in 1954 it established a national committee to inquire into the federal loyalty-security program. Reflecting the tenor of the times, this report did not reject the program as a whole but rather sought to restrict its scope and improve the fairness of its procedures. Published as a book in 1956, the ABCNY's report contributed to the growing doubts about the usefulness and fairness of the entire loyalty-security effort.[18] Although in retrospect it is clear that the

---

18. Association of the Bar of the City of New York, *The Federal Loyalty-Security Program* (New York: Dodd, Mead, 1956).

ABCNY did too little too late, it went farther than any other local association, or the ABA, in attempting to insert some reason and procedural protections into the national anticommunist witch-hunt of the time. Even Auerbach, generally so critical of the corporate legal elite, recognized that the ABCNY was "among the most responsible bar associations during this period."[19]

Moreover, the ABCNY was usually successful in getting its reform proposals on the agendas of the relevant decision-making bodies. Even though local, nonelite bar groups frequently were able to limit the outcomes of these proposals, they were not able to prevent the initiatives from being considered. The influence resources of the elite association are such that decision makers cannot simply ignore it. Rather, they must take into account and respond to its proposals. As recent analysts of power relations have pointed out, concentration on who determines outcomes of decision-making processes ignores an earlier, and perhaps more important, exercise of power in the selection of appropriate alternatives for consideration.[20] The analysis of power must pay attention not only to outcomes but to what does and does not get onto the agenda in the first place. Potential alternatives may be excluded from consideration from the outset. From this perspective it is an important indication of power to be able to place items on the agendas of decision-making bodies; in so doing, the elite association is able to influence the content and direction of professional and political discourse even if it is unable to determine outcomes in the short term. That the elite ABCNY was constantly bringing merit selection of the judiciary before legislators and the public facilitated its eventual partial adoption when the time was ripe.

THE COLLECTIVE INFLUENCE OF THE BAR

We have already noted the distinct limits placed on the influence of the large-firm elite over professional policy by the heterogeneous and pluralistic character of the legal profession. But what about the elite bar's influence over broader public policy issues, over the direction and content of legal change? When professional associations move outside their primary spheres of influence—in this case, the legal profession and the court system—into the wider public policy arena, they have to contend with not only competing professional interests but also multiple other organized interests. Some commentators have suggested that

19. Auerbach, *Unequal Justice*, p.255.
20. See, for example, Steven Lukes, *Power: A Radical View* (London: Macmillan, 1974).

the collective influence of lawyers, even elite lawyers, in the public policy-making arena is very limited indeed. Heinz, for example, contends that the collective action of lawyers "does not bring about an allocation of the society's scarce resources that differs in any substantial way from the distribution that would have been willed by the lawyers' clients or by the polity" quite apart from that action.[21]

Heinz bases his provocative contention upon two observations. First, he argues that sharp internal divisions within the bar itself prevent the organized bar from taking decisive stands on any but the most inconsequential of issues; and, second, he finds little evidence to indicate that lawyers are able or willing to support policies that run contrary to the interests of their clients. In other words, when lawyers do take public positions on policy issues having to do with the allocation of scarce resources, their positions reflect the interests of their clients and so do not represent the distinctive influence of lawyers.

Internal veto groups were not a serious problem for the ABCNY, even after its membership became more diversified. Rather than obstructing bar association action from within, the opposition of local bar groups to ABCNY reform proposals surfaced in the external political process, as demonstrated in the debate over no-fault automobile insurance. The eventual outcome was the same whether the debate took place within or outside the bar association: The collective influence of the bar was significantly impaired by intraprofessional dissensus. On many other issues that had either a positive or a negligible impact on the interests of specific segments of the bar, however, there was no significant opposition from diverse bar groups to ABCNY proposals.

A more telling judgment is that lawyers, individually or collectively, are rarely willing to challenge the policy interests of their clients and therefore are unable to make an independent professional contribution to legal change on major issues affecting the distribution of wealth and political power. Robert Nelson, in his in-depth analysis of the social structure and client relations of large Chicago law firms, found a decided reluctance on the part of large-firm lawyers to assert autonomous professional or personal values in the face of client demands.[22] The extreme rarity with which the lawyers in Nelson's study report ever refusing an assignment on the grounds of a conflict in values suggests that there is little divergence between their professional and personal values and the business interests of their clients.

---

21. John P. Heinz, "The Power of Lawyers, *Georgia Law Review* 17 (1983): 911.
22. Robert L. Nelson, *Partners with Power: The Social Transformation of the Large Law Firm* (Berkeley: University of California Press, 1988), pp. 251–259.

Perhaps the unquestioning acceptance of client demands is understandable in the hurly-burly of everyday practice, especially given the high value placed on zealous advocacy and the competitive marketplace within which large-firm lawyers work. When the reward structure of the large firm is tied closely to bringing in business to the law firm, then few lawyers will be willing to risk losing a client by inquiring into the justness of the client's cause or pressing ethical considerations very far. Certainly, in daily practice the professional value of commitment to the client far outweighs that other professional value of commitment to equal justice.

But if this lack of separation between client and professional values characterizes the practices of individual lawyers and their firms, what about their collective representations through their professional associations? The bar association represents an arena of professional action quite separate from that of daily practice where client interests must prevail. Thus the ideology of the organized bar stresses that lawyers leave their clients at the door when they enter the bar association and participate in its deliberations. In large part, of course, the validity of the claim on the organized bar to be more than just another interest group depends upon public acceptance of this professional ideology. That is, the bar association must not only appear to be above narrow partisan politics but its deliberations must also reflect the disinterested application of autonomous professional expertise to legislative change. Only then can its recommendations be taken as representing independent professional judgment in the public interest.

Basic to Terence Halliday's thesis that the collective action of lawyers makes a significant contribution to modern governance is his contention that bar associations are able to transcend sectional professional and client interests in bringing expert knowledge to the service of the embattled state.[23] His detailed analysis of the CBA's contribution to judicial and constitutional change in Illinois assumes the independent application of autonomous professional knowledge to the determination of which legislative proposals further the public good. In other parts of his analysis, however, Halliday leans toward a rather different argument, which accepts the close identity of lawyers with their client and practice interests in their bar association activities. His contention that bar associations are still able to exercise influence comes to rest, paradoxically, on the very heterogeneity of the bar that Heinz finds so debilitating. The presence of diverse groups of lawyers within the inclusive association necessitates its reaching compromises or transcend-

---

23. Halliday, *Beyond Monopoly*, chapters 11 and 12.

ing narrow professional or client interests. He found this to be the case in the CBA's active involvement in the revision of the revenue article of the Illinois Constitution.[24] The initial position adopted by the CBA was seen to be too closely aligned to particular economic interests and was opposed by representatives of other interests within the CBA, leading to the eventual modification of the CBA's original position. To exercise any influence on the shape of the new revenue article, the CBA had to reconcile or transcend the competing interests within it.

In additional research on the CBA, Charles Cappell also demonstrates the close similarity between positions supported within the CBA and the practice and client interests of its members. Identifying the typical clients and practices of members of the CBA's board of governors, Cappell found that "the advocacy profiles of board members were partisan for the most part, and in most instances, consistent with the board member's set of clients and practice characteristics."[25] It was the absence of relevant client ties that freed a board member to take a more general, nonpartisan approach to an issue. There was not much evidence of the disinterested application of autonomous professional knowledge to proposals for legislative change within the CBA.

ABCNY committees also tended to recommend policies or adopt positions in line with the interests of the clients of their members. For instance, perceiving that the time had come to revise the New York State corporation law in the late 1950s, the ABCNY and NYCLA established a joint committee largely composed of corporate lawyers, which pressed the legislature to replace the existing regulatory approach with an enabling act that would encourage incorporation in the state rather than discourage businesses with burdensome requirements and excessive liabilities.[26] Its position was clearly pro-business and did not take into account the interests of labor and consumers. Notwithstanding the cumulative expertise of this joint committee, and the support of the business community, the bar committee failed to dissuade the legislature from retaining the regulatory orientation in the revised corporation law.

Similarly, the report of an ad hoc committee established by the ABCNY in the mid-1970s to examine proposed legislation imposing sanctions on corporations making illegal foreign payments was consistent with the interests of the giant corporations. There was strong sen-

---

24. Ibid., chapter 9.

25. Charles L. Cappell, *Professional Projects and the Private Production of Law* (Ph.D. dissertation, University of Chicago, 1982), p. 344.

26. See Michael J. Powell, *Social Change and an Elite Professional Association: The Politics of Inclusion* (Ph.D. dissertation, University of Chicago, 1982), pp. 405–412.

timent in Congress to impose not only reporting requirements with civil penalties on offending corporations but also criminal sanctions on corporate leaders. The ABCNY's committee questioned the need for additional legislation at all, but in the eventuality of legislation strongly opposed the inclusion of criminal penalties.[27]

In both these instances of proposed legal change, ABCNY committees advocated positions in line with the general interests of the corporate clients of their members. In the mid-1970s, the Committee on Trade Regulation did begin to diverge from its traditional pro-business stance and supported increased sanctions for violations of the antitrust laws. This apparent aberration, however, is explained by the changing composition of this committee noted in Chapter 4. It did not reflect corporate antitrust lawyers taking positions contrary to the interests of their clients, but rather the increased presence of law professors, government lawyers, and lawyers who represented consumer groups.

Without question, the preponderance of the evidence suggests that lawyers even in their collegial associations find it difficult to distance themselves from their clients' interests. I not wish, however, to advance a crude interest theory of collective professional action. The explanation lies less in the proclivity of lawyers to advance consciously their clients' interests in their professional associations than in their close identification with, and sharing in, those interests. Although lawyers may leave their immediate clients at the door of the bar association committee room, they are unable to leave behind the common culture and values they share with their clients in general.

Nelson's research on large-firm lawyers in Chicago finds that they strongly identify with the economic interests of their clients even to the point of putting clients' long-term interests over their own short-term interests.[28] Thus, large-firm lawyers will support deregulation of an area of business activity even if it ultimately threatens to reduce substantially their own legal work because deregulation is in the long-term interests of their clients and they share with their clients a general distaste for government regulation.[29] The values of lawyers, like those of other people, are largely shaped by what they do and with whom they interact on an ongoing basis. As Karl Llewellyn observed more than fifty years ago: "The practice of corporation law not only works

---

27. Ibid., pp. 441–447. The ABCNY was unsuccessful in having its position adopted. The Foreign Corrupt Practices Act enacted by Congress in 1977 included both reporting requirements and criminal sanctions.

28. Nelson, *Partners with Power,* pp. 243–249.

29. Heinz presents an example of such behavior. See Heinz, "The Power of Lawyers," pp. 901–902.

for business men toward business ends, but develops within itself a business point of view."[30] It seems reasonable, then, to agree with Nelson, who concludes from his examination of large-firm lawyers' values and attitudes that it is "unlikely that their law reform activities will depart to any significant extent from the positions that they advocate for their clients."[31]

In this sense there would seem to be ample grounds to support Heinz's ready dismissal of any independent collective influence of the bar over important allocative decisions. However, his test of lawyers' collective influence is framed too narrowly. For one thing, it ignores the broader institutional and ideological roles of the organized bar. Nelson argues persuasively that large law firms have a considerable impact "not because they bring about an allocation of society's scarce resources which differs from that willed by clients but precisely because they maintain and make legitimate the current system for the allocation of rights and benefits."[32] The same argument could be made even more strongly for major bar associations such as the ABCNY, which are not involved in the immediate adversarial representation of clients. Their support for, or opposition to, particular legislative proposals is presented as the considered opinion of independent, disinterested legal experts, thereby garbing the positions represented in those proposals in the symbols of justice and the language of rights. This claim to an independence from particular interests and a commitment to the transcendent rule of law allows them to intervene in a wide range of issues and endows their pronouncements with unusual normative force.[33] Bar associations, then, can play a significant legitimating, or delegitimating, role in the process of legal change.

Furthermore, Heinz does not consider the influence of the organized bar on important issues that do not involve, at least not directly, major distributive questions. Yet Halliday recounts the CBA's active defense of individual rights through its emphasis on procedural protections and its consistent efforts to rationalize the Illinois court system. He also points out that the Illinois legislature delegated virtually complete responsibility for the revision and codification of the Illinois criminal law

30. Karl N. Llewellyn, "The Bar Specializes—With What Results?" *Annals of the American Academy of Social and Political Sciences* 167 (1933): 177.

31. Nelson, *Partners with Power*, p. 249.

32. Ibid., p. 264.

33. For development of the conception of the legal profession as a "normative" profession with unusual legitimacy, see Terence C. Halliday, "Knowledge Mandates: Collective Influence by Scientific, Normative, and Syncretic Professions," *British Journal of Sociology* 36 (1985): 421–447.

to a joint committee of the Chicago and Illinois bar associations in the 1950s. The new criminal code enacted by the Illinois legislature in 1960 was almost entirely the handiwork of the bar associations.[34]

The contributions of the ABCNY to general law reform were no less noteworthy. In Chapter 6, I outlined the critical role played by the ABCNY in the 1960s in the substantial revision of New York's mental health and divorce laws. A decade later, the ABCNY played a pivotal role in the evaluation and revision of the New York drug laws. Joining forces with the Drug Abuse Council, Inc., the ABCNY undertook an examination of the impact of the harsh drug laws enacted during Governor Rockefeller's administration in New York in 1973.[35] Popularly known as "the nation's toughest drug law," the Rockefeller laws imposed stiff mandatory sentences on those convicted of drug offenses. Funded by the Law Enforcement Assistance Administration, a joint committee of the ABCNY and the Drug Abuse Council studied the effect of these laws on drug use and availability, and on the arrest, conviction, and sentencing of drug offenders. After three years of research, it reported that the tough laws did not seem to have the intended deterrent effect. The use and availability of drugs were not reduced, and the already overburdened New York courts were further overloaded because those charged with offenses had no motivation to plead guilty as they faced severe mandatory prison sentences. Shortly after the publication of the joint committee's report, the legislature revised the New York Drug Law, reducing the mandatory penalties considerably. The widely reported study initiated by the ABCNY provided the data and justification for significant legislative reform in a very sensitive area of the criminal law.

In these successful excursions into law reform, the bar associations mobilized their organizational, financial, and knowledge resources to initiate and inform statutory change. Despite the apparent importance of these law reform efforts to the social-control powers of the state, the bar associations experienced relatively little opposition. Although New York psychiatrists made representations with respect to reform of the mental health law, they approved its general direction, and there was no organized group of mental health lawyers with vested interests in the status quo to oppose it. Neither law enforcement agencies nor the judiciary opposed the relaxation of the draconian Rockefeller drug laws which had placed the entire criminal justice system of New York under

---

34. Halliday, *Beyond Monopoly*, pp. 245–53.

35. The report of the joint committee was published as a book entitled *The Nation's Toughest Drug Law: Evaluating the New York Experience* (New York: Association of the Bar of the City of New York, 1977).

extra pressure. Once the ABCNY–Drug Abuse Council report demonstrated the apparent failure of the laws to achieve their stated goals, thereby providing legitimacy for their revision, the legislature was quite willing to amend them.

While the success of the bar on these issues does not provide a good test of its ability to have its way despite the mobilized opposition of others, these were not inconsequential issues and in each instance involved more than mere technical law reform. Halliday suggests that as the boundaries are blurred between what is technical and what is normative in the law, "the legal profession has an unusual opportunity to exercise moral authority in the name of technical advice."[36] This might have been the case in the revision of the Illinois criminal law, but was certainly not so in the other examples where the normative and substantive implications of changes proposed by the bar were apparent. Reform of the New York drug law promised to increase judicial discretion over sentencing and reduce the severity of penalties for drug offenses; the new mental health law would take commitment proceedings out of the courtroom and place them completely in the hands of medical experts; and revision of the New York divorce law offered to make divorce more readily available. The statutory changes in the criminal, divorce, and mental health laws advocated by the ABCNY had important, and apparent, consequences for social behavior and for the social-control powers of the state.

Although this study indicates that the collective influence of the elite bar was generally unable to prevail over strong, organized opposition even in areas in which the elite bar had considerable expertise, it was able to get its proposals onto decision-making agendas in the first place and thereby influence the discourse of legal change. It was also able to initiate and shape legislative developments in important areas upon which there was agreement about the need for, and the general direction of, change. The existence of a broad consensus on the need for change does not guarantee that change will in fact occur, however, or determine the direction of change. There first need to be change agents who take up the cause of reform and mobilize support for change.[37]

In the revision of New York's mental health, divorce, and drug laws, committees of the ABCNY initiated the process of legal change, either by undertaking research and publishing its results or by actually drafting new statutes and having them introduced into the state legislature. In the case of divorce law reform, the ABCNY committee

---

36. Halliday, *Beyond Monopoly*, p. 41.

37. For a discussion of the role of change agents in the initiation and diffusion of innovations, see Everett M. Rogers, *Diffusion of Innovations* (New York: Free Press, 1983).

worked closely with legislative leaders in guiding the reform through the legislature and in mobilizing support at critical junctures. We have no way of knowing whether legal change in these areas would have occurred without the goading of the ABCNY, or taken a different direction without its active involvement, but with its ample resources, its access to decision makers, and its moral authority as a repository of legal expertise, the ABCNY served as an important change agent in the broader legal system.

SYMBOLIC POLITICS, CIVIC PROFESSIONALISM, AND ELITE RESPONSIBILITY

Critical views of the collective action of the modern professions emphasize either its self-interested monopolistic intent or its subservience to the interests of powerful clients or patrons. In the first view, the collective entities of the profession seek to expand or protect its boundaries, exclude outsiders, and stimulate demand for its services. Codes of ethics, for instance, are seen as merely ideological camouflage that legitimate the profession's self-interested exploitation of its market.[38] In the second view, the profession's collective action reflects the dominant client interests of the bar's leadership. For Heinz, client characteristics determine the positions particular segments of the bar take on public policy issues, whereas for Melone the ABA is little more than "the spokesman of big business."[39]

Although it could be argued that some of the ABCNY's activities advance the generalized interests of the clients of its members, others clearly do not. The reform of the criminal, divorce, and mental health laws were not issues from which any immediate professional or client advantages could be inferred. Similarly, the immense energy expended by the organized bar over the last forty years in court-reform activities does not have any immediate apparent advantage to lawyers or particular client interests. Why, then, does the organized bar commit its resources to such reform efforts? In particular, why would the elite ABCNY expend considerable resources on reformist activities in areas of law in which few of its members and none of its leaders practice?

---

38. See, for example, Jeffrey L. Berlant, *Profession and Monopoly: A Study of Medicine in the United States and Great Britain* (Berkeley: University of California Press, 1976); Richard L. Abel, "Why Does the ABA Promulgate Ethical Rules?" *Texas Law Review* 59 (1981): 639–688.

39. Heinz, "The Power of Lawyers"; Alfred P. Melone, *Lawyers, Public Policy, and Interest Group Politics* (Washington, D.C.: University Press of America, 1977), pp. 200–201.

Mental health, divorce, and drug law were far removed from the practices of the corporate legal elite of the ABCNY, as were the local criminal, civil, and domestic relations courts. Yet it committed its prestige, money, and organizational resources to reform in these areas throughout the postwar period.

One possible answer to this paradox of elite collective action in nonelite areas of practice is what might be described as moral displacement on the part of the elite bar. Developed to explain the enthusiasm the Victorian middle and upper classes exhibited for the moral improvement of the lower classes, all the while ignoring their own moral lapses, the displacement theory suggests that it is easier, and indeed even therapeutic, for elites to reform the institutions and behaviors of the nonelite than of their own.[40] Accordingly, elite corporate lawyers, unwilling or unable to address problems in their own practices, displace their reformist energies onto nonelite activities where the need for reform is only too apparent and the implications for their own conduct negligible.

A more likely, although not unrelated, explanation would hold that the paradoxical involvement of the elite bar in nonelite reform was one way by which the elite emphasized its separation from the lower and dirtier world of ambulance chasing, contingent fees, plea bargaining, and custody fights. Andrew Abbott argues that the status of a particular specialty or area of practice within a profession is largely a function of its distance from the more unpleasant professional tasks.[41] Thus lawyers who deal with the rarified, abstracted legal problems of corporate law enjoy higher standing within the bar than their colleagues who defend nasty criminals or represent parties to messy divorces.

By directing its reform efforts at nonelite areas of practice, the large-firm elite of the bar was suggesting that this was where reform was most needed and at the same time implying that its own areas of practice were characterized by rationality and integrity. The ABCNY committed much more energy to the reform of local and state courts and procedures than to the reform of the federal system. The clear implication was that federal practice, the practice of the elite of the bar, was

---

40. This explanation for elite reformism is discussed in Robert W. Gordon, "The Ideal and the Actual in the Law: Fantasies and Practices of New York City Lawyers, 1870–1910," pp. 55–56 in Gerard W. Gawalt, ed., *The New High Priests: Lawyers in Post–Civil War America* (Westport, Conn.: Greenwood Press, 1984). For its development with respect to the Victorians, see Walter Houghton, *The Victorian Frame of Mind, 1830–1870* (New Haven, Conn.: Yale University Press, 1957).

41. Andrew Abbott, "Status and Status Strain in the Professions," *American Journal of Sociology* 86 (1981): 819–835.

morally superior to local and state practice, which was infested with political, particularistic, and commercial considerations. From this perspective, the symbolic significance of the ABCNY's reform efforts is what is critical.[42] Reform activities are best understood as a means by which the elite of the bar symbolically reasserts its superiority over nonelite groups by maintaining its distance from them.

There clearly is some basis to these accounts of elite lawyers' reform interests, but they fail to explain why the ABCNY committed so much of its time and energy to reform activities. Surely, it could have achieved the same end with periodic forays in the direction of reform that did not require the expenditure of vast amounts of its scarce resources. Yet it devoted considerable effort to court and judicial reform over a large number of years, far in excess of what would have been necessary for merely symbolic purposes. Similarly, the ABCNY did not simply wave a symbolic flag at divorce law reform but made two major attempts spanning almost twenty years until a new divorce law was enacted in 1966. Certainly, the ABCNY benefited from its identification with reform, which usually enabled it to occupy the high moral ground, and allowed its members to bask in its reflected glory; but the extent of its commitment to achieving actual legal change far exceeded that required for mere symbolic purposes.

An alternative explanation is that of civic professionalism proffered by Halliday, who argues that established professions such as law and medicine are in a position to contribute their expertise to the service of the state.[43] On the one hand, mature professions no longer need to focus their collective energies on monopolistic concerns and are able to commit their resources in other areas; on the other hand, governments increasingly suffer from overload and crisis and look to the professions for assistance in meeting the many demands made upon them. According to Halliday, the professions can, and do, contribute to the adaptive upgrading of state agencies and institutions by "bringing their knowledge to the service of power."[44]

The legal profession is particularly suited to bring its talents to the aid of the state because it is partly a "state-constitutive" profession, straddling the boundary between the state and civil society. Halliday suggests it is motivated to offer its services because of the "civic consciousness" of bar elites and a collective sense of obligation.[45] Halliday tempers this idealist view with the recognition that the strain toward

---

42. Recall the discussion at the end of chapter 5 of the symbolic significance of the ABCNY's attempts at controlling the practices of nonelite segments of the bar.
43. Halliday, *Beyond Monopoly*, pp. 368–376.
44. Ibid., p. 376.
45. Ibid., p. 370.

materialist self-interest is always present, but the overall impression is of a profession collectively animated by concerns of public service.

Civic professionalism requires that the professions do not simply respond to state requests for assistance, but actually precipitate state action by drawing attention to the areas in which adaptation is required and by presenting specific proposals to state agencies calling for change. The proactive legal profession reviews existing statutory law and initiates reform in areas where it appears to be archaic, inconsistent, disorganized, or otherwise ineffective in achieving its ends. Utilizing their concentrated expertise, and professing disinterested motives, bar committees draft and propose rationalized legislation for enactment. Thus the Illinois bar associations initiated the codification of the Illinois criminal law and drafted a new criminal code that then became the basis for debate and eventual legislative action. Similarly, the ABCNY determined that the statutes governing divorce and commitment procedures for the mentally ill were archaic and needed substantial revision. It established special committees to study the existing law and draw up recommendations for reform. In so doing, the ABCNY drew the legislature's attention to the need for legislative change in these areas and developed proposals upon which the legislature could act.

Halliday's depiction of a proactive profession eagerly coming to the aid of an overburdened state may appear rather Pollyanna-ish at first glance, endowing the organized bar with too much civic virtue, but it does provide a tenable explanation for the initiation of legislative change by the organized bar on issues that are irrelevant to its collective self-interest and immaterial to the interests of its clients. Moreover, some of the initiatives of the bar have undoubtedly contributed to the adaptability and legitimacy of state institutions and agencies. The revised federal conflict-of-interest statutes, modeled on those the ABCNY proposed, greatly facilitated the movement of experts between the private and public sectors, enabling the state to draw more effectively on expertise from the private sector. By launching an examination of the impact of the harsh Rockefeller drug laws, the ABCNY was able to present the legislature with the data necessary to justify revision of the controversial laws, thereby relieving it of the burden of undertaking such research itself. These are instances of the ABCNY's contributing its resources and expertise to the strengthening and adaptation of the state.

Civic professionalism provides a timely corrective to the popular debunking of professionalism as mere ideology masking occupational self-interest. One must take seriously the ideal interests of bar elites as well as their materialist concerns, as Robert Gordon suggests in his examination of the tension between the ideal and the actual in the professional lives of the elite New York lawyers who founded the ABCNY.[46] A solely materialist, or monopolistic, interpretation of the collective action of the profession cannot explain the full range of reform activities of the ABCNY.

Of course, the ABCNY could afford to be in favor of professional or legal change on issues that did not affect in any way the interests of its members or their clients. It could afford to support proposals for federal funding of legal services, neighborhood legal clinics, and lawyer advertising because these changes in the provision of legal services involved little risk for the large-firm elite, whereas they impinged directly on the practices of solo and small-firm general practitioners. It could also afford to support vigorously civil rights legislation as its leaders were safely ensconced in corporate law firms and affluent suburbs where integration was not likely to have much of an impact. Yet lack of an interest at stake in these proposed changes is not in itself an adequate explanation of the ABCNY's action. Although it might, perhaps, explain lack of opposition on the part of the elite ABCNY to proposed changes such as these, it does not elucidate its strong, positive support. The ABCNY did not simply withhold opposition to federal funding of legal services for the indigent, or civil rights legislation. It actively campaigned for them. Nor does the absence of interest help us understand why the ABCNY involved itself in the revision of the New York divorce and mental health laws. Narrow interest theories, then, are not sufficient to explain the law-reform activities of the large-firm elite of the bar.

Ultimately driving civic professionalism in the bar, according to Halliday, are strongly held collective value commitments to an efficient and rational legal system, to the legitimacy of law as an institution, and to the merits of procedural justice.[47] Undoubtedly, members of the bar hold to these values to varying degrees, but one need not have recourse to ultimate values to understand the elite bar's reform agenda. The ABCNY's considerable involvement in law and legal-system reform certainly reflects the high value its leadership places on the rule of law, but may be more usefully viewed as a manifestation of the large-firm elite's perception of its responsibility for the maintenance of the larger system of which it is part and from which it ultimately benefits.

The leadership of the ABCNY was very much aware of its prominent place in the profession and the wider legal system. Representing

---

46. Robert Gordon, "The Ideal and the Actual."
47. Halliday, *Beyond Monopoly*, p. 369.

the large-firm elite of the bar, the leaders of the ABCNY clearly felt they had a particular responsibility for the moral order of the profession and the legitimacy of the legal system. Such a view was a recurring theme in presidents' reports and innumerable bar association speeches. Advocates of particular issues of concern to the bar and the legal system more generally would refer to this obligation as a means of mobilizing the ABCNY. The ABCNY's ongoing concern with questions of professional self-regulation reflects this elite self-perception, and its reform activities can be understood as attempts by the elite to shore up the legal system and restore respect for the law. Thus its vigorous support for civil rights legislation reflected the general apprehension that the continued denial of rights to a substantial minority of the American population undermined the legitimacy of the law; its advocacy of federal funding of legal services represented its concern about the consequences of lack of access to justice; and its sustained efforts to achieve divorce law reform revealed its awareness that a law so out of touch with social reality as New York's outmoded divorce law engendered widespread disrespect for the law in general.

Representing an important strategic elite in contemporary American society, the leadership of the ABCNY committed its resources to uphold the legitimacy of the law and to improve the efficiency of the legal system. Ultimately, the advantaged position of the corporate legal elite, and of lawyers in general, depends on the continued recognition and acceptance of legal institutions as effective and necessary integrative mechanisms in the political economy and social order.

Index